Backyard
Grilling

For your grill, smoker, turkey fryer and more

Jim & Ann Casada

Kate Fiduccia

Teresa Marrone

CREATIVE
PUBLISHING
international

CHANHASSEN, MINNESOTA

www.creativepub.com

Jim and Ann Casada have written several books, including *Wild Bounty* and *The Complete Venison Cookbook*. Both are freelance writers and frequent contributors to a variety of outdoor magazines and other publications. They live in Rock Hill, South Carolina.

Kate Fiduccia has written several cookbooks, including *Cooking Wild in Kate's Kitchen* and *Cooking Wild in Kate's Camp*. She also shares her knowledge and love of cooking through her cooking segment on the Woods N' Waters TV series. She lives in Warwick, New York.

Teresa Marrone is a freelance writer and editor, who has authored several cookbooks, including *Abundantly Wild*, *The Back-Country Kitchen*, *The Seasonal Cabin Cookbook* and *Cookin' Wild Game*. She lives in Minneapolis, Minnesota.

Copyright © 2005 by Creative Publishing international, Inc.
18705 Lake Drive East
Chanhassen, MN 55317
1-800-328-3895
www.creativepub.com

President/CEO: Ken Fund
Vice President/Publisher: Linda Ball
Vice President/Retail Sales & Marketing: Kevin Haas
Executive Editor, Outdoor Group: Barbara Harold
Creative Director: Brad Springer
Editor: Teresa Marrone
Project Manager: Tracy Stanley
Photo Editor: Angela Hartwell
Studio Services Manager: Jeanette Moss McCurdy
Photographer: Tate Carlson
Assistant Photographer: Michael Karns
Food and Prop Stylist: Abigail Wyckoff
Assistant Food Stylist: Susan Telleen
Director, Production Services: Kim Gerber
Production Manager: Stasia Dorn

Printed on American paper by: R. R. Donnelley
10 9 8 7 6 5 4 3 2 1

Backyard Grilling
by Jim and Ann Casada, Kate Fiduccia, Teresa Marrone

Contributing Photographers:
©Brand X Pictures (p. 7BL); Jim Casada (all shots on p. 100); Ariel Skelley/Corbis (p. 14); Owen Franken/Corbis (p. 96); Peter Fiduccia (all shots on p. 28); Teresa Marrone (all shots on p.95); Christine Nesheim (p. 108).

Contributing Illustrator: Tom Wallerick

Contributing Manufacturers:
Brinkmann Corporation, Broilmaster Premium Gas Grills, Eastman Outdoors, Little Chief Smoker/Luhr-Jensen, Lodge Manufacturing.

Library of Congress Cataloging-in-Publication Data

Backyard grilling : for your grill, smoker, turkey fryer and more / Jim Casada ... [et al].
    p. cm.
  Includes index.
  ISBN 1-58923-148-1 (hardcover)
  1. Barbecue cookery. I. Casada, James A.
  TX840.B3B29 2004
  641.5'784--dc22
                                    2004017474

Backyard Grilling

TABLE OF CONTENTS

CHAPTER ONE

What Is Outdoor Cooking?

4

CHAPTER TWO

Grilling Meat, Poultry & Fish

14

CHAPTER THREE

Smoking Meat, Poultry & Fish

72

CHAPTER FOUR

"Low & Slow" Techniques

96

CHAPTER FIVE

Deep-Frying & Boiling

108

CHAPTER SIX

Rubs, Marinades, Sauces & Butters

116

CHAPTER SEVEN

Vegetables, Sides & Desserts

128

Nutrition .138

Index 140

What Is Outdoor Cooking?

n a sense, cooking outdoors is as old as man's use of fire, but as we think of it today, it really belongs to the last two or three generations. Prior to the 1950s or 1960s, with the advent of hibachis, small charcoal grills and the like, this type of meal preparation usually involved community barbecue events or maybe huge pots of soup or hash cooked for a family reunion, fund-raiser or other special event. Gradually, though, realization dawned that a grill, smoker or deep-fryer could bring welcome diversity to family meals; provide a break from kitchen drudgery as food cooked while family or friends relaxed in an outdoor setting; or offer strikingly different approaches to food preparation. This book celebrates outdoor cooking in its many guises, and in doing so offers approaches sure to appeal to anyone who revels in cooking under the open sky.

With today's choices of grills, barbecues, smokers, fryers and more, the cook can easily prepare an entire meal—from appetizers and vegetables, to main-dish items and breads, and even dessert—in a pleasant outdoor setting. It's an easy, fun method to prepare food in a healthy way. Best of all, depending on the method and equipment, dinner can be on the table in less than an hour—or, cooking can be a leisurely, all-day affair suited to lawn games or sitting in the shade with a tall glass of lemonade.

Fuel Choices and Other Fundamentals

The type of fuel is the first basic decision. Grills are available in charcoal or gas models; most gas models use liquid propane (LP), but a few use butane or natural gas. Bullet-style smokers can be charcoal-fueled or electric, with a rare few adapted for the use of gas; box-style smokers are electric. Specialty units such as offset firebox smokers and free-standing barbecue units burn charcoal or natural wood, while trailer-style barbecues and roasters may use gas, charcoal or natural wood. Outdoor deep-fryers use liquid propane. If you plan to have several types of outdoor cooking appliances, such as a grill and a deep-fryer, it may make sense to use the same type of fuel for both (for example, an LP gas canister can easily move from grill to deep-fryer and back). If your choice is electricity or natural gas, remember that the appliance will either have to be near the house, or will require special utility lines run to the area where it will be used.

Charcoal is widely available, convenient and portable. Two forms of charcoal are available: manufactured briquettes and natural-wood, or lump, charcoal. Briquettes are made from burned wood trimmings and chemical additives that are pressed into regularly sized lumps. They're easy to light, make a good fire, and offer a steady source of heat. Some people, however, can detect a chemical aftertaste in foods that have been cooked with briquettes. Lump charcoal is large chunks of hardwood that have already been burned. It burns much cleaner, and a bit hotter, than charcoal briquettes, and leaves no chemical aftertaste. Lump charcoal burns more quickly than briquettes, however, so your fire will not last as long.

Opinions often run strong when comparing gas to charcoal, particularly for grills. Many cooks enjoy the push-button convenience of a gas grill, which can be ready for use in as little as 10 minutes and does not produce a pile of ash to be cleaned up. Others feel that charcoal grills provide superior grilled flavor, and don't mind the 30-minute wait while the coals burn down—or the subsequent clean-up. Some smoking enthusiasts are adamant that gas or manufactured charcoal briquettes provide an unnatural taste to foods, and will use only natural lump charcoal or actual hardwood as fuel. In truth, many people can't tell the difference between, say, a steak cooked over gas and one cooked over charcoal; the meat isn't over the fuel long enough to make that much of a difference. If you're a purist with a fine-tuned palate, stick to natural lump charcoal or, better yet, actual hardwood; otherwise, the differences between gas and charcoal probably won't be that noticeable, particularly for foods that cook relatively quickly.

When shopping for a grill, smoker or other backyard appliance, remember that the unit will be exposed to temperature extremes as well as the vagaries of the weather; quality materials and workmanship will extend the life of the appliance. Heavy-gauge metal lasts longer, holds heat better, and is less likely to warp from high temperatures than thin metal. A baked-on enamel finish lasts far longer than a spray-painted coating. If you're comparing models at a store, put your hands on top of the closed appliance and gently rock it from side-to-side to check for

wobble; remember that over time, any such defects will be amplified.

The grates that will hold food (and coals, in the case of a charcoal grill) should be heavy steel, preferably stainless; some quality gas grills have grates that are coated with porcelainized enamel, while specialty units like hibachis have cast-iron grates. Thicker grates hold heat and provide nice searing marks. Thin grates lose heat quickly when cold food is added, causing the food to stick; they also warp and twist over time from exposure to heat. Some charcoal grills come with a special hinged grate that allows you to add more coals without lifting off the entire grate; this is a great feature for lengthy cooking.

About Grills and Barbecue Units

Grills and barbecue units are the most common tools in the arsenal of the backyard chef. They range from small cast-iron hibachis to elaborate barbecue systems with multiple heat zones, separate burners for preparing sauces and side dishes, built-in thermometers and a host of other amenities. The most common grill is probably the covered grill—often a charcoal-fired kettle-style grill or simple two-burner gas grill. Here is information on some grills and barbecue units, ranging from the simple to the elaborate.

Hibachi—In North America, the term "hibachi" is used for a small, charcoal-fueled, cast-iron unit that consists of a rectangular or oval firebox with one or two metal grates to hold food; some have a reflecting hood that helps retain heat. They are portable, and are ideal for high-heat cooking for two or three people at a time. Lodge Manufacturing, which has been manufacturing cast-iron cookware in Tennessee

Portable Gas Grill—Also called wagon or trolley grills, these units are available in a wide variety of styles, ranging from simple to extremely elaborate. Larger units allow you to cook with two or more heat zones. Many come with side burners, warming shelves, swing-up work tables and storage areas. Most are fueled with liquid propane, although some can also be fitted to burn natural gas. Some manufacturers of gas grills, including Kenmore and Holland, offer special add-on panels to convert a portable gas grill to a more permanent island-style grill. All gas grills can be used for the same cooking methods as covered charcoal grills (above).

Gas grills come in a dizzying array of configurations and price points. To begin the selection process, first consider the size of the actual cooking area and the number of burners. Common configurations range from 350 to 750 square inches (8.9 to 19 square

since the late 1890s, has a nice unit called the Sportsman's Grill that is perfect for quick, small-volume grilling.

Covered Kettle or Square Charcoal Grill—The covered kettle charcoal grill was pioneered by Weber-Stephens Co., and remains the standard to this day for the many backyard cooks who prefer charcoal. Square covered charcoal grills can be found at many discount stores, and offer a less expensive—but generally less durable—alternative. Covered charcoal grills can be used for direct cooking at any heat level required; indirect cooking; covered roasting or barbecuing; and even as a basic smoker. Temperature is controlled by the amount of charcoal used and by adjusting vents on the bottom and in the lid.

meters), with two to six burners; even larger units are available if you need to cook for a crowd on a regular basis. A unit with three or more burners is better than a two-burner unit for indirect cooking; however, a quality two-burner unit can be used for indirect cooking as long as the grill is well insulated and tightly built.

Gas grills are rated by the amount of BTUs (British Thermal Units) they produce, but this can be deceptive. A high-BTU grill that is loosely built will cook less efficiently than a well-constructed model with lower BTUs. The heat can be uneven across the cooking area as well, and the BTU rating will not reflect that problem; in addition, some grills can't be adjusted to cook at the low temperatures required for barbecuing or smoking.

Some gas grills have used lava rocks or ceramic briquettes to distribute heat and catch drippings, which otherwise fall onto the burners and cause flare-ups. Many newer models use V-shaped bars rather than rocks to trap the drippings; in some models such as the Weber series, the bars are designed to vaporize the drippings to provide flavor, while in others the drippings are channeled into a drip pan.

Steel-Drum Barbecue—Many professional barbecuers prefer the steel-drum barbecue, which works well for low-and-slow cooking and has a large capacity. The basic form comes from an old homemade design—a 55-gallon (200-liter) drum that has been cut in half lengthwise and fitted with legs, a chimney, a grate and a hinged lid with handles. These types of grills are ideal for indirect cooking, as the charcoal or natural-wood fire can be set on one side of the grill and the food can be placed on the other side to create ideal conditions for slow-roasting barbecue.

Lyfe Tyme is a well-known manufacturer of steel-drum barbecues. Their product originates from the oil fields of Texas (the first ones were made from leftover pieces of pipeline). Like all things in Texas, these barbecue units are big; their largest unit weighs in at 2,000 pounds (907 kg)! Brinkmann also offers several configurations of steel-drum barbecues. Steel-drum barbecues are generally used for indirect cooking, but they can also be used for direct cooking and smoking.

BRING IT ON HOME

In our part of the world (South Carolina and surrounding area), you can find a sort of cottage industry specializing in homemade grilling units just about anywhere you live. These are usually big units, typically utilizing propane but sometimes designed specifically with charcoal in mind. Often they feature a hitch and sit atop an axle and two tires so they can be towed behind a truck. These are likely made of heavy-duty material and will be designed according to the dictates of the owner. Typical features include a small smoke outlet, removable grill tops, hinged lids that can be propped open much like the hood of an automobile, thermometers and special utensils designed for handling large pieces of meat or special items. Smaller grills are often built from a large barrel that has been cut in half, fitted with hinges, welded as needed and equipped with a grill top. In truth, give someone with a fair degree of ingenuity who knows welding a general design and the appropriate selection of metal, and chances are he or she can create a grill precisely fitted to your own needs.

—Jim and Ann Casada

About Smokers

With the steel-drum barbecue units noted above, we cross over into the area where barbecuing intersects with smoking. Barbecuing, or low-and-slow cooking, calls for temperatures in the range of 175°F to 275°F (80°C to 135°C). When smoking wood is added to the heat source during barbecuing, or if the fuel is natural wood, the process is often called smoke-cooking. Some refer to this simply as "smoking"; however, smoking can be done at a variety of temperatures.

In reality, any grill can be used for smoking by adding chunks of smoking wood to the heat (small wood chips or sawdust must be used for gas or electric appliances; see page 75 for more information). This is particularly effective when moderate to low heat is used because the longer cooking times allow the smoke flavor to permeate the food. However, if you plan to do a lot of smoking, it is worthwhile to get a unit that is specifically built to function as a smoker; you'll be able to use lower temperatures, and it is usually easier to burn the wood needed to produce smoke. Following is information on some units that are designed primarily for smoking.

Bullet-Style Water Smoker—Here's another unit that acts as a crossover between barbecuing and smoking. The bullet-style smoker is an upright cylinder with a charcoal firebox or electric coils at the bottom. A water pan sits over the heat source; grates above the water pan hold the food; and a rounded dome cover holds in the heat and moisture. The unit can be used as a plain barbecue; it's more effective than a covered grill because with the firebox at the bottom and a separate door to access the fuel, it's easier to control the heat. Smoking wood can be added to the heat to use the unit as a water smoker; during cooking, vapor from the heated water combines with the smoke particles from the wood and these

condense on the food item. In this manner, the food is infused with a savory, sweet smoke flavor. The water vapor also helps to maintain the ideal cooking temperature. Water is not the only liquid that can be used in the water pan; experiment with apple juice, cider, wine, vinegar water, beer or broth. The Weber Smokey Mountain is widely available, as are similar models from Brinkmann.

Offset Firebox Smoker—The classic offset firebox smoker is a steel-drum barbecue with a separate fire chamber that is attached to the side. Wood or charcoal is burned in the firebox; the heat and vapors travel through the drum (which becomes the central cooking chamber) and out the vent stack, which is connected to the cooking chamber at the end opposite the firebox. Some of the Lyfe Tyme units have offset fireboxes; Char-Broil also offers similar smokers, as well as a vertical unit with an offset firebox. Brinkmann Corporation offers a number of offset firebox smokers, ranging from backyard units costing a few hundred dollars to trailer-mounted pull-behind units designed for professionals. Since these units are typically large and

heavy, it may pay to investigate local manufacturers; a quick Internet search for "offset firebox smokers" will provide information on numerous smaller manufacturers.

Box-Style Electric Smoker—These units range from a simple aluminum box with a hotplate at the bottom, to more elaborate insulated units that offer reliable temperature control. The Luhr Jensen Little Chief is probably the first smoker that most people use (particularly hunters and anglers). It works well in a protected situation, where it is not exposed to wind or cold weather; its effectiveness drops off dramatically in cold weather because the thin aluminum walls don't hold the heat well. (A large cardboard box, inverted over the smoker, can help hold the heat; make sure the box is large enough that it does not touch the actual smoker, to avoid the possibility of a fire.)

For more serious smoking, an insulated box-style smokehouse is a great choice. These offer fairly precise temperature controls, at ranges from 80°F to 325°F (27°C to 163°C). The Sausage Maker, at www.sausagemaker.com, offers several different sizes of well-insulated electric smokehouses; Cookshack,

at www.cookshackamerica.com, also has some excellent units.

Match the Food to the Cooking Method

Whether you're cooking domestic meat or wild game, you must use the proper cooking method for the particular cut to ensure success. Direct high-heat grilling works great for tender, smaller cuts such as steaks, chops, fish fillets or boneless chicken breasts. If you tried to cook a roast or a whole chicken by this method, however, the outside would be charred and inedible long before the interior was cooked through. Tough cuts such as pork shoulder and beef brisket require long, slow cooking, and are best prepared with the low, indirect heat used for barbecue or smoking.

Fat content affects the way that meat cooks. A well-marbled strip steak can be cooked at a higher temperature than a lean skirt steak. Unlike beef, venison has no internal marbling and can withstand only a limited amount of high heat before the protein in the meat shrinks and toughens. This is why most choice venison cuts are cooked quickly and only to a medium-rare state; larger or less-choice cuts require slow cooking with indirect heat. The same is true of wild game birds, which generally have far less fat than domestic poultry or farm-raised game birds. Brining before cooking (page 53), as well as basting with sauces during cooking, adds moisture and succulence to poultry of all sorts, and is a particularly good idea when grilling wild game birds. Pork has little marbling, but larger cuts generally have enough external fat to baste the meat during cooking. Basting or brining is helpful for smaller cuts of pork such as chops.

The tenderness of a piece of meat is also related to the amount of connective tissue in the cut. The general rule is that the closer the particular cut is to the ground, the more connective tissue it has. Thus, beef shanks have more connective tissue—and therefore are tougher—than loin steaks or rump roast. Animals also develop stronger connective tissue as they get older, so meat from older animals is tougher than that from younger animals. Most store-bought chickens and turkeys are young, so they have tender meat that can be cooked easily and quickly by a dry-heat method such as grilling. Older, tougher birds should be cooked by slower methods (such as low-and-slow barbecuing) that will break down the connective tissue. The same holds true for venison; a choice cut from the top round section of a young deer will be more tender than the same cut from a much older deer. Venison from older animals will benefit much more from a marinade than venison from a younger animal, and works well for barbecue and slow smoking.

Fish has very little connective tissue; it is naturally tender and cooks quickly. Fish falls into two categories: lean or oily. Lean fish include catfish, bass, perch, grouper, haddock, halibut, striped bass, pike, walleye, flounder, sole, cod and red snapper. Oily fish include salmon, trout, tuna, Chilean sea bass, swordfish, bluefish, steelhead, char, shad and mackerel. Lean fish tend to cook very well in foil packets or wrapped in leaves to prevent direct contact with the heat source. Oily fish do better when grilled directly over the heat; a medium or medium-low setting cooks the fish through without charring the outside.

Judging Doneness of Meat, Poultry and Fish

There is no substitute for an instant-read meat thermometer when it comes time to judge the doneness of meat and poultry—particularly larger cuts such as a roast or a whole chicken. Insert the thermometer into the meat so that the tip is in the center of the meat; in the case of a steak, this may mean inserting the thermometer sideways through the edge of the meat. The tip shouldn't touch any bone, which may give a false reading. See sidebar on page 12 for the temperatures at which various foods are properly cooked.

Meat, fish and poultry—particularly larger cuts—continue to cook even after they are removed from the grill; this carryover cooking can raise the temperature by 5°F–10°F (3°C–6°C). When judging doneness of a larger cut, remove it from the grill when it is not quite to the final temperature; cover the meat loosely with a tent of foil and let it stand for 5 to 15 minutes, during which time the temperature should rise to the desired level.

Although it is often helpful to check the color of the meat, this is not always a reliable way to judge doneness. For example, common wisdom says that hamburgers are medium-rare when pink in the middle, and well-done when the meat is gray all the way through. However, a phenomenon known as premature browning may cause the meat to lose its pink color before it is cooked to the well-done stage (160°F/71°C). At the other end of the spectrum, sometimes hamburger and other meats remain pinkish even when well-done. This can be caused by particular seasoning blends (those containing a cure will give a pink color to meat, even when it is fully cooked—think of corned beef, which is bright pink even though it is fully cooked), or even by the exact makeup of the ground meat. An instant-read thermometer inserted into the center of the burger takes the guesswork out of cooking.

Some cuts, such as beef brisket, pork shoulder or ribs, aren't judged by temperature; they are cooked until they reach the desired level of tenderness. For example, if you can easily insert a fork into a brisket or shoulder, it is tender. Ribs are generally cooked until the meat shrinks away from the ends of the bone tips. Even in meats that are best judged by temperature, such visual clues can be helpful in determining doneness. The leg of a chicken or turkey will wriggle freely when the bird is properly cooked, for example, and juices will no longer be tinged with pink when the thigh is pierced with a fork. Note that occasionally, chicken will appear reddish at the bone even when properly cooked; this is another example of why temperature is a better guide to appearance than doneness.

Some experienced cooks prefer to judge doneness of steaks by feel rather than poking a thermometer into the meat (which does allow juices to escape). A steak that is cooked rare should feel like the flesh between your thumb and pointer finger when your hand is held limp. Medium-rare meat will feel a bit firmer, but not hard; it will be slightly resistant to your touch. Medium steak feels firm in the center and springs back from your touch. Another method is to

JUDGING DONENESS

FOOD	FAHRENHEIT	CELSIUS
Poultry and Game Birds		
Chicken or Turkey		
Breast	160°F	71°C
Thighs	170°F	77°C
Ground	165°F	74°C
Duck or Goose		
Medium-rare (breast only)	145°F	63°C
Well-done (parts)	170°F	77°C
Pheasant, Partridge, Quail	160°F	71°C
Dove	155°F	68°C
Meat		
Beef Roast or Steak		
Rare	130°F	55°C
Medium	140°F	60°C
Well-done	155°F	68°C
Ground Beef or Lamb*		
Rare	135°F	57°C
Medium	150°F	66°C
Well-done	160°F	71°C

The USDA recommends that ground beef or lamb be cooked to 160°F (71°C) for safety.

FOOD	FAHRENHEIT	CELSIUS
Lamb Roast or Chops		
Rare	135°F	57°C
Medium	150°F	66°C
Well-done	160°F	71°C
Pork, any cut	160°F	71°C

Note: Many people prefer pork cooked slightly less done, 150°F or 155°F (66°C to 68°C). The trichinosis parasite is killed at 137°F (58°C). The USDA recommends cooking all pork to an internal temperature of 160°F (71°C) for safety.

FOOD	FAHRENHEIT	CELSIUS
Venison, Elk, Moose, etc.		
Rare	130°F	55°C
Medium	140°F	60°C
Well-done	155°F	68°C
Fish		
Fish, General	140°F	60°C
Tuna or Salmon		
Rare**	125°F	52°C

***See note on page 62 about safety and rare fish.*

observe the color of the juices that run from the steak when it's pricked. If the juices run red, then the steak is probably cooked medium-rare. Once the juice turns pink, the steak has cooked to medium and should be removed immediately to avoid overcooking.

Although fish can be tested with an instant-read thermometer, it is easier in most cases to judge doneness with visual clues. To check for doneness, gently separate the flesh at the thickest point with a fork; the fish is perfectly cooked when the flesh has just turned from translucent to opaque. This is a more reliable indicator than the traditional flake test, which states that fish is done when it flakes; by the time the flaking is noticeable, the fish may be overcooked and dry. Remember that fish cooks quickly—much more quickly than the red meats we may be accustomed to grilling—and is easily overcooked.

Due to their small size, shellfish are judged by visual clues rather than temperature to determine doneness. Shrimp are done when they are creamy white throughout and no longer translucent; they generally turn pink on the outside. Clams, mussels and oysters should be removed from the grill when they open. Throw away any that do not open in a reasonable amount of time; these were dead before they hit the grill, and should not be eaten.

Thoughts on Health Issues

In recent years, some grilled foods have been implicated as possible health risks. According to the American Institute for Cancer Research (AICR), when fats from meat and poultry fall onto the hot coals and are burned, the vapors which are deposited onto the meat may be carcinogenic. In addition, high-heat dry cooking methods such as grilling and broiling may cause other carcinogenic compounds to form in muscle meats (poultry, red meat and even fish).

However, the studies also show that marinating meat, even for short periods, reduces the formation of these troublesome compounds. Certainly, it is prudent advice—from both a health and a taste standpoint—to prevent flare-ups and burning while grilling. Lean meats will cause fewer flare-ups, and are a more healthy choice anyway. Fruits, vegetables and blackened foods (in which only the seasoning is charred) also present a lower risk, according to the AICR.

Doubtless in part because of the setting, cooking outdoors has always had a special appeal for those who hunt and fish. In many cases they already have experience in preparing shore lunches or hunting-camp dinners. That brings to the forefront some of the health issues connected with wild game, and to a lesser degree, fish. Basically, wild game is healthier and better for you than domestic meats. For starters, it contains none of the chemicals that can come from inoculations, growth supplements, medicines and the like regularly used in domestic animals. Of course, care does need to be taken in the dressing, handling and preparation of wild game, but even there a reliable processor (or doing your own preparation) likely guarantees a far higher sanitary level than you get with meat purchased at a local market.

Another health-related benefit from wild game focuses on fat and cholesterol. To take just one comparison, beef versus venison, the latter is virtually fat free (and any fat found in the dressing process should be removed). It also has much lower cholesterol levels and is the only red meat some heart patients are allowed to eat. Of course, when eating fish you have caught you do need to be aware of any problems—mercury, lead, PCBs or the like—in waters where they were taken. Local agencies monitor this quite closely, and if there are warnings you can find them in fishing regulations.

Grilling Meat, Poultry & Fish

O f all backyard cooking methods, grilling is the most familiar and most popular. Most grilling takes place fairly quickly; dinner can often be ready in less than an hour from the time you start the grill.

Whether you're working with a charcoal or gas grill, there are two distinct styles of grilling: direct heat and indirect heat. With direct heat, the food is placed on the grill grate directly over the heat source; this works well for tender cuts that are less than 1 inch (2.5 cm) in thickness or those that take less than 30 minutes to cook, such as most steaks, chops, sausages and kabobs. Direct heat is also used to sear foods that require longer cooking; after searing, the food is moved to an area of the grate that is away from the heat for slower cooking.

With indirect heat, the grill acts as an outside oven. The heat source is off to the sides of the grill, and the food is placed on the grate over an area with no heat underneath. The grill lid is closed and the heat circulates as it reflects off the lid to cook the food evenly from all sides. Food items most often used with indirect cooking are those that take more than 30 minutes to cook: roasts, whole chicken or turkey, slabs of ribs, and whole fish. A drip pan is often placed on the coal grate underneath the food to catch drips, which keeps the grill clean and prevents flare-ups. With longer cooking methods, the pan is sometimes filled with water to add humidity to the cooking process.

Preparing a Charcoal Grill for Cooking

Before you put fresh coals in the grill, it should be cleared of ash and residue from the previous fire. Pile the coals in a rough pyramid, saturate with lighter fluid and carefully ignite (or, use one of the more environmentally friendly options discussed in the sidebar on page 17). When the flames die down and the coals are glowing red and covered with gray ash, arrange them as required for the cooking method you're using. Put the cooking grate in position, and allow it to heat up for a few minutes before adding the food.

• **For direct cooking,** spread the coals out in an even layer that is 2 to 3 inches (5 to 7.5 cm) larger than the food you'll be cooking. A thick layer of coals provides a hotter fire; a thin layer of coals provides a cooler fire.

• **For indirect cooking,** there must be an area on the cooking grate that has no coals below it. It's best to arrange the coals in two banks at opposite sides of the grill, leaving the center clear of fire; some quality grills

come with charcoal rails or baskets to hold the coals along the sides. You can also pile all the coals along one side and place the food on the grate at the opposite side, but the food will not cook as evenly as it would if surrounded on both sides by hot coals.

To use a water pan with indirect cooking, place an old metal baking dish or a disposable aluminum baking pan between the banks of coals, or on the opposite side of the coal grate from the lit coals. Fill the pan with water, beer or other liquid. Add the cooking grate, and place the food on the cooking grate above the pan, not above the heat.

For longer cooking methods, you'll need to add additional coals partway through the cooking time. It's best to start the additional coals in a chimney starter (or in a separate grill) and add them to the fire after they are ready. If you add

unstarted coals directly to an already started fire, you may get uneven heat as the fresh coals start up (and, if you are using manufactured briquettes, they may impart a chemical taste to your food as the chemicals burn off). Natural lump charcoal is the best choice if you plan to add unstarted coals directly to an already started fire. Be sure to give the fire plenty of air as the new coals are starting up.

Preparing a Gas Grill for Cooking

Before starting the fire, clean out any residue such as drippings from the previous fire. Start the burners on high, cover the grill, and allow it to heat for about 10 minutes (or as directed by manufacturer); then, adjust the temperature as required for the individual recipe.

• **For direct cooking,** simply use as many burners as needed to provide a grilling area large enough for the food. In gas grills with two or three burners, this probably means using all of them; with larger grills containing more burners, you will probably need just two or three burners for most foods. If you have a grill with more than three burners, you can actually cook several types of food that require different heat levels at the same time, simply by adjusting the levels of the various burners to create multiple heat zones.

• **For indirect cooking,** light the outer two burners of a three-burner grill, leaving the central burner unlit. If your grill has more than three burners, simply use enough of the outer burners for the size of the food, leaving one or two burners in the middle unlit. If your grill has just two burners, light only one and place the food over the unlit burner; you'll need to rotate the food more frequently to get even cooking.

To use a water pan with indirect cooking on a gas grill, follow the manufacturer's recommendations for the placement of the pan; fill it with water, beer or other liquid and put the food on the cooking grate above the pan, not above the heat. Some grills have a special water-pan attachment, or a pan that is underneath the burners.

Judging and Adjusting the Heat Level

Whether you're cooking with charcoal or gas, you need to monitor the heat level. Each grilling recipe in this book includes a recommended heat level, as well as noting whether the recipe requires direct or indirect heat. To judge the heat level, hold your hand about 5 inches (12.5 cm) above the cooking grate, and begin counting ("one-thousand-one, one-thousand-two" works well for most people). If you can hold your hand there for a count of eight to ten before it becomes too uncomfortable, your heat level is low. A count of four or five indicates a medium fire, while a count of one or two means your fire is hot.

To adjust the heat level of a gas grill, simply increase or decrease the gas flow, or turn burners on or off as needed to get the proper heat level. Charcoal grills are more complicated; the heat level is controlled by the amount and arrangement of the coals, as well as the amount of air that the fire receives. Obviously, more coals make a hotter fire; but you can also control the heat level by adjusting the thickness of the charcoal layer. For low-heat cooking, spread out the lit coals in a single layer; for high-heat cooking, pile up a thick layer of coals—three or four deep. To cool down a too-hot fire, close the vents partway; to warm up the fire, open all the vents (and add fresh coals as needed).

In cold or windy weather, you'll need to use more fuel to maintain the proper temperature. Yes, you can grill in Minnesota in January; it just takes a whole lot more charcoal (or gas) to get the job done. Keep the grill covered except when it's absolutely necessary to open it; and if the grill just can't maintain the heat long enough to cook the food, there is no shame in finishing the food in the oven.

ENVIRONMENTALLY FRIENDLY ALTERNATIVES TO LIGHTER FLUID

CHIMNEY STARTER. This aluminum canister requires no chemical starters. Fill the perforated bottom of the canister with several sheets of crumpled newspaper. Add coals to the canister and place on a flameproof surface. Ignite the newspaper, which will eventually start the coals; you'll be ready to cook in about 20 minutes. Chimney starters hold only a somewhat limited number of coals.

ELECTRIC STARTER. This is a loop made of a sturdy electrical rod. Place the starter loop onto the coal grate and pile coals over it. Plug the starter in; it will soon be red-hot, and will start the coals. When they are well started, carefully remove the starter and set it down on a flameproof surface until completely cool.

SOLID FUEL LIGHTER CUBES. These waxy cubes can be found at specialty outdoor stores. Tuck a few around the edges of your pyramid of coals, then light the cubes. The starter cubes burn hotly, and will ignite the coals.

ALCOHOL-BASED FIRESTARTING GEL. This odorless product is used like petroleum-based starter fluid, but is non-toxic and does not add any objectionable flavor. Look in a camping store for this product; you can also order it at www.bmfp.com or www.hasty-bake.com.

Grilling Accessories

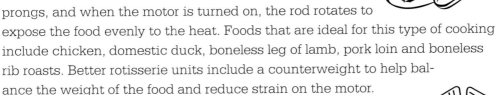

Rotisserie or Spit—This is an add-on appliance that makes it easy to grill-roast larger food items such as whole chickens or roasts. A long rod is attached to an external electric motor that hangs above the grill (generally attached to a hood); food is secured to the rod with special prongs, and when the motor is turned on, the rod rotates to expose the food evenly to the heat. Foods that are ideal for this type of cooking include chicken, domestic duck, boneless leg of lamb, pork loin and boneless rib roasts. Better rotisserie units include a counterweight to help balance the weight of the food and reduce strain on the motor.

Hinged Grilling Basket—This wire or perforated metal basket prevents smaller or fragile items from falling through the grate, or from breaking up during turning. It is ideal for delicate items like vegetables, hamburgers, fish and small potatoes. Lightly oil the insides of the basket, then add the food and close the hinged cover. Place it on the grill and when one side is done, flip the basket over to cook the other side.

Fish Grilling Basket—Similar to the hinged grilling basket above, this specialty grilling basket is shaped like a whole fish. With this, you can cook an entire fish without worrying about it breaking when you turn it over. Fish grilling baskets work best when the size matches that of the fish to be cooked, and so are somewhat limited in their use.

Grilling Wok—These specialty woks come in several types and sizes. A perforated grilling wok is a flat-bottomed wok with flared sides and small holes throughout that allow the heat and flavor of the grill to come through. It is a unique and fun way to stir-fry foods over direct heat on the grill. Other grill woks are like traditional solid woks; some, from China, are made of porcelain enamel for stick-free cooking.

Instant-Read Meat Thermometer—Helps you accurately gauge doneness.

Long-Handled Tongs—These protect hands and prevent piercing meat (which causes precious juices to be lost).

Long-Handled Metal Spatula—LamsonSharp makes a 6-inch-wide (15.25-cm-wide) stainless-steel spatula with a heatproof resin handle that is great for turning or moving large burgers, fragile fish or foil packets around on the grill.

Long-Handled Meat Fork—Great for lifting large roasts and aids in carving.

Long-Handled Basting Brush or Mop—It keeps heat away from your hands as you baste (wear long-sleeved heatproof mitts when basting in case there are flare-ups from oily basting liquid).

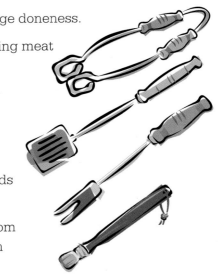

Mesh or Wire Grill Screen—This round mesh wire screen is primarily designed to cook pizzas in the oven, but it can also be used for a variety of items on the grill. It supports whatever food is being cooked and prevents pieces of food from falling through the grate. It can also be used to grill pizzas, toast bread or heat hamburger buns.

Skewers—Metal skewers offer more rigidity, can hold heavier food items, and are often longer than bamboo skewers. The flat, metal type keeps food from spinning as you turn the skewers on the grill. Bamboo skewers cool much more quickly than metal skewers.

Small Spray Bottle of Water—Helps control flare-ups when using charcoal (don't use water on gas grills unless directed to do so by the manufacturer). You may wish to keep a fire extinguisher handy in case a fire gets out of control.

Heatproof Mitts—Heavy-duty, long-sleeved ones are especially good for handling metal items such as skewers or cast-iron skillets, and to protect hands and arms from heat.

Stiff Wire Brush/Scraper—It's a must to clean food residue from the grill grates. A brass-bristled brush won't rust and is gentle on porcelain enamel. A steel-bristled brush works better on cast-iron grates.

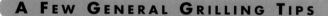

A FEW GENERAL GRILLING TIPS

• Check a gas grill for leaks at the beginning of the season, or any time you switch gas canisters. Make a mixture of liquid dish detergent and water, then spray or brush it over all connection joints and turn on the gas. If there are any leaks, you will see bubbles; turn the gas off immediately and correct the problem (or don't use the grill).

• For best results, let the food stand at room temperature for a time before placing it on the hot grill. This will ensure that the food is cooked evenly and quickly throughout.

• Keep the cooking grate clean; food sticks to a dirty grate. Before adding the food, oil the clean grate lightly (unless the food is already coated with oil, or is very fatty); use a long-handled brush dipped in oil, or rub an oil-dampened paper towel over the grate with long tongs (wear barbecue mitts, move quickly to avoid lighting the towel on fire, and don't use so much oil that the towel is dripping).

• If the recipe calls for use of a drip pan, simply put an old metal baking pan or a disposable aluminum pan underneath the cooking grate below the area where the food will be placed. You could also create a homemade drip pan with heavy-duty foil.

• Cover the grill to smother a flare-up, or move the food to a cooler area of the grate until the flames die down.

• Because nearly all grilled foods taste best hot off the grill, it's important to have all other dishes ready, the table set to eat, the proper utensils at hand to remove the food from the grill, and a clean platter to hold the cooked food. Never re-use the same platter that held raw meat, fish or poultry unless it has been washed in hot, soapy water.

• It's easiest to clean the cooking grate while it is still warm. If your eating schedule permits, do this shortly after removing the food, before the grill has a chance to cool completely.

Elk Tenderloin Grilled <u>with</u> Asian Spices

3 servings
Preliminary preparation: Under 15 minutes initial prep, 2 to 4 hours marinating
Grilling: Direct medium-high heat, under 15 minutes

1 elk tenderloin or venison loin portion
  (about 12 ounces/340 g)

4 cloves garlic

2 shallots, quartered

1 fresh red chile pepper, seeds and veins removed

1x1-inch (2.5x2.5-cm) piece of lemon zest

1 tablespoon (15 ml/12 g) sugar

1/2 teaspoon (2.5 ml/3 g) coarse salt

2 tablespoons (30 ml/18 g) sesame seeds

1 tablespoon (15 ml) dark sesame oil

1 tablespoon (15 ml) canola oil

2 teaspoons (10 ml) soy sauce

Spicy Vietnamese Dipping Sauce, optional
  (see below)

Vietnamese serving accompaniments, optional
  (see below)

Pat tenderloin dry. With sharp knife, score in a diamond pattern on all sides, cutting about 1/8 inch (3 mm) deep and 1/2 inch (1.25 cm) apart. Place in glass baking dish; set aside. With mortar and pestle, pound garlic, shallots, pepper, lemon zest, sugar and salt to a smooth paste. Stir in sesame seeds, sesame oil, canola oil and soy sauce. Pour mixture over tenderloin, turning to coat all sides. Cover and refrigerate for 2 to 4 hours, turning once or twice.

30 minutes before you're ready to cook, remove tenderloin from refrigerator and allow to stand at room temperature. Prepare grill for direct medium-high heat; lightly oil grate. Drain tenderloin; place directly on grate over heat. Cook to medium-rare or medium doneness, about 15 minutes, turning several times. Slice thinly before serving. Serve with dipping sauce, with or without Vietnamese serving accompaniments.

Spicy Vietnamese Dipping Sauce

1 clove garlic

Half of a fresh red chile pepper, seeds and veins
  removed

1 tablespoon (15 ml/12 g) sugar

2 tablespoons (30 ml) rice vinegar

2 tablespoons (30 ml) Vietnamese fish sauce
  (<u>nuoc mam</u>)

2 tablespoons (30 ml) water

1 tablespoon (15 ml) freshly squeezed lime juice

With mortar and pestle, pound garlic, chile and sugar to a smooth paste. Transfer to small bowl and add remaining ingredients; stir well to blend.

Vietnamese Serving Accompaniments

To serve this in true Vietnamese style, present the tenderloin—very thinly sliced—with the following accompaniments, arranged attractively on a platter. Each diner places a few pieces of meat on a lettuce leaf, along with green onions, fresh cilantro, bean sprouts and a few cooked noodles. The parcel is rolled up and dipped into the Spicy Vietnamese Dipping Sauce, then eaten out-of-hand with the cucumber and carrot on the side.

Half of a head of Boston lettuce with large leaves,
  leaves separated

3 green onions, sliced 1/4 inch (6 mm) thick

A handful of fresh cilantro leaves

4 ounces (115 g) fresh bean sprouts

4 ounces (115 g) thin rice vermicelli, cooked
  according to package directions and drained

1 cucumber, peel scored and seeds removed, cut
  into wedges about 2 inches (5 cm) long

1 cup (130 g) baby carrots

Mustard-Pepper Grilled Tenderloin

3 or 4 servings
Preliminary preparation: Under 30 minutes initial prep, 30 minutes marinating
Grilling: Direct medium-high heat, under 15 minutes

If you have any leftover sauce, store it in the refrigerator for up to a week, and use it to perk up pork, lamb or other meats.

1 tablespoon (15 ml/6 g) whole mixed-color peppercorns

1 cup (240 ml) chicken broth

1 teaspoon (5 ml) coarsely chopped fresh rosemary, or 1/2 teaspoon (2.5 ml) coarsely crushed dried

1/4 cup (60 ml/60 g) Dijon mustard

1 tablespoon (15 ml) olive oil

2 teaspoons (10 ml) balsamic or red wine vinegar

1 teaspoon (5 ml/2 g) mustard seeds

2 whole venison tenderloins (8 to 12 ounces/ 225 to 340 g each) or 1 1/2 pounds (680 g) elk, moose or beef tenderloin, trimmed as necessary

Crush peppercorns coarsely with mortar and pestle (or, place peppercorns on work surface and place a heavy skillet on top, then press and twist the skillet to crush the peppercorns). Combine crushed peppercorns, chicken broth and rosemary in small saucepan. Heat to boiling over high heat, and cook until reduced to 1/3 cup (80 ml), about 15 minutes. Remove from heat. Add mustard, oil, vinegar and mustard seeds; stir well and set aside to cool to room temperature.

Place tenderloins in nonreactive dish and pour about 3 tablespoons (45 ml) of the mustard sauce over the tenderloins; brush evenly on all sides of tenderloins. Let stand at room temperature for 20 or 30 minutes. Set remaining sauce aside until serving time.

When you're ready to cook, prepare grill for direct medium-high heat; lightly oil grate. Place tenderloins on grate over heat. Grill for about 5 minutes per side, or to desired doneness. Slice tenderloins across the grain into inch-thick (2.5-cm) pieces and serve with mustard-pepper sauce.

Barbecued Pork Tenderloin

4 to 6 servings
Preliminary preparation: Under 15 minutes initial prep, 8 to 12 hours marinating
Grilling: Initial searing, followed by indirect high heat, under 30 minutes

Barbecue Marinade

1/4 cup (55 g/half of a stick) unsalted butter

1 small rib celery, minced

1 cup (240 ml/200 g) finely chopped onion

3 cloves garlic, minced

1 cup (240 ml) red wine vinegar

1 cup (240 ml) Worcestershire sauce

2 tablespoons (30 ml/10 g) dry mustard powder

2 tablespoons (30 ml/12 g) paprika

1 tablespoon (15 ml/15 g) brown sugar (packed)

1 tablespoon (15 ml) molasses

2 teaspoons (10 ml/4 g) cayenne pepper

1 1/2 pounds (680 g) pork tenderloin

1 tablespoon (15 ml) dark sesame oil

In small saucepan, melt butter over medium-high heat. When butter is foamy, add celery, onion and garlic; sauté until soft. Stir in remaining marinade ingredients and heat to boiling, stirring occasionally. Remove from heat and let cool. This can be done a day ahead of time. You should get about 3 cups (690 ml).

Place pork in glass baking dish (or zipper-style plastic bag). Add cooled marinade, turning pork to coat. Cover and refrigerate for 8 to 12 hours, or overnight.

When you're ready to cook, prepare grill for indirect high heat. Drain pork, transferring marinade to small saucepan. Heat marinade to boiling. Cook until marinade is thick and syrupy, 5 to 8 minutes. Pat pork dry with paper towels and brush with sesame oil. Place pork on grate directly over heat. Grill until seared on all sides, about 3 minutes per side. Move pork to area away from heat. After a few minutes, begin basting pork with reduced marinade. Continue cooking, basting frequently, until center of pork reaches 155°F (68°C). Transfer pork to serving platter and let stand for 5 minutes. Slice pork on the diagonal and serve hot.

Grill-Roasted Rosemary Pork Loin

8 servings
Preliminary preparation: Under 15 minutes
Grilling: Initial searing, followed by indirect high heat, about an hour

2 pounds (900 g) boneless pork loin, trimmed of excess fat

3 fresh rosemary sprigs

4 cloves garlic

Freshly ground black pepper

4 to 6 tablespoons (55 to 90 g) unsalted butter, softened

A piece of heavy kitchen string (about 3 feet/90 cm long), soaked in water

Slice loin down the middle vertically, about three-quarters of the way through. Open loin up. Remove leaves from rosemary sprigs and mince them with the garlic. Mix together well. Season rosemary mixture with pepper to taste. Sprinkle about half of the rosemary mixture inside the loin. Dot with 2 to 3 tablespoons (30 to 45 g) butter. Close loin, then tie together in several places with wet kitchen string. Rub outside of loin with an additional 2 to 3 tablespoons (30 to 45 g) butter, and then with remaining rosemary mixture.

Prepare grill for indirect high heat. Position drip pan between coal banks, or away from heated area of gas grill.

Place loin on grate directly over heat. Grill until seared on all sides, about 3 minutes per side; watch for flare-ups, and squirt with water as necessary. Move loin to grate over drip pan. Cover grill and cook until internal temperature reaches 155°F (68°C), about 45 minutes. Transfer loin to serving platter; tent lightly with foil and let stand for 10 minutes before slicing. The internal temperature of the loin will rise during this time; final temperature should be 160°F (71°C).

Grilled Lamb Loin

4 servings
Preliminary preparation: Under 15 minutes initial prep, 1 to 2 hours marinating
Grilling: Direct high heat, under 15 minutes

<u>Marinade</u>
1 cup (240 ml) olive oil
1/2 cup (120 ml/80 g) finely chopped onion
1/2 cup (120 ml/50 g) chopped green onions (white and green parts)
2 tablespoons (30 ml/2.5 g) minced fresh parsley
2 tablespoons (30 ml) fresh lemon juice

1 tablespoon (15 ml/10 g) minced shallots
1 teaspoon (5 ml/6 g) kosher salt
1 teaspoon (5 ml/2 g) freshly ground black pepper

2 boneless lamb loins (8 ounces/225 g each), trimmed

In nonreactive dish, whisk together all marinade ingredients. Add lamb, turning to coat. Cover and let marinate at room temperature for 1 to 2 hours, turning lamb in marinade several times.

When you're ready to cook, prepare grill for direct high heat. Drain lamb, discarding marinade. Place lamb on

grate over heat and sear all sides, 1 to 2 minutes per side. At this stage the lamb should be rare to medium-rare. If you want the meat more well-done, continue to cook to desired doneness, turning as needed. Remove from heat and let stand for 5 minutes before slicing.

If you took a survey of people's favorite barbecued foods, ribs would come up pretty high on the list. The ideal technique for preparing the perfect rack of ribs is a matter of some debate, however. Certainly, the most classic method for preparing ribs is slow-cooking in a smoker or wood-burning barbecue; purists insist on natural wood as a fuel, but you can get good results by adding smoking-wood chunks to a charcoal or propane fire. Please see page 85 for information on smoking ribs, and page 88 if you're interested in cooking ribs with natural wood.

For the backyard cook who doesn't have a smoker or wood-burning barbecue, there are several approaches that produce good results—although the purist would point out that these are not "barbecue" in the classic sense. A popular method is to slow-cook the ribs by roasting in the oven or simmering on the stovetop; the cooked, tenderized ribs are then slathered with sauce and finished on the grill. (This method is used at many restaurants, by the way.) Another option involves a short par-boil followed by a lengthy soak in a flavorful sauce; the ribs are then cooked over moderate heat on the grill. Here are some recipes to get you started; once you work with these recipes, you'll probably come up with your own variations.

Spicy Roasted Pork Ribs

2 servings
Preliminary preparation: 2½ hours oven-roasting
Grilling: Direct medium heat, under 15 minutes

While baby back ribs are the most tender, spareribs or racks of ribs from wild hogs also work well with this approach. Roasting in the oven makes the grilling process quick and easy. The roasting can be done a day ahead if you like.

1 rack pork back ribs (about 2 pounds/900 g), or substitute as noted above

Dry Spice Rub
1 tablespoon (15 ml/5 g) chili powder
1½ teaspoons (7.5 ml) dried cilantro
1½ teaspoons (7.5 ml/3 g) paprika
1½ teaspoons (7.5 ml/7.5 g) dark brown sugar (packed)

1 teaspoon (5 ml/2 g) ground cumin
1 teaspoon (5 ml/3 g) kosher salt
½ teaspoon (2.5 ml/1 g) freshly ground pepper

Prepared barbecue sauce as needed (about 1 cup/240 ml, plus additional for serving)

Heat oven to 300°F (150°C). Line bottom of broiler pan with foil; spray broiler-pan rack with nonstick spray. Peel membrane from back side of ribs if you like (see page 26); cut rack in half to fit broiler pan if necessary. In small bowl, stir together all rub ingredients. Sprinkle and press all of the rub into both sides of rib rack. Place ribs on broiler-pan rack, meaty-side up. Bake until tender, 2 to 2½ hours, rotating pan after the first hour and every 30 minutes thereafter. If ribs are

prepared in advance, cool, wrap and refrigerate until ready for final cooking.

When you're ready for final cooking, prepare grill for direct medium heat; lightly oil grate. Place ribs on grate over heat. Baste with barbecue sauce until ribs are well coated; grill until nicely glazed and heated through, 10 to 15 minutes, turning ribs frequently and brushing with sauce. Cut into individual ribs and serve with additional barbecue sauce for dipping.

Pork and beef ribs are available in a number of cuts. Pork spareribs are cut from the lower portion of the ribs; this is the same area from which bacon is cut. St. Louis-style ribs are pork spareribs that have had the breastbone, or brisket, removed; the separated breastbone portion is marketed as rib tips. If the skirt muscle is removed from the inside of a rack of St. Louis-style ribs and the ends are squared off, the resulting cut is sometimes called Kansas City ribs. Back ribs—also called loin ribs or Canadian ribs—come from higher up on the pig, next to the backbone; they're leaner and thinner, with a more pronounced curve than spareribs. Country-style pork ribs are actually butterflied pork blade chops with the rib bone still attached.

A rack, or slab, of spareribs contains 11 to 14 bones, depending on how it was trimmed; a rack of back ribs contains 8 to 14 bones. A full rack of spareribs generally weighs from 3 to 4 pounds (1.36 to 1.8 kg), and will serve 2 to 4 people. Back ribs are trimmed in two widths; a rack of 3¾-inch-wide (9.5-cm) back ribs will generally weigh about 1½ pounds (680 g), while a rack of 5½-inch-wide (14-cm) back ribs will weigh anywhere from 1¾ to 2½ pounds (790 g to 1.125 kg). A slab of wide back ribs will serve 2 people; if you're cooking the narrower racks, plan on 2 racks to serve 3 people. Country-style ribs vary quite a bit; depending on how the butcher trims, there will be 3 to 6 country-style ribs per side. Generally, 6 ribs will weigh about 2 pounds (900 g) and will serve 2 or 3 people.

Beef is cut in a similar fashion to pork, but the cuts are named differently. The ribs from the lower section are called short ribs; they're meaty, but require slow cooking to become tender. Beef back ribs—which are sometimes called beef spareribs, although they are from a different part of the animal than pork spareribs—are the leftovers created when a beef loin is boned to make a boneless prime rib roast. They're more tender than short ribs, but are less meaty. There are 6 or 7 beef back ribs per side; a 6-bone rack is generally 2 to 3 pounds (900 g to 1.36 kg), and will serve 2 or 3 people. Short ribs are usually cut into shorter lengths, so there are as many as 14 per side. Short ribs are sold by weight, not by the rack; plan on ¾ to 1 pound (340 to 454 g) per serving.

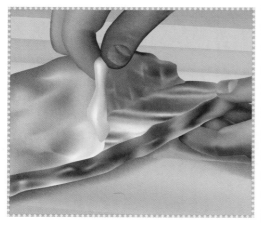

The back (inside) of a rack of pork spareribs is covered with a thin, translucent, flexible sheet of tissue, or membrane. The ribs will be more tender and easier to eat if this is removed before seasoning or cooking; in addition, removing the membrane allows any rub, as well as the smoke or grilling flavor, to penetrate the meat better.

Lift the corner of the membrane from the ribs, using a blunt knife to help you start. Once it's started, grasp the membrane with a paper towel for better grip. Peel away and discard the membrane. It may come off in a single piece; if it tears, peel away smaller pieces individually.

Ribs in Beer

Succulent Pork Spareribs

3 or 4 servings
Preliminary preparation: Under an hour initial prep, 6 to 12 hours marinating
Grilling: Initial searing, followed by indirect medium heat, under 30 minutes

1 rack pork spareribs (about 3½ pounds/ 1.6 kg)

¼ cup (60 ml) **peanut oil**

1 teaspoon (5 ml/3 g) **dry mustard powder**

1 teaspoon (5 ml/2 g) **paprika**

½ teaspoon (2.5 ml/1 g) **cayenne pepper**

½ teaspoon (2.5 ml) **dried oregano**

½ teaspoon (2.5 ml/1 g) **ground cumin**

1 cup (240 ml) **ketchup**

⅓ cup (80 ml/80 g) **tomato paste**

¼ cup (60 ml) **honey**

2 tablespoons (30 ml) **Worcestershire sauce**

1 tablespoon (15 ml) **cider vinegar**

2 cloves garlic, chopped

TIP: Leftover ribs can be wrapped in foil and reheated in a 250°F (120°C) oven for 20 to 30 minutes.

Begin heating a stockpot full of water to boiling. Peel membrane from back side of ribs if you like (see page 26); cut rack as necessary to fit into stockpot. When water is boiling, add ribs; return to boiling and cook for 3 or 4 minutes. Remove ribs and set aside until cool. Meanwhile, combine oil, mustard, paprika, cayenne pepper, oregano and cumin in saucepan; mix well. Cook over medium heat until hot, stirring several times. Add ketchup, tomato paste, honey, Worcestershire sauce, vinegar and garlic; stir to blend. Cook for 5 to 10 minutes longer, stirring occasionally. Remove from heat; set aside until cool.

In nonreactive dish or large zipper-style plastic bag, combine ribs and about half of the sauce (or enough to coat), turning to coat; reserve remaining sauce. Refrigerate ribs and remaining sauce for at least 6 hours, or as long as overnight.

When you're ready to cook, prepare grill for indirect medium heat; lightly oil grate. Remove ribs from marinade; discard marinade. Place ribs on grate directly over heat; sear on both sides. Move ribs to area away from heat. Baste with reserved sauce. Cook until well-done throughout, about 20 minutes, turning and basting with sauce several times. Cut into individual ribs and serve with remaining sauce for dipping.

Ribs in Beer

4 or 5 servings
Preliminary preparation: 1 to 1½ hours stovetop simmering
Grilling: Direct medium heat, under 15 minutes

4 to 5 pounds (1.8 to 2.3 kg) **beef, venison or pork ribs**

2 large **onions,** quartered

3 or 4 cans **beer** (12 ounces/350 ml each), or enough to cover ribs

1 tablespoon (15 ml/6 g) **black pepper,** or to taste

Salt

Prepared barbecue sauce as needed (about 1 cup/ 240 ml, plus additional for serving)

Peel membrane from back side of ribs if you like (see page 26); cut rack as necessary to fit into Dutch oven. In Dutch oven, combine ribs and onions. Add beer to cover; add pepper and salt to taste. Simmer over medium heat until tender, 1 to 1½ hours. Remove from Dutch oven and drain well. Prepare grill for direct medium heat; lightly oil grate. Place ribs on grate over heat. Baste with barbecue sauce until ribs are well coated; grill until nicely glazed and heated through, 10 to 15 minutes, turning ribs frequently and brushing with sauce. Cut into individual ribs and serve with additional barbecue sauce for dipping.

As an owner of a restaurant, a chef and a cookbook author, I have attended innumerable food fairs and festivals over the years. I especially enjoy the annual BBQ cook-offs held throughout Texas as well as some of the chili competitions that pop up all across the country. But the one food fair that I anticipate with bated breath is the annual Feast of San Gennaro, held in New York City's Little Italy each September. The history behind the

festival says San Gennaro was a bishop of Naples who was beheaded in 305 A.D. when he refused to worship pagan idols. Ever since 1389, his dried blood, which is stored in a vial in a silver reliquary topped by a crown and cross, liquifies and sometimes even "boils." And it is said that if the blood doesn't boil, disaster is to follow. San Gennaro is the Patron Saint of Napoli and is very dear to descendants from the southern part of Italy, as well as to the thousands of other Italians in New York City.

The first Feast took place in New York City on September 19, 1926, when new immigrants had settled into the section of Manhattan now known as Little Italy. These folks decided to carry on the tradition they had celebrated in Italy. Since that time, the one-day Feast has grown into an eleven-day event. One of the highlights of the Feast is the religious procession where the statue of San Gennaro is carried down the street between the vendors along Mulberry Street. This procession follows a celebratory Mass held at the Most Precious Blood Church on the same street.

While there is a wonderful party atmosphere during the eleven days (when over one million people come to visit), there is a serious purpose behind it as well. In recent years, Figli di San Gennaro, Inc. (Children of San Gennaro), a not-for-profit community organization, has produced the festival, and more than one million dollars has been donated to numerous worthy organizations in the five boroughs of New York City and the tri-state area to help the needy and children.

The stimulating sights and celebratory sounds of the Feast of San Gennaro are captivating. There are parades, live entertainment, pastries, pastas, seafood, meats galore and even a cannoli eating contest! Each block is lined with hundreds of vendors grilling countless pounds of pungent hot and sweet Italian sausages, steak, lamb, fish, London broil, chicken, and mountains of green and red peppers, onions and garlic. The enticing aromas of grilled meats can be smelled from blocks away. Inevitably, I find myself tempted by each and every booth ... even the sinful pastry concessions with offerings like zeppolis, cannolis, chocolate-dipped strawberries, deep-fried Oreos and more, where the calorie count is never less than 5,000! But who's counting?

The best part of attending the festival, of course, is sampling the wide array of grilled foodstuffs. In addition to the grilled meats and vegetables, there are grilled shish kabobs of fruit and grilled ears of corn-on-a-stick. Some food items are good, others are exquisite, and most are just plain mouthwatering. Each and every sample is a taster's delight. I don't eat for a full day before attending this wonderful assault on my taste buds.

Another thing I really enjoy about going to the Feast of San Gennaro is talking to so many of the wonderful Italian Americans about their special grilling techniques, spices and recipes. Over the years, I have even had a few vendors provide me with some of their family's most guarded recipes.

The Feast of San Gennaro is certainly a celebration for the spirit, eyes and stomach. If your travels permit, be sure to come to New York City's biggest and most famous street party!

— *Kate Fiduccia*

Dijon-Style T-Bone Steak

6 servings
Preliminary preparation: Under 15 minutes initial prep, 2 hours marinating
Grilling: Direct high heat, under 15 minutes

6 T-bone steaks (about 12 ounces/340 g each), trimmed of excess fat

1/3 cup (80 ml/85 g) Dijon mustard

2 tablespoons (30 ml) Italian-style vinaigrette dressing

1 tablespoon (15 ml) lemon juice

1 tablespoon (15 ml/7 g) chopped green onions

1 tablespoon (15 ml/15 g) minced fresh garlic

1 tablespoon (15 ml) honey

1 teaspoon (5 ml/2 g) cayenne pepper

Kosher salt to taste

Score edges of steak to prevent them from curling while cooking; place in shallow, nonmetallic dish or zipper-style plastic bag. In small bowl, whisk together mustard, dressing, lemon juice, green onions, garlic, honey and pepper. Pour mustard mixture over steaks, turning to coat. Cover and refrigerate for about 2 hours, turning several times so marinade penetrates steaks evenly.

When you're ready to cook, prepare grill for direct high heat; lightly oil grate. Remove steaks from marinade, discarding marinade. Place steaks on grate over heat and sear for 2 to 3 minutes per side. Check for doneness; depending upon thickness of steaks, they may need only a few minutes more cooking for medium-rare. When done, remove from grill, season with salt and let stand for a few minutes before serving.

Grill up any of the following over direct medium heat:

• Bacon-wrapped shrimp, scallops, water chestnuts and/or mushrooms (secure bacon with toothpicks for grilling)

• Smoked sausages, cut into bite-sized pieces (serve with mustard dipping sauce)

• Seasoned vegetable chunks

• Hearty bread brushed with olive oil; grill and top with a mixture of chopped tomatoes and olives

• Cheese quesadillas (top flour tortilla with shredded cheese, then with a second tortilla; grill until cheese melts)

• Miniature kabobs: Marinate bite-sized pieces of chicken or pork and grill on small skewers

**Make the Children Happy:
Grilled Pita Pizzas**

If you are serving something a bit too sophisticated for a child's palate, this is a quick and easy alternative.

Set the kids up at their own table with pita bread, jarred pizza sauce, shredded mozzarella or cheddar cheese, and bowls of toppings, such as sliced pepperoni, mushrooms, chopped ham, sliced grilled chicken, olives, onions or crumbled cooked bacon.

Let children spoon a few tablespoons (30 to 40 ml) of sauce on top of each pita and sprinkle on their favorite toppings and shredded cheese. Have an adult place the pizzas on a preheated grill at medium heat. Cover grill and cook for 2 to 4 minutes, or until cheese melts and crust bottom browns. Use a wide spatula to remove from grill.

Grilled Lamb Chops with Mint Cream Sauce

2 servings
Preliminary preparation: Under 15 minutes initial prep, 1 hour marinating
Grilling: Direct high heat, under 15 minutes

Marinade

$1/2$ cup (120 ml) olive oil

3 tablespoons (15 ml) lemon juice

1 teaspoon (5 ml) dried rosemary, or 1 tablespoon (15 ml/3 g) chopped fresh

1 teaspoon (5 ml) dried oregano, or 1 tablespoon (15 ml/5 g) chopped fresh

1 teaspoon (5 ml) dried thyme, or 1 tablespoon (15 ml/2.5 g) chopped fresh

$1/2$ teaspoon (2.5 ml/3 g) salt

$1/2$ teaspoon (2.5 ml/1 g) freshly ground black pepper

$1/4$ teaspoon (1.25 ml) finely grated fresh lemon zest

4 lamb chops, 1 inch (2.5 cm) thick (about $1^{1}/4$ pounds/570 g total)

Mint Cream Sauce

$1/3$ cup (80 ml/76 g) sour cream

2 tablespoons (30 ml/8 g) finely chopped fresh mint leaves

$1/4$ teaspoon (1.25 ml) finely minced garlic

TIP:
Mint is among the easiest of all herbs to grow, and there are a number of varieties from which to choose. It is a perennial, and once established, rest assured it is there to stay.

In nonreactive dish, whisk together all marinade ingredients. Add lamb chops, turning to coat. Cover and marinate at room temperature for about an hour, turning chops in marinade once or twice. Meanwhile, combine all sauce ingredients in small bowl; stir together. Cover and refrigerate until needed.

When you're ready to cook, prepare grill for direct high heat; lightly oil grate. Drain chops, discarding marinade. Place chops on grate over heat and cook for about 3 minutes per side (medium-rare) or until desired doneness. Serve with Mint Cream Sauce.

Paprika Pork Cutlets

3 or 4 servings
Preliminary preparation: Under 15 minutes
Grilling: Direct medium heat, under 15 minutes

We had a paprika epiphany many years ago when Jim played on a semi-professional soccer team with a number of Hungarians. Many of their dishes featured paprika, and we fell in love with both these gregarious people and their foods. Since then, we've frequently tried paprika in new dishes, almost always to our delight. This one is a prime example.
—A. and J. C.

1 pound (454 g) pork tenderloin

Spice Rub
1 tablespoon (15 ml) olive oil
2 teaspoons (10 ml/4 g) sweet Hungarian paprika
1 teaspoon (5 ml) dried Italian herb blend, well crushed

1/2 teaspoon (2.5 ml/3 g) salt
1/2 teaspoon (2.5 ml/1.25 g) garlic powder
1/2 teaspoon (2.5 ml/1.25 g) dry mustard powder
1/2 teaspoon (2.5 ml/1 g) freshly ground black pepper

Trim fat from pork. Cut crosswise into 8 slices. Place pork slices between 2 sheets of heavy-duty plastic wrap, and flatten each slice to 1/4-inch (.6-cm) thickness using a meat mallet or rolling pin. In small bowl, combine spice-rub ingredients and mix well. Rub spice mixture evenly over both sides of pork slices.

Prepare grill for direct medium heat; lightly oil grate. Place pork slices on grate over heat. Cook for 3 to 4 minutes per side, or until just done. Let stand for 5 minutes before serving.

Grilled Pork Chops

2 servings
Preliminary preparation: Under 15 minutes initial prep, 1 hour marinating
Grilling: Initial searing, followed by direct medium heat, under 15 minutes

TIP:
For additional juiciness and flavor, brush chops with your favorite barbecue sauce during the last 5 minutes, if you like.

Brining is the secret to moist, succulent grilled chops. An instant-read meat thermometer helps you avoid overcooking and dryness.

Brine

1/3 cup (80 ml/73 g) light brown sugar (packed)

1/4 cup (60 ml/38 g) Diamond Crystal kosher salt (see pages 53 and 79 for information on using other types of salt)

3 cups (690 ml) water, divided

2 cloves garlic, crushed

2 bay leaves, crumbled

4 whole cloves

1 teaspoon (5 ml/2 g) whole black peppercorns, crushed

2 pork loin chops, 1 to 1 1/2 inches (2.5 to 3.8 cm) thick (6 to 8 ounces/170 to 225 g each)

1 tablespoon (15 ml) olive oil

Freshly ground black pepper

In nonmetallic mixing bowl, dissolve sugar and salt in 1 cup (240 ml) hot water. Add garlic, bay leaves, cloves, peppercorns, and 2 cups (470 ml) cold water. Add pork chops and weight down with plate (or, combine brine and chops in large zipper-style plastic bag; press to remove as much air as possible and seal). Refrigerate for 1 hour.

Near the end of brining time, prepare grill for direct high heat; you'll also need an area of the grill that is cooler, so bank the coals appropriately if using charcoal. Remove chops from brine, discarding brine. Rinse chops briefly and pat dry with paper towels. Rub chops with oil; sprinkle with pepper to taste. Place chops on grate directly over high heat and cook for about 3 minutes per side, or until nicely browned. Move chops to cooler area of grill, or reduce heat if using gas grill. Cook until center of chops reaches 155°F (68°C), 8 to 10 minutes longer. Transfer chops to platter and cover with foil; let stand for 5 minutes. The internal temperature of the chops will rise during this time; final temperature should be 160°F (71°C).

London Broil

4 to 6 servings
Preliminary preparation: 4 to 8 hours marinating
Grilling: Direct medium heat, under 15 minutes

This works equally well with venison.

1 flank steak (1 1/2 to 2 pounds/680 to 900 g)

Marinade

1/4 cup (60 ml) canola oil

1/4 cup (60 ml) lemon juice

2 tablespoons (30 ml) soy sauce

2 teaspoons (10 ml/8 g) sugar

2 garlic cloves, crushed

Place steak in shallow, nonreactive dish. In mixing bowl, whisk marinade ingredients together; pour over steak. Cover and refrigerate for 4 to 8 hours, turning occasionally. When you're ready to cook, prepare grill for direct medium heat; lightly oil grate. Drain steak, discarding marinade; place on grate over heat and cook until desired doneness, 12 to 14 minutes, turning once. Allow steak to rest for 5 minutes to redistribute juices before slicing thinly across the grain.

Wright Sweet Venison Kabobs

4 servings
Preliminary preparation: Under 15 minutes initial prep, 4 to 6 hours marinating
Grilling: Direct medium heat, under 30 minutes
Special equipment: Metal skewers

This recipe, named for the longtime friend who shared it with us, is delicious with venison but beef or pork can be used. Serve it with yellow rice and a side salad.
—A. and J. C.

Marinade

1/2 cup (120 ml) soy sauce

1/2 cup (120 ml/110 g) brown sugar (packed)

1/4 cup (60 ml) olive oil

2 to 2 1/2 pounds (900 g to 1.125 kg) venison loin (substitute lean beef or pork if you like)

1 1/2 jars (8 ounces/225 g each) button mushrooms, drained

1 pint (470 ml) cherry tomatoes

1 can (20 ounces/567 g) pineapple chunks, drained

In saucepan, combine marinade ingredients; heat over medium heat, stirring constantly, until sugar dissolves. Set aside to cool. Cut venison into 2-inch (5-cm) cubes; transfer to nonmetallic bowl. Pour cooled marinade over venison, tossing to coat. Cover and refrigerate for 4 to 6 hours, stirring several times.

When you're ready to cook, prepare grill for direct medium heat; lightly oil grate. Thread venison, mushrooms, tomatoes and pineapple alternately on skewers. Place skewers on grate over heat and cook for 20 to 30 minutes, or until steak has reached desired doneness, turning several times.

Fabulous Fajitas

4 servings
Preliminary preparation: Under 15 minutes initial prep, 6 to 8 hours marinating
Grilling: Direct medium heat, under 15 minutes
Special equipment: Perforated grill wok

Marinade

2 tablespoons (30 ml) fresh orange juice

1 tablespoon (15 ml) white vinegar

1 teaspoon (5 ml/4 g) sugar

1/2 teaspoon (2.5 ml/1 g) ground cumin

1/2 teaspoon (2.5 ml) dried oregano

1 large clove garlic, chopped

Salt and pepper to taste

1 pound (454 g) venison, beef or buffalo steak, cut into thin strips

1 green bell pepper, cored and cut into strips

1 red bell pepper, cored and cut into strips

1 onion, thinly sliced

8 flour tortillas

Condiments

1 cup (240 ml/115 g) shredded cheddar or Monterey Jack cheese

1 cup (240 ml) salsa

1 cup (240 ml/235 g) guacamole (or sliced avocado)

1 cup (240 ml/240 g) refried beans

1 cup (240 ml/180 g) chopped tomato

1 cup (240 ml/55 g) shredded lettuce

Combine marinade ingredients and pour over steak in zipper-style plastic bag. Refrigerate for 6 to 8 hours, turning occasionally.

When you're ready to cook, prepare grill for direct medium heat. Place grill wok on grate over heat for about a minute, then add green and red peppers and onion. Stir-fry until vegetables are tender-crisp. Transfer vegetables to a dish; set aside. Drain steak, discarding marinade. Add steak to wok; stir-fry for 2 to 4 minutes. Return vegetables to wok and toss to combine. Serve on warmed tortillas with desired condiments.

Blue Cheese Venison Steak

4 servings
Preliminary preparation: Under 15 minutes
Grilling: Initial searing, followed by indirect medium heat, under 15 minutes

**4 venison steaks (about 6 ounces/170 g each),
trimmed of all fat and connective tissue**
Freshly ground black pepper

5 ounces (142 g) blue cheese, crumbled
**1/2 cup (120 ml/50 g) minced green onions (white
and green parts)**

Season steaks with pepper. In a small bowl, combine blue cheese and green onions. Mix with a fork and set aside.

Prepare grill for indirect medium heat; lightly oil grate. Place steaks on grate directly over heat and sear each side quickly. Move steaks to area away from heat; cook until almost desired doneness. Keep a close eye on the steaks; venison cooks quickly and must not be over-cooked. When steaks are almost done, top each steak with some of the blue cheese mixture and cook until done to taste. Serve hot.

Rubbed-Hot Venison Steaks

4 servings
Preliminary preparation: Under 15 minutes initial prep, up to 30 minutes standing
Grilling: Direct high heat, under 15 minutes

2 tablespoons (30 ml/12 g) paprika

2 teaspoons (10 ml/6 g) kosher salt

2 teaspoons (10 ml/10 g) brown sugar (packed)

2 teaspoons (10 ml/4 g) freshly ground black pepper

1 teaspoon (5 ml/2 g) ground dried chile pepper, such as ancho or chipotle

1/2 teaspoon (2.5 ml/1 g) ground cumin

1/4 teaspoon (1.25 ml/.5 g) cayenne pepper

4 elk or venison steaks (about 6 ounces/170 g each), trimmed of all fat and connective tissue

2 tablespoons (30 ml) olive oil

In small bowl, combine paprika, salt, brown sugar, black pepper, chile pepper, cumin and cayenne pepper; mix very well. Sprinkle spice mixture over both sides of steaks, rubbing in gently with your fingertips. Let steaks stand at room temperature for up to 30 minutes while the grill heats up.

Prepare grill for direct high heat; lightly oil grate. Drizzle oil over steaks, then place on grate over heat. Cook for 3 to 5 minutes per side, depending upon the thickness of the steaks (do not cook beyond medium-rare). Remove from grill and let stand for about 5 minutes before serving.

Backstrap in Bacon

4 to 6 appetizer servings
Preliminary preparation: Under 15 minutes initial prep, 6 to 8 hours marinating
Grilling: Direct medium heat, under 15 minutes

Try this with folks who say they do not care for venison. It will produce an attitude adjustment. It's also delicious prepared with any tender beef or buffalo cut.

1/2 cup (120 ml) Dale's Steak Seasoning*

1/2 cup (120 ml) water

1 pound (454 g) venison loin, cut into 1-inch (2.5-cm) chunks

Bacon slices, cut in half (about 1/2 pound/225 g)

In mixing bowl, blend together seasoning and water. Add venison, stirring to coat. Cover and refrigerate for 6 to 8 hours, stirring occasionally. Near the end of the marinating time, soak a handful of wooden toothpicks (1 for each venison chunk) in water for 30 minutes.

When you're ready to cook, drain venison, discarding marinade. Wrap each chunk in bacon and secure with a toothpick. Prepare grill for direct medium heat. Place bacon-wrapped chunks on grate over heat and cook for 8 to 10 minutes, or until desired doneness is reached. Do not overcook; the center should still be pink. Serve hot.

*Dale's Steak Seasoning is a soy sauce-based blend that is available at grocery stores and even places such as Wal-Mart; it's common throughout the South and Southeast. It really adds a special flavor, and is worth searching out. If you can't find it in your area, visit www.dalesseasoning.com.

Ham Steak with Peach-Mustard Glaze

2 or 3 servings
Preliminary preparation: Under 15 minutes
Grilling: Direct medium-high heat, about 15 minutes

2 tablespoons (30 ml) peach preserves

1 tablespoon (15 ml) bourbon or dark rum, optional

1 teaspoon (5 ml) dry mustard powder

1 teaspoon (5 ml) canola oil

A good pinch of ground ginger

1 ham steak (1 to 1 1/2 pounds/454 to 680 g)

Prepare grill for direct medium-high heat; lightly oil grate. In small bowl, combine preserves, bourbon, mustard, oil and ginger; stir to blend. Pat ham steak dry with paper towels. Make small cuts at 1-inch (2.5-cm) intervals around edges of ham; this prevents curling during cooking.

Place ham on grate over heat; cook for about 4 minutes. Turn ham and brush half of the preserve mixture over the ham. Cook for about 4 minutes longer. Turn ham and brush with remaining preserve mixture. Cook for about 3 minutes, then turn and cook for about 3 minutes longer, or until ham is heated through and nicely glazed.

Variations

Dieter's Burgers

Follow Basic recipe, substituting 1 pound (454 g) extra-lean ground meat (90 to 92% lean) for the 1½ pounds (680 g) ground meat; reduce salt to ¾ teaspoon (3.75 ml/ 3.5 g). Shape into 4 patties that are ½ inch (1.25 cm) thick. Grill as directed; cooking time will be reduced slightly.

Cheese-Stuffed Burgers

Follow Basic recipe, but divide seasoned meat into 8 equal portions. Shape each portion into a patty that is about ⅜ inch (.8 cm) thick, or a bit thinner. Top half of the patties with a generous tablespoon of blue cheese crumbles, or with a thin slice of cheddar or American cheese (use a 1-ounce/28-g slice of sandwich cheese, trimming the corners); keep the edges of the patty free of cheese. Top each patty with a second patty, then seal edges very well. Grill as directed; cooking time may need to be increased slightly.

Barbecue-Onion Burgers

Follow Basic recipe, adding ¼ cup (60 ml/45 g) finely diced onion to meat mixture before shaping patties. Grill first side as directed, then turn and brush 1 teaspoon (5 ml) barbecue sauce over the browned side of each burger. Just before burgers are done, gently turn burgers and brush second side of each burger with an additional teaspoon of barbecue sauce; cook for a minute longer, or until done.

Pizza Burgers

Follow Basic recipe, adding ½ teaspoon (2.5 ml) dried oregano, ½ teaspoon (2.5 ml) dried marjoram and 1 minced clove garlic to meat mixture before shaping patties. Grill as directed; when burgers are almost done, top each with 1 tablespoon (15 ml) prepared marinara sauce and 1 slice (1 ounce/28 g) mozzarella cheese. Cook for a minute or 2 longer, until sauce is hot and cheese melts.

Thai-Style Burgers

Follow Basic recipe, adding 3 tablespoons (45 ml/10 g) finely chopped fresh cilantro, 2 tablespoons (30 ml/5 g) finely chopped basil leaves, 1 tablespoon (15 ml) lime juice, ¼ teaspoon (1.25 ml) hot red pepper flakes and 1 minced clove garlic to meat mixture before shaping patties. Grill as directed, brushing patties with Asian fish sauce or soy sauce after turning (use about 2 tablespoons/30 ml fish sauce total).

Basic Grilled Burgers

4 servings
Preliminary preparation: 15 minutes
Grilling: Direct medium-high heat, under 15 minutes

Grilled burgers are one of the classic American backyard foods. You can jazz up the basic recipe with seasonings of your choice. You can even stuff them. See the variations at right for some ideas. —T.M.

1½ pounds (680 g) ground beef, buffalo, lamb or venison (85% lean works well)

1 teaspoon (5 ml/4 g) salt, garlic salt or seasoned salt

¼ teaspoon (1.25 ml) black pepper or cayenne pepper

4 split hamburger rolls, toasted if you like

Condiments of your choice (ketchup, sliced pickles, mustard, diced onion, etc.)

In mixing bowl, combine ground meat, salt and pepper; mix gently but thoroughly with your hands. Divide into 4 equal portions; shape each portion into ¾-inch-thick (1.9-cm) patty, patting meat just enough to hold together (for rare burgers, shape into 1-inch-thick [2.5-cm] patties).

Prepare grill for direct medium-high heat; lightly oil grate. Place burgers on grate over heat. Cook to desired doneness, 4 to 5 minutes per side for medium-rare (see Judging Doneness of Grilled Burgers); a covered grill helps reduce flare-ups, and helps cook the meat more evenly. Serve immediately, with buns and condiments.

JUDGING DONENESS OF GRILLED BURGERS

With a little experience, it's easy to judge the doneness of grilled burgers. Press lightly on the center of a burger with your finger. If the meat yields easily and seems soft, it is rare. As the burger continues to cook, it becomes more firm to the touch. A burger cooked to medium doneness will feel somewhat springy to the touch. For well-done, cook the burger until it feels firm when pressed with your finger. (Don't press down on burgers with a spatula; this causes juice loss, resulting in a dry burger.)

Until you become accustomed to judging burger doneness by touch, you can check the temperature of the burger with an instant-read meat thermometer inserted into the center of the burger. Rare burgers will read 135°F (57°C). At 150°F (66°C), burgers will be cooked to medium doneness, while well-done burgers have an internal temperature of 160°F (71°C). Remember that the temperature will rise a few degrees after the burger is removed from the grill.

Note: The United States Department of Agriculture recommends cooking all ground-beef or ground-lamb products to 160°F/71°C (165°F/74°C for ground chicken or turkey), to eliminate harmful *E. coli* bacteria. If you want to eat rare burgers, it is safest to custom-grind meat (well cleaned first), rather than using purchased pre-ground meat. Irradiated ground beef is also becoming more available; this meat is safe to eat even when cooked to lower temperatures.

BURGER TIPS

• When shaping patties, try making the center slightly thinner than the edges. As the burger shrinks during cooking, it will remain flatter; if the burger is thicker in the middle to start, it can become very rounded during cooking.

• A hinged grilling basket works great for grilling burgers, making them easy to flip. Be sure to lightly oil the basket before arranging the burgers in it.

• The grate should be very hot when the burgers hit it; this creates nice grilling marks, and also helps prevent sticking.

• For an attractive presentation, put the burgers on the grate and cook until nicely marked, then rotate the burgers 90 degrees and cook a bit longer to create cross-hatch marks; turn the burgers and finish cooking. It's best to turn burgers just once.

• If the grill flares up from dripping fat, move the burgers off to a cooler area while you extinguish the flames with a water bottle (charcoal grill) or wait for the flames to subside (gas grill).

Spiced Pork or Boar Burgers

> **3 servings**
> **Preliminary preparation:** Under 15 minutes initial prep, 1 to 8 hours refrigerating
> **Grilling:** Direct medium-high heat, under 15 minutes

See page 39 for some general burger-grilling tips.

Spice Mixture

1 1/4 teaspoons (6.25 ml/3 g) fennel seeds

3/4 teaspoon (3.75 ml/3 g) mustard seeds

3 tablespoons (45 ml) broth (any kind), wine or water

1 1/2 teaspoons (7.5 ml/5 g) finely chopped garlic

1/2 teaspoon (2.5 ml/3 g) salt

1/2 teaspoon (2.5 ml/1 g) paprika

1/4 teaspoon (1.25 ml/.5 g) freshly ground black pepper

1/4 teaspoon (1.25 ml) hot red pepper flakes, optional

1 pound (454 g) ground pork or boar burger

3 rye or whole wheat hamburger buns

Condiments of your choice (ketchup, sliced pickles, mustard, diced onion, etc.; caramelized onions are particularly good with these burgers)

Make the spice mixture: With mortar and pestle, crush fennel and mustard seeds coarsely (or, crush the seeds in a small bowl using a spoon). Combine crushed seeds with broth in small microwave-safe bowl and microwave until just boiling; or, heat broth to boiling on stovetop and combine with seeds in small bowl. Cool broth completely, then combine with garlic, salt, paprika, black pepper and red pepper; mix well. Add to ground pork; mix gently but thoroughly with your hands. Cover and refrigerate for at least 1 hour, or as long as 8 hours.

When you're ready to cook, divide into 3 equal portions; shape each portion into 3/4-inch-thick (1.9 cm) patty, patting meat just enough to hold together. Prepare grill for direct medium-high heat; lightly oil grate. Place burgers on grate over heat. Cook until internal temperature reaches 160°F (71°C), 5 to 7 minutes per side; a covered grill helps reduce flare-ups, and helps cook the meat more evenly. Serve immediately, with buns and condiments.

Chili Venison Burgers

> **8 to 10 servings**
> **Preliminary preparation:** Under 15 minutes initial prep, 2 hours refrigerator time
> **Grilling:** Direct medium-high heat, under 15 minutes
> **Special equipment (optional):** Hinged grilling basket

A hinged grilling basket makes it easy to turn 8 burgers all at once. See page 39 for additional burger-grilling tips.
—K.F.

2 pounds (900 g) ground venison (substitute beef or buffalo if you like)

4 small onions, minced

1 cup (240 ml/110 g) seasoned bread crumbs

1/4 cup (60 ml/15 g) finely chopped fresh parsley

2 tablespoons (30 ml) soy sauce

1 tablespoon (15 ml) dried oregano

1 tablespoon (15 ml) tomato paste

1 tablespoon (15 ml) rice vinegar

1 tablespoon (15 ml) chili sauce, such as Heinz

2 teaspoons (10 ml/4 g) ground cumin

1 teaspoon (5 ml/2.5 g) garlic powder

1 egg, lightly beaten

8 to 10 split hamburger rolls, toasted if you like

Garlic Herb Butter (page 127), optional

In mixing bowl, combine all ingredients except hamburger rolls and herb butter; mix gently but thoroughly with your hands. Cover with plastic wrap and refrigerate for about 2 hours; this allows the flavors to blend.

Shape into patties that are sized the way you like them; as a starting point, divide the mixture into 8 portions and shape each portion into a 3/4-inch-thick (1.9-cm) patty, patting meat just enough to hold together (for rare burgers, shape into 1-inch-thick [2.5-cm] patties). Let stand at room temperature while you prepare grill.

Prepare grill for direct medium-high heat; lightly oil grate (or inside of hinged grilling basket, if using; after oiling, arrange burgers in a single layer and close basket). Place burgers on grate over heat. Cook to desired doneness, 4 to 5 minutes per side for medium-rare (see sidebar on page 39 for information on judging doneness); a covered grill helps reduce flare-ups, and helps cook the meat more evenly. Serve immediately, with buns and Garlic Herb Butter.

Italian Turkey Burgers

4 servings
Preliminary preparation: Under 15 minutes
Grilling: Direct medium heat, under 15 minutes

Ground venison or ground beef can replace the ground turkey in this scrumptious recipe. Please see page 39 for some general burger-grilling tips.

1 pound (454 g) ground turkey

1/2 cup (120 ml) tomato-and-basil pasta sauce

1/3 cup (80 ml/67 g) finely chopped onion

1/4 cup (60 ml/28 g) Italian-seasoned bread crumbs

1/4 cup (60 ml/30 g) freshly grated Parmesan cheese

1 tablespoon (15 ml) dried parsley flakes

1/2 teaspoon (2.5 ml) onion salt

1/4 teaspoon (1.25 ml) finely minced garlic

4 slices mozzarella cheese (1 ounce/28 g each)

4 onion rolls or buns

1 clove garlic, halved

Lettuce and tomato for serving, optional, or additional pasta sauce

In mixing bowl, combine ground turkey, sauce, onion, bread crumbs, Parmesan cheese, parsley, salt and garlic; mix gently but thoroughly with your hands. Divide into 4 equal portions; shape each portion into 3/4-inch-thick (1.9-cm) patty, patting meat just enough to hold together.

Prepare grill for direct medium heat; lightly oil grate. Place burgers on grate over heat. Cook until center reaches 165°F (74°C), 6 to 7 minutes per side. Top with cheese slices; cover grill to melt cheese. Rub rolls with garlic clove and toast on grill. Serve burgers on buns with lettuce and tomato, or with additional pasta sauce.

Barbecued Meatloaf

6 servings
Preliminary preparation: Under 15 minutes
Grilling: Indirect medium heat, about an hour
Special equipment: 8- or 9-inch-square (20- or 23-cm) metal baking dish

1/2 cup (120 ml/55 g) Italian-seasoned or plain bread crumbs

1/4 cup (60 ml) barbecue sauce

1/4 cup (60 ml/45 g) finely chopped onion

1 egg

1 teaspoon (5 ml/4 g) garlic salt, seasoned salt or plain salt

1/2 teaspoon (2.5 ml/1.5 g) dry mustard powder

1 pound (454 g) lean ground beef, buffalo or venison

8 ounces (225 g) ground pork

8 ounces (225 g) ground veal

2 tablespoons (30 ml) ketchup

1 tablespoon (15 ml) maple syrup or brown sugar (packed)

1/4 teaspoon (1.25 ml) chipotle powder or paprika

Cover metal baking dish inside and out with foil (make sure seam is on the outside, so inside of pan is protected from burning juices); set aside. In large mixing bowl, combine bread crumbs, barbecue sauce, onion, egg, salt and mustard powder; mix very well and let stand for 5 minutes. Add beef, pork and veal; mix gently but thoroughly with your hands. In prepared baking dish, pack meat mixture firmly into a rounded loaf that is about 5 inches (13 cm) wide and 7 or 8 inches (18 to 20 cm) long.

Prepare grill for indirect medium heat. Place meatloaf on grate away from heat; cover grill and cook for 30 minutes, rotating pan once or twice. Meanwhile, combine ketchup, syrup and chipotle powder; mix well. When meatloaf has cooked for 30 minutes, brush ketchup mixture on top of meatloaf; re-cover grill and cook for 30 to 40 minutes longer, or until center of meatloaf reaches 160°F (71°C). Use spatula to transfer meatloaf to serving plate; let stand for 10 minutes before slicing.

Chicken under a Brick
(Pollo al Mattone)

poultry

4 or 5 servings
Preliminary preparation: Under 15 minutes initial prep, 1 to 8 hours marinating
Grilling: Indirect medium-high heat with water pan, under 45 minutes
Special equipment: 1 or 2 clean garden bricks

This classic Italian recipe produces incredibly juicy, flavorful chicken with a crispy skin.

1 whole skin-on chicken (3 to 4 pounds/1.36 to 1.8 kg)
Salt and freshly ground black pepper
3/4 cup (180 ml) olive oil
2 tablespoons (30 ml/3 g) fresh rosemary leaves, or 1 tablespoon (15 ml) dried
1/2 teaspoon (2.5 ml) hot red pepper flakes, optional
Juice from 1 lemon
4 to 6 cloves garlic, minced

Split chicken by cutting along the backbone with kitchen shears or knife. Open chicken up flat, like a book. With the split chicken skin-side up, press over the breastbone firmly with your hands to flatten as much as possible (if you like, you may cut the chicken along the breastbone also so it is in 2 halves); salt and pepper to taste. Place in large nonreactive dish. In small bowl, combine oil, rosemary, pepper flakes, lemon juice and garlic; stir to mix. Pour mixture over chicken, turning to coat. Cover and refrigerate for at least 1 hour, and as long as 8 hours (turn several times if marinating over an hour).

When you're ready to cook, prepare grill for indirect medium-high heat. Wrap a brick completely in foil (if you've cut chicken in half, wrap 2 bricks). Position filled water pan between coal banks, or away from heated area of gas grill. Drain chicken, discarding marinade. Place chicken, skin-side down, on grate over water pan. Place foil-wrapped brick on top of chicken, turning brick sideways to weight down both halves (for halved chicken, place 1 brick on each half). Cover grill and cook for 20 minutes. Remove brick(s), then flip chicken and replace brick(s). Continue cooking for about 20 minutes longer, or until juices run clear and thigh reaches 170°F (77°C). Transfer chicken to platter; tent loosely with foil and let stand for 5 to 10 minutes before cutting into serving pieces.

Honey-Grilled Pheasant

4 or 5 servings
Preliminary preparation: Under 15 minutes
Grilling: Indirect high heat, under an hour

2 whole dressed, skin-on pheasants
1/2 teaspoon (2.5 ml/1 g) freshly ground black pepper
Kosher salt
1 whole head garlic, loose papery skin rubbed off
2 small bunches of fresh rosemary
4 to 6 baby carrots, peeled

Honey Baste
1/4 cup (55 g/half of a stick) unsalted butter
2 tablespoons (30 ml) canola oil
2 teaspoons (10 ml) honey
1 teaspoon (5 ml/3 g) kosher salt

Wipe pheasants dry, inside and out, with paper towels. Season cavities with pepper, and salt to taste. Cut off the top of the garlic head, then split the head in half from top to bottom. Place half into the cavity of each pheasant, along with a bunch of rosemary and 2 or 3 baby carrots. Close cavities with small skewers.

Prepare grill for indirect high heat; lightly oil grate. Position drip pan between coal banks, or away from heated area of gas grill. To make the baste: Melt butter in small saucepan over low heat. Stir in oil, honey and salt. Brush the outside of the pheasants with some of the honey baste. Place pheasants on grate over drip pan. Cover grill and cook for 45 minutes to an hour, brushing occasionally with honey baste. To check for doneness, pierce thigh of pheasants; juices should run clear. Transfer pheasants to plate and let stand for 5 to 10 minutes before carving; remove vegetables and herbs from cavities as you carve. Serve carrots and garlic with pheasant.

Chicken under a Brick (left)

Rolled Stuffed Turkey Breast

6 to 8 servings
Preliminary preparation: Under an hour
Grilling: Indirect high heat with water pan, about an hour

3/4 cup (180 ml/120 g) diced onion

1/2 cup (120 ml/60 g) thinly sliced celery

1/2 cup (120 ml/65 g) coarsely chopped carrots

1 tablespoon (15 g) butter

1/2 cup (120 ml/20 g) fresh bread crumbs*

2 tablespoons (30 ml) white wine or water

1 teaspoon (5 ml) mixed dried herb blend of your choice

1 boneless turkey breast half (about 2 1/2 pounds/ 1.125 kg), skin-on or skinless

Salt and freshly ground black pepper

6 pieces heavy kitchen string (each about 18 inches/46 cm long), soaked in water

1/2 cup (120 ml) chicken broth

1 tablespoon (15 ml) olive oil or canola oil

In medium skillet, sauté onion, celery and carrots in butter over medium heat until tender, about 7 minutes. Remove from heat. Stir in bread crumbs, wine and herbs; set aside. Butterfly turkey breast by slicing horizontally through the breast (parallel to the cutting board), almost but not quite all the way through. Open turkey breast up like a book. Cover with a sheet of plastic wrap, then pound thicker areas to even out thickness as much as possible. Remove plastic wrap; sprinkle turkey with salt and pepper to taste. Place turkey on work surface with the seam parallel to you; if the turkey has the skin on, place the half with the skin farthest from you (skin-side down). Spread vegetable mixture over turkey, leaving the last 2 inches (5 cm) at the edge away from you clear of stuffing. Starting with the edge closest to you, roll breast up, tucking edges in as much as possible. Tie the roll with kitchen string at 1-inch (2.5-cm) intervals, keeping skin stretched and smooth underneath string if using skin-on breast. Some filling will fall out of the ends

during rolling and tying, and this is unavoidable. Combine chicken broth and oil in measuring cup.

Prepare grill for indirect high heat; lightly oil grate. Position filled water pan between coal banks, or away from heated area of gas grill. Place turkey roll on grate over water pan, skin-side up. Brush with broth mixture. Cover grill and cook until center of turkey roll reaches 170°F (77°C), brushing every 15 minutes with broth mixture and rotating roll once or twice (don't turn the roll, just rotate it, keeping the skin-side up). Total cooking time will be about an hour. Transfer to serving platter; tent loosely with foil and let stand for 10 minutes before slicing.

*To make fresh bread crumbs: Remove crusts from day-old French or Italian-style bread; cut each slice of bread into several pieces. Start blender, and drop bread pieces into running blender; be ready to cover the blender quickly, as the bread will pop out the top. Process until chopped into evenly sized crumbs.

Apple-Ginger Quail

2 servings
Preliminary preparation: Under 15 minutes initial prep, 1 hour marinating
Grilling: Direct medium heat, under 15 minutes

4 whole dressed quail

1/4 cup (60 ml) applesauce

1 tablespoon (15 ml) soy sauce

1 teaspoon (5 ml/5 g) finely minced fresh gingerroot

1/2 teaspoon (2.5 ml/1.5 g) dry mustard powder

Rinse quail; pat dry. Arrange in glass baking dish. In small bowl, combine remaining ingredients, stirring to blend. Pour over quail, then brush the applesauce mixture over all sides of the quail with a pastry brush. Cover dish and set aside to marinate at room temperature for 30 minutes, or up to 1 hour refrigerated.

When you're ready to cook, prepare grill for direct medium heat; lightly oil grate. Drain quail, reserving apple-

sauce mixture. Place quail on their sides on grate over heat and cook for 3 to 4 minutes. Turn so the other side faces the heat; brush reserved applesauce mixture over the grilled side. Turn and brush again after 3 or 4 minutes, then continue cooking with no additional brushing, turning several times, until the quail are just cooked through; total cooking time will be about 15 minutes.

Teriyaki Chicken <u>with</u> Mustard Dipping Sauce

8 servings
Preliminary preparation: Under 15 minutes initial prep, 1 to 2 hours marinating
Grilling: Direct medium heat, under 15 minutes

8 boneless, skinless chicken breast halves (about 6 ounces/170 g each)

Marinade

¹/₂ cup (120 ml) dry sherry

¹/₂ cup (120 ml) soy sauce

¹/₄ cup (60 ml) canola oil

¹/₄ cup (60 ml/50 g) brown sugar (loosely packed)

¹/₄ teaspoon (1.25 ml) freshly ground black pepper

Mustard Dipping Sauce

¹/₂ cup (120 ml/128 g) mayonnaise

¹/₃ cup (80 ml/85 g) Dijon mustard

1 teaspoon (5 ml) Worcestershire sauce

¹/₄ to ¹/₂ teaspoon (1.25 to 2.5 ml) hot pepper sauce

Place chicken breasts in zipper-style plastic bag. Mix marinade ingredients well and pour over chicken, turning to coat. Refrigerate for 1 to 2 hours, turning several times. Meanwhile, blend together all sauce ingredients in small bowl; cover and refrigerate.

When you're ready to cook, prepare grill for direct medium heat; lightly oil grate. Drain chicken breasts, discarding marinade; place on grate over heat. Cook for 6 to 7 minutes per side, or until internal temperature reaches 160°F (71°C) and juices run clear. Let chicken stand for 5 minutes before serving with prepared Mustard Dipping Sauce.

Lemon Herb Chicken

4 servings
Preliminary preparation: Under 15 minutes initial prep, 8 hours marinating
Grilling: Direct medium heat, under 15 minutes

If you prefer, freeze the chicken breasts in the marinade (using a freezer-weight plastic bag), then defrost in the refrigerator and have ready for a quick meal. The chicken will be even more flavorful.

4 boneless, skinless chicken breast halves (about 6 ounces/170 g each)

Marinade

¹/₃ cup (80 ml) lemon juice

¹/₃ cup (80 ml) canola oil

1 teaspoon (5 ml) Worcestershire sauce

³/₄ teaspoon (3.75 ml) onion salt

¹/₂ teaspoon (2.5 ml) dried thyme

¹/₂ teaspoon (2.5 ml/1 g) pepper

1 or 2 cloves garlic, minced

Place chicken breasts in zipper-style plastic bag. In small bowl, whisk marinade ingredients together; pour over chicken breasts. Marinate in refrigerator for 8 hours, turning occasionally.

When you're ready to cook, prepare grill for direct medium heat; lightly oil grate. Place drained chicken breasts on grate over heat. Cook for 6 to 7 minutes per side, or until internal temperature reaches 160°F (71°C) and juices run clear. Let chicken stand for 5 minutes before serving.

Teriyaki Chicken with Mustard Dipping Sauce

Grilled Balsamic Chicken and Salad

2 servings
Preliminary preparation: Under 30 minutes
Grilling: Direct medium heat, under 15 minutes

Serve with garlic toast or blueberry muffins.

Dressing and Marinade

1/3 cup (80 ml) balsamic vinegar

1/3 cup (80 ml) olive oil

1 tablespoon (15 ml) Dijon mustard

1/4 teaspoon (1.25 ml) seasoned salt

1/4 teaspoon (1.25 ml) sugar

1/8 teaspoon (.6 ml) black pepper

2 boneless, skinless chicken breast halves (about 6 ounces/170 g each)

1 medium Vidalia onion, cut into slices and placed on skewers

1 medium zucchini or yellow summer squash, cut in half lengthwise

Salad

4 cups (1 liter/220 g) mixed young greens

2 tablespoons (30 ml/5 g) chopped fresh basil

1/2 cup (120 ml/75 g) halved grape tomatoes

1/4 cup (60 ml/25 g) raw cauliflower, broken into small flowerets before measuring

1/4 cup (60 ml/33 g) sliced olives

1/4 cup (60 ml/30 g) sliced celery

1/4 cup (60 ml/40 g) crumbled feta cheese

1/4 cup (60 ml/10 g) croutons

4 small fresh, water-packed mozzarella cheese balls

Half of a medium cucumber, sliced

In small bowl, blend together all dressing ingredients. Pour 3 to 4 tablespoons dressing into small bowl and brush over chicken, onion and squash; reserve remaining dressing. Let chicken stand for 10 to 15 minutes before grilling. Combine all salad ingredients in large bowl.

Prepare grill for direct medium heat. Place chicken, onion and squash on grate over heat. Cook, turning sev-eral times, for 12 to 15 minutes, or until vegetables are tender and chicken is done (internal temperature should be 160°F/71°C, and juices should run clear).

Toss salad with desired amount of dressing. Separate onion into rings and chop squash; add to salad and toss gently. Slice chicken 1/4 inch (6 mm) thick and arrange over tossed salad.

Herbed Turkey Strips

4 or 5 servings
Preliminary preparation: Under 15 minutes initial prep, 2 hours marinating
Grilling: Direct medium heat, under 15 minutes

TIP: This method also works well with chicken or pheasant breast strips.

1 1/2 pounds (680 g) boneless, skinless turkey breast meat (from wild or domestic turkey)

1/2 cup (120 ml) canola oil

1/2 cup (120 ml) lemon juice

1 teaspoon (5 ml/4 g) seasoned salt

1 teaspoon (5 ml/2 g) paprika

1 teaspoon (5 ml) dried basil

1/2 teaspoon (2.5 ml) dried thyme

1/2 teaspoon (2.5 ml/1 g) black pepper

1/4 teaspoon (1.25 ml) hot red pepper flakes

2 green onions, minced

1 clove garlic, minced

Cut turkey meat into lengthwise strips, about 1 inch (2.5 cm) wide. In mixing bowl, whisk together remaining ingredients. Pour over turkey and marinate in refrigerator for 2 hours.

When you're ready to cook, prepare grill for direct medi-um heat. Drain turkey, discarding marinade. Place on grate over heat and cook until no longer pink in the cen-ter, 10 to 15 minutes, turning occasionally.

Apricot-Glazed Grilled Chicken Breasts

4 servings
Preliminary preparation: Under 30 minutes
Grilling: Direct medium heat, under 15 minutes

Brine

1 quart (950 ml) water

½ cup (120 ml/70 g) Diamond Crystal kosher salt or substitute (see pages 53 and 79 for information on using other types of salt)

½ cup (120 ml/100 g) sugar

4 boneless, skinless chicken breast halves (about 6 ounces/170 g each)

1 tablespoon (15 ml) olive oil

Freshly ground black pepper

Apricot Glaze

2 tablespoons (30 g) butter

1 tablespoon (15 ml) olive oil

2 tablespoons (30 ml) apricot preserves

1 tablespoon (15 ml) orange marmalade

⅛ to ¼ teaspoon (.6 to 1.25 ml) ground nutmeg

In large nonreactive bowl or pot, combine water, salt and sugar; stir until salt and sugar dissolve completely. Add chicken breast halves; weight down with small plate or bowl to submerge completely. Refrigerate for 20 to 30 minutes.

Meanwhile, prepare apricot glaze. In small saucepan, melt butter in oil over medium heat. Add preserves, marmalade and nutmeg. Stir until preserves have melted. Set aside.

Prepare grill for direct medium heat. Rinse chicken and pat dry with paper towels. Drizzle oil over chicken and sprinkle with freshly ground pepper to taste. Place chicken on grate over heat; cover grill and cook for 5 minutes. Turn breasts; re-cover grill and cook for 5 to 6 minutes longer, or until internal temperature reaches 160°F (71°C) and juices run clear; brush glaze on chicken during the last 3 or 4 minutes of cooking.

Grilled Goose Breast Fillets

6 main-dish servings; 10 to 12 appetizer servings
Preliminary preparation: 4 to 24 hours marinating
Grilling: Direct medium heat, under 30 minutes

With resident Canadas being so plentiful in many areas as to have become a nuisance, obtaining the basic raw material for this dish has become relatively simple. When cooking this, remember that goose breast should be cooked rare or medium-rare. —A. and J.C.

2½ to 3 pounds (1.125 to 1.36 kg) boneless, skinless goose breast meat*

2 to 3 cups (470 to 690 ml) merlot, burgundy or other hearty red wine

1 clove garlic, minced

½ cup (110 g/1 stick) butter, melted

Poultry seasoning to taste

Salt and pepper to taste

Place goose breasts in nonreactive bowl or deep dish. Add enough wine to barely cover goose; sprinkle garlic over. Refrigerate for 4 to 24 hours, turning several times.

When you're ready to cook, prepare grill for direct medium heat; lightly oil grate. Drain goose, discarding wine. Place goose on grate over heat; brush with butter and sprinkle with poultry seasoning, salt and pepper to taste. Cook for 8 to 10 minutes per side, basting with butter and sprinkling several times. Transfer goose to serving platter; tent loosely with foil and let stand for 5 minutes. Slice breasts on diagonal and drizzle with remaining melted butter.

*The boneless, skinless breast meat from 1 mature Canada goose will be about the right amount. If preparing snows or smaller geese, you may need meat from 2 geese.

Oven-Roasted and Grilled Chicken

6 to 8 servings
Preliminary preparation: 1½ hours roasting
Grilling: Direct medium heat, under 15 minutes

Chicken can be roasted ahead, refrigerated, and then grilled when needed. Precooking makes the grilling process much quicker and easier. Such preparation allows you to prepare for guests in a timely, trouble-free fashion.

6 to 8 bone-in, skin-on or skinless chicken breast halves (about 10 ounces/284 g each)

¼ cup (55 g/half of a stick) butter, melted

Garlic salt

Dried parsley flakes

Freshly ground black pepper

Prepared barbecue sauce as needed (about 1¼ cups/290 ml)

Heat oven to 325°F (164°C). Place chicken breasts in baking dish large enough to hold them without overlapping. Drizzle melted butter over each breast and sprinkle breasts with garlic salt, parsley and pepper to taste. Cover dish with foil. Bake for 1½ hours, or until chicken is tender and cooked through.

When you're ready for final cooking, prepare grill for direct medium heat; lightly oil grate. Place chicken on grate over heat. Baste with barbecue sauce until chicken is well coated; grill until nicely glazed and heated through, 8 to 10 minutes, turning chicken frequently and brushing with sauce.

Crab-Stuffed Chicken Breast

4 servings
Preliminary preparation: Under 45 minutes initial prep, 1 hour refrigerator time if possible
Grilling: Indirect medium-high heat, under 30 minutes

¼ cup (60 ml/45 g) finely diced onion

3 tablespoons (45 g) butter, divided

3 ounces (80 g) mushrooms, chopped fairly fine (about 1 cup/240 ml after chopping)

4 boneless, skinless chicken breast halves (about 6 ounces/170 g each)

Salt and black pepper

4 ounces (113 g) shredded crabmeat (about ¾ cup/180 ml)

¼ cup (60 ml/60 g) mayonnaise

¼ cup (60 ml/28 g) bread crumbs

4 pieces heavy kitchen string (each about 18 inches/46 cm long)

1 tablespoon (15 ml/4 g) chopped fresh herbs (a mix of parsley, marjoram and thyme works well)

In medium skillet, sauté onion in 1 tablespoon (15 g) of the butter over medium heat for about 5 minutes. Add mushrooms; cook, stirring frequently, until liquid released by mushrooms has been re-absorbed, about 7 minutes. Remove from heat; set aside to cool completely.

Place each chicken breast half between 2 sheets of plastic wrap. Pound with meat mallet until a uniform ¼ inch (6 mm) thick; it will be about 6x7 inches (15x17.75 cm). Sprinkle 1 side with salt and pepper to taste. In mixing bowl, combine cooled mushroom mixture with crabmeat, mayonnaise and bread crumbs; mix gently but thoroughly. Divide mixture evenly between 4 breast halves, mounding in the center of each breast half. Fold ends over filling, tucking edges up as much as possible. Tie each bundle with a cross of kitchen string (as though putting a cross of ribbon on a gift-wrapped box). Wrap each tied breast half tightly in plastic wrap to make a smooth bundle. If possible, refrigerate for an hour or longer, to allow the bundles to firm up; if you like, the chicken can be prepared earlier in the day and refrigerated until you're ready to cook it.

When you're ready to cook, prepare grill for indirect medium-high heat; lightly oil grate. In small saucepan or microwave-safe dish, melt remaining 2 tablespoons butter. Mix in herbs. Unwrap chicken bundles; place on grate away from heat. Brush with herb butter; turn and brush second side. Cover grill; cook for 25 minutes or until internal temperature reaches 160°F (71°C), turning twice and brushing with herb butter. Cut strings and remove before serving.

Greek Pheasant Skewers

4 servings
Preliminary preparation: Under 30 minutes initial prep, 1 hour marinating
Grilling: Direct medium heat, under 15 minutes
Special equipment: Metal skewers

Feel free to substitute chicken, turkey or the meat from any other upland gamebird for the pheasant in this delicious dish.

Greek Marinade

1/3 cup (80 ml) freshly squeezed lemon juice

2 tablespoons (30 ml) dry vermouth or water

2 tablespoons (30 ml) olive oil

1 clove garlic, pressed or finely minced

1/2 teaspoon (2.5 ml) dried oregano

1/4 teaspoon (1.25 ml) dried thyme

1/8 teaspoon (.6 ml) coarsely ground black pepper

1¼ pounds (570 g) boneless, skinless pheasant meat, cut into 1-inch (2.5-cm) chunks

2 medium carrots

Half of a red bell pepper, cored and cut into 1-inch (2.5-cm) chunks

Half of a green bell pepper, cored and cut into 1-inch (2.5-cm) chunks

Half of a medium red onion, cut into 1-inch (2.5-cm) chunks

Hot cooked orzo or rosamarina pasta*, optional

In nonreactive mixing bowl, whisk together all marinade ingredients. Spoon about half the mixture into a small bowl and set aside. Add pheasant to mixing bowl with marinade, stirring to coat. Cover and refrigerate for 30 minutes to 1 hour, stirring occasionally. Meanwhile, peel carrots and cut into 1-inch (2.5-cm) lengths. Microwave, steam or boil just until tender-crisp. Refresh under cold running water; drain and set aside.

When you're ready to cook, drain pheasant, discarding marinade. Arrange pheasant, carrots, peppers and onion on skewers; fold over thinner or irregularly shaped

pheasant pieces to form a thicker chunk. Prepare grill for direct medium heat. Place skewers on grate over heat. Cook until pheasant is cooked through and vegetables are tender-crisp, 12 to 15 minutes, turning and brushing occasionally with reserved marinade. Serve over a bed of orzo, if you like.

*Orzo and rosamarina are small pasta shapes. Orzo is shaped like rice, while rosamarina is a bit thicker and wider—like a cantaloupe seed.

Twice-Grilled Chicken Burritos

4 servings
Preliminary preparation: Under 15 minutes initial prep, 1 to 2 hours marinating
Grilling: Direct medium-high heat, under 30 minutes

1 pound (454 g) boneless, skinless chicken breasts or thighs

Half of a red bell pepper, cored and cut into 1/2-inch (1.25-cm) strips

Half of a green bell pepper, cored and cut into 1/2-inch (1.25-cm) strips

1 small onion, sliced vertically into 1/2-inch (1.25-cm) slivers

1/4 cup (60 ml) canola oil, divided

2 tablespoons (30 ml) freshly squeezed lime juice

2 cloves garlic, minced

1 teaspoon (5 ml/3 g) chili powder blend

4 burrito-sized flour tortillas

1 cup (240 ml/115 g) shredded Monterey Jack cheese

Salsa and sour cream for garnish, optional

Place chicken in 11x7-inch (28x18-cm) glass baking dish. Scatter bell peppers and onion slices over chicken. In small glass jar, combine 3 tablespoons (45 ml) of the oil, the lime juice, garlic and chili powder blend; cover tightly and shake to blend. Pour mixture over chicken and vegetables, stirring to coat. Cover and refrigerate for 1 to 2 hours.

When you're ready to cook, prepare grill for direct medium-high heat. Place a 12x18-inch (30x46-cm) sheet of heavy-duty foil on work surface, shiny-side up; transfer peppers and onion to foil, letting excess marinade drip back into dish with chicken. Seal packet as shown on page 132. Place packet on grate over heat and cook for 10 minutes, turning once (do not pierce foil when turning). Move foil packet to side of grate, turning it as you move it. Drain chicken and place on grate over heat. Cover and cook for 6 to 7 minutes per side, or until internal temperature reaches 160°F (71°C) for breasts or 170°F (77°C) for thighs and juices run clear, turning chicken and vegetable packet once. Remove chicken and vegetables from grill, but keep grill going for final cooking.

Slice chicken across the grain into thin strips. Place one-quarter of the strips at the base of a flour tortilla. Add about one-quarter of the vegetables (but don't overfill the burrito); top with 1/4 cup (60 ml/28.75 g) cheese. Fold up the bottom of the tortilla over the filling. Fold in the sides, then roll tortilla up tightly. Repeat with remaining ingredients. Brush rolled burritos with remaining 1 tablespoon (15 ml) oil. Place on grate over heat, seam-side down. Cook for about 2 minutes, or until burritos are firm and lightly browned. Carefully turn burritos and cook for about 2 minutes longer. Serve immediately, with salsa and sour cream on the side.

Basic Grilled Chicken

4 or 5 servings
Preliminary preparation: Under 15 minutes
Grilling: Indirect high heat with water pan, under 45 minutes

1 whole skin-on chicken (4 to 5 pounds/1.8 to 2.3 kg), or about 4 pounds (1.8 kg) skin-on parts

Garlic salt, seasoned salt or plain salt

Lemon pepper, other seasoned pepper or plain pepper

Prepare grill for indirect high heat; lightly oil grate. Position filled water pan between coal banks, or away from heated area of gas grill. Cut chicken into serving pieces. Sprinkle generously with salt and pepper of your choice, rubbing seasonings in with your fingertips. Place chicken on grate over water pan. Cover grill and cook for 35 minutes, turning chicken about every 10 minutes. Now transfer chicken to the grate over heat. Re-cover and cook for 10 to 15 minutes longer, turning chicken every 5 minutes, until chicken is crispy and cooked through; internal temperature of the thigh should read 170°F (77°C) and juices should run clear.

Flavor Variations for Basic Grilled Chicken

• Omit salt and pepper; rub the chicken with about 2 tablespoons (30 ml) Basic Dry Rub (page 118) or any other rub.

• Rub chicken pieces with 3/4 cup (180 ml) barbecue sauce before grilling. When chicken is almost done, brush with an additional 1/4 cup (60 ml) barbecue sauce and cook, turning once, for 5 minutes.

• Rub chicken pieces with 3/4 cup (180 ml) prepared pesto before grilling. During cooking, baste chicken each time you turn it with additional pesto (you will need about 1/2 cup/120 ml for the basting).

• Marinate chicken in the refrigerator in bottled Italian-style salad dressing for 1 to 4 hours. Drain, discarding dressing; grill as directed.

Lemonade-Glazed Wings

4 main-dish servings; 8 appetizer servings
Preliminary preparation: Under 15 minutes initial prep, 3 to 5 hours marinating
Grilling: Direct medium-high heat, under 30 minutes

These wings acquire a shiny, golden-brown finish from the lemonade concentrate. Serve with plenty of napkins to clean up sticky fingers.

Lemonade Marinade

1/4 cup (60 ml) frozen lemonade concentrate, thawed

1/4 cup (60 ml) soy sauce

3 tablespoons (45 ml) vegetable oil

2 tablespoons (30 ml) honey

2 teaspoons (10 ml) Dijon mustard

1/2 teaspoon (2.5 ml) finely minced garlic

1/2 teaspoon (2.5 ml) chopped fresh thyme leaves, or 1/4 teaspoon (1.25 ml) dried

2 to 3 pounds (900 g to 1.36 kg) chicken wings or drumettes

In small saucepan, combine all marinade ingredients. Heat just to boiling over medium heat, stirring occasionally. Remove from heat and set aside until completely cool.

Place wings in large zipper-style plastic bag. Add half of the cooled marinade, turning to coat. Refrigerate for 3 to 5 hours, turning bag occasionally. Refrigerate remaining marinade also.

When you're ready to cook, prepare grill for direct medium-high heat; lightly oil grate. Drain wings, discarding marinade. Place on grate over heat. Cover grill and cook for 20 to 25 minutes, turning wings and brushing with reserved marinade every 5 to 10 minutes. Wings are done when they are nicely browned and cooked through. If wings are getting too browned before they are cooked through, move to cooler area of grill to finish cooking.

Dove Breast Appetizers

8 to 10 appetizer servings
Preliminary preparation: At least 4 hours marinating
Grilling: Direct high heat, under 15 minutes

We are fortunate enough to live where doves are plentiful and where a three-segment season embraces more than 60 days. That means these wonderful game birds grace our table with regularity. —A. and J.C.

20 boneless, skinless dove breast halves (about 1 pound/454 g total)

1 cup (240 ml) Italian-style vinaigrette dressing

10 slices bacon, cut in half

In large zipper-style plastic bag, combine dove breasts and dressing, turning to coat. Refrigerate for at least 4 hours, turning bag occasionally. Meanwhile, pre-cook bacon slices for a few minutes in the microwave; bacon should be about half cooked but still quite pliable. Refrigerate until needed. Soak 20 toothpicks in cold water for the last 30 minutes of marinating.

When you're ready to cook, wrap a strip of bacon around each dove breast and secure with a toothpick. Prepare grill for direct high heat. Place doves on grate over heat and cook for 8 to 10 minutes, turning often. Do not overcook; the meat should be pink inside.

Variations: Insert a jalapeño pepper half and onion slice, water chestnut or piece of pepper cheese before wrapping bacon around dove breasts.

Oriental Chicken Breasts

4 servings
Preliminary preparation: Under 15 minutes initial prep, 30 minutes standing
Grilling: Direct high heat, under 15 minutes

2 tablespoons (30 ml) mirin*

2 tablespoons (30 ml) sake (Japanese rice wine)

2 tablespoons (30 ml/13 g) chopped fresh green onions

1 tablespoon (15 ml) dark sesame oil

1 tablespoon (15 ml/15 g) minced fresh gingerroot

4 boneless, skin-on chicken breast halves (about 6 ounces/170 g each)

In small bowl, combine mirin, sake, green onions, sesame oil and gingerroot; mix well. Place chicken breasts in shallow dish and pour marinade over chicken, turning to coat. Let stand at room temperature for 30 minutes.

Prepare grill for direct high heat; lightly oil grate. Remove breasts from marinade, reserving marinade; place chicken on grate over heat. Cook for 4 to 6 minutes per side, or until internal temperature reaches 160°F (71°C) and juices run clear. While chicken is cooking, boil remaining marinade in small pan for 5 to 7 minutes. Drizzle cooked marinade over chicken before serving.

*Mirin is sweetened Japanese cooking wine. Look for it in the Asian section of large supermarkets, or in specialty Asian stores.

BRINING: THE SECRET TO MOIST GRILLED POULTRY & PORK

Unlike a well-marbled beef steak, poultry has no internal fat to baste the meat as it cooks, so overcooking by even a few minutes may produce a dry, tough result. Brining—soaking the poultry in a saltwater solution—enhances juiciness by reducing moisture loss and softening proteins in muscle fibers. It works great for chicken and other domestic birds, and is particularly helpful for pheasant.

Kosher salt is the standard for brining, but canning/pickling salt also works fine; table salt is acceptable for the short brining times used to add moisture to poultry, but it does not work well for longer brining used for smoking (see page 79). For precision and consistency, salt used in a brine is calculated by weight, not by volume; conversions to U.S. standard measure are a bit confusing because various types of salt measure differently due to varying flake size and structure. For a standard brine, recommended strength is 70 grams of salt per quart (950 ml) of cold water. If you're using Diamond Crystal kosher salt, 70 grams is 1/2 cup (120 ml by metric volume measure). For Morton kosher salt, 70 grams is 5 tablespoons (75 ml by metric volume measure). For canning/pickling salt, or regular table salt, 70 grams is 1/4 cup (60 ml by metric volume measure). As a general rule, most references recommend using half as much canning/pickling salt as kosher salt when measuring salt by volume (the standard U.S. system). Obviously, this simple conversion works best with Diamond Crystal.

Always make up enough brine (following the basic proportions above) to completely cover the food. Sugar, herbs and spices are often added for more flavor; for another variation, substitute apple juice for the water. Chicken or pheasant pieces can be brined for up to 2 hours (refrigerated); larger items such as turkey parts or a whole chicken can sit in the brine for 3 to 4 hours. Pork also benefits from brining; soak chops for 2 to 3 hours, or a roast for up to 4 hours. After brining, rinse the meat in cold water and pat dry with paper towels, then season if you like before grilling.

Crab-Stuffed Rainbow Trout

2 servings
Preliminary preparation: Under 15 minutes
Grilling: Direct medium heat, under 15 minutes
Special equipment: Hinged grilling basket

Trout abound in the nearby mountain streams of North Carolina, and we enjoy them at every opportunity. Small to medium-sized trout (8 to 14 inches/20 to 36 cm) taste better than larger ones. —A. and J. C.

1 tablespoon (15 ml) olive oil, plus additional for rubbing fish

1 tablespoon (15 ml/10 g) finely diced onion

1 tablespoon (15 ml/8 g) finely diced celery

2 tablespoons (30 g) butter

1 cup (240 ml/142 g) shredded crabmeat (about 5 ounces)

¼ cup (60 ml) Italian-seasoned bread crumbs

¼ cup (60 ml/18 g) crushed saltine crackers

1 tablespoon (15 ml) lemon juice

¼ teaspoon (1.25 ml) Old Bay Seasoning

¼ teaspoon (1.25 ml) black pepper, plus additional for seasoning trout

5 or 6 small wild rainbow trout, or 2 farm-raised rainbow trout (about 1½ pounds/680 g total)

Kosher salt and freshly ground black pepper

Prepare grill for direct medium heat. In saucepan, heat oil over medium heat. Add onion and celery; sauté for about 2 minutes. Add butter, crabmeat, bread crumbs, cracker crumbs, lemon juice and seasonings; mix gently but thoroughly. Spoon stuffing into the cavity of each fish. Rub both sides of each fish with additional olive oil and place in grilling basket. Sprinkle fish with salt and pepper to taste. Place on grate over heat and cook for about 10 minutes, or until fish are golden and flake when tested with a fork; turn basket several times during cooking. Serve immediately.

TIP: Using a grilling basket makes turning the fish easy and the stuffing remains inside the trout. Remember to brush the basket with olive oil to prevent sticking.

Whole Fish with Chinese Flavors

4 servings
Preliminary preparation: Under 15 minutes initial prep, up to 2 hours marinating
Grilling: Direct medium heat, under an hour

Whole dressed 18- to 20-inch (46- to 51-cm) lake trout, salmon or similar fish (about 2 pounds/900 g dressed weight)

3 tablespoons (45 ml) soy sauce

3 tablespoons (45 ml) hoisin sauce

2 tablespoons (30 ml) black bean sauce with garlic

1 tablespoon (15 ml) dark sesame oil

1 tablespoon (15 ml) dry sherry

1 teaspoon (5 ml/5 g) finely minced fresh gingerroot

Rinse fish inside and out; pat dry. Make deep slashes through the skin on both sides, cutting parallel with the gill edge and spacing the slashes about 2 inches (5 cm) apart; you will have 4 or 5 slashes per side. Tear off a piece of heavy-duty foil that is 4 inches (10 cm) longer than the fish. Fold foil in half lengthwise; turn up edges slightly, forming a shallow rim. Place foil on a baking sheet, and place the fish on the foil.

In small bowl, mix together remaining ingredients. Pour one-quarter of the mixture over 1 side of the fish and rub it into the slits with your fingers. Turn fish over and pour a similar amount over the second side, rubbing it into the slits. Cover and refrigerate for 15 minutes to as long as 2 hours; reserve remaining soy-sauce mixture.

When you're ready to cook, prepare grill for direct medium heat, placing coals in a line up the center of the grill or along one side, so there is an area of the grill with no coals (for gas grill, leave one bank unlit). Carefully lift the foil-cradled fish onto the grate over heat. Pour half of the remaining soy-sauce mixture over the fish. Cover grill and cook for 15 minutes. Pour remaining soy-sauce mixture over the fish; re-cover grill and cook for 10 minutes longer. Now, carefully pull the foil-cradled fish to the side of the grill so the back part of the fish is still partially over the heat; the belly side should not be over the hot area. Re-cover grill and cook until the fish is just cooked through, 10 to 15 minutes longer.

Crab-Stuffed Rainbow Trout (left)

Grilled Marinated Fish Fillets

3 servings per pound
Preliminary preparation: Under 15 minutes, plus 10 to 45 minutes marinating
Grilling: Direct medium-high heat, under 15 minutes
Special equipment (optional): Hinged grilling basket, or 2 cake-cooling racks (page 58)

Marinating fish fillets adds flavor, and helps keep the fish moist. Here are a few different marinades and a basic technique to get you started; feel free to vary the marinade to suit your tastes. Salmon, trout, char, tuna and other oily fish are most commonly used with this method, although you may substitute other fish such as grouper, mahi-mahi, tilapia, perch or sea bass.

Boneless skin-on or skinless salmon fillets, or substitute

Marinade of your choice (each marinade recipe below works for 1 pound/454 g fish fillets)

Sauce of your choice, optional

Parsley-Ginger Marinade

2 tablespoons (30 ml/8 g) minced fresh parsley

2 tablespoons (30 ml) olive oil

2 tablespoons (30 ml) lemon juice

1 teaspoon (5 ml/5 g) minced fresh gingerroot

1 teaspoon (5 ml/3.5 g) minced shallot

Sweet Lemon-Dill Marinade

1/4 cup (60 ml) freshly squeezed lemon juice

2 tablespoons (30 ml/25 g) light brown sugar (packed)

1/2 teaspoon (2.5 ml/.5 g) snipped fresh dill weed

1/4 teaspoon (1.25 ml) kosher salt

1/8 teaspoon (.6 ml) pepper

Dill Sour Cream Sauce (page 125) is particularly good when using this recipe

Vermouth-Maple Marinade

1 cup (240 ml) sweet (red) vermouth, boiled until reduced to 1/3 cup (80 ml)

2 tablespoons (30 ml) maple syrup

2 teaspoons (10 ml) soy sauce

1 teaspoon (5 ml/3 g) dry mustard powder

1/4 teaspoon (1.25 ml) ground ginger

A few grindings of black pepper

In small bowl, whisk together marinade ingredients, stirring until any sugar or salt dissolves. Place fish in shallow nonreactive dish. Pour marinade over fish, turning to coat. Cover and let stand for 10 to 45 minutes (don't overmarinate fish, especially if the fillets are thin; acids in the marinade will begin to "cook" the fish after too long).

When you're ready to cook, prepare grill for direct medium-high heat. If you like, place trout fillets in lightly oiled hinged grilling basket, or between 2 cake-cooling racks (page 58); this is particularly helpful if cooking skinless or thin fillets (if you're not using a basket or racks, lightly oil grate). Place on grate over heat and cook until fish is just opaque (see sidebar on page 62).

Stir-Fried Marlin and Peppers

4 servings
Preliminary preparation: Under 45 minutes
Grilling: Direct medium-high heat, under 15 minutes
Special equipment: Perforated grilling wok

This easy grilled stir-fry is great served with buttered noodles or rice. You could substitute any firm-fleshed oily fish such as swordfish, tuna, wahoo or cobia for the marlin.

2 tablespoons (30 ml) hot pepper oil or dark sesame oil

1 teaspoon (5 ml/3.5 g) chopped garlic

1/2 teaspoon (2.5 ml/3 g) salt

1/2 teaspoon (2.5 ml/1 g) ground cumin

1/4 teaspoon (1.25 ml) coarsely ground pepper

1 small orange, peeled and sectioned

3/4 to 1 pound (340 to 454 g) skinless marlin steaks, cut into 3/4-inch (1.9-cm) cubes

1 red or orange bell pepper, cored and cut into 3/4-inch (1.9-cm) squares

1 green or yellow bell pepper, cored and cut into 3/4-inch (1.9-cm) squares

1 small white onion, cut into 3/4-inch (1.9-cm) pieces

1 small zucchini, halved lengthwise and sliced 1/4 inch (6 mm) thick

2 tablespoons (30 ml/5 g) chopped fresh cilantro, optional

In large nonreactive bowl, combine oil, garlic, salt, cumin and pepper. Break or cut orange segments into bowl in 1/2-inch (1.25-cm) pieces, holding segments over bowl to allow juices to drip into oil mixture. Stir to blend. Add cubed marlin, bell peppers, onion and zucchini; stir to coat. Set aside at room temperature to marinate for about 30 minutes, stirring occasionally.

Prepare grill for direct medium-high heat. Place perforated grilling wok on grate; heat for about a minute. Add marlin mixture. Cover grill and cook for about 15 minutes, stirring every few minutes with wooden spatula. Transfer mixture to serving bowl; sprinkle with cilantro.

Coconut-Basted Fish

4 servings
Preliminary preparation: Under 30 minutes
Grilling: Direct medium-high heat, under 15 minutes
Special equipment: 2 cake-cooking racks (below)

4 boneless, skinless walleye or other mild fish fillets (4 to 6 ounces/113 to 170 g each)

¼ cup (60 ml) freshly squeezed lime juice (from about 1 lime)

¼ cup (60 ml) Asian fish sauce (<u>nuoc</u> <u>mam</u> or <u>nam</u> <u>pla</u>)

½ cup (120 ml) thick coconut milk (canned, unsweetened)

3 tablespoons (45 ml/40 g) brown sugar (packed)

1 tablespoon (15 ml/15 g) finely minced fresh gingerroot

¼ cup (60 ml/18 g) flaked unsweetened coconut, lightly toasted*

Arrange fillets in glass baking dish. In measuring cup, combine lime juice and fish sauce; pour over fillets, turning to coat. Set aside to marinate at room temperature for 15 to 30 minutes. Combine coconut milk, brown sugar and gingerroot in small bowl, stirring to blend; set aside.

Prepare grill for direct medium-high heat. Remove fish from marinade; pat dry. Place fish between cake-cooling racks as directed below; secure edges. Place rack of fish on grate over heat. Cook for about 1 minute, then flip rack and brush fish with coconut-milk mixture. Cook for about 1 minute longer, then flip rack and brush second

side of fish with coconut-milk mixture. Continue cooking, flipping rack every 2 minutes and brushing fish with coconut-milk mixture, until fish is cooked through and beginning to brown in spots; total cooking time will be about 10 minutes. Open rack carefully, loosening fish from top rack as you open. Loosen fish from bottom rack; transfer to serving plate. Sprinkle with toasted coconut; serve immediately.

*To toast coconut, spread on baking sheet. Bake at 375°F (190°C), stirring frequently, until lightly toasted and fragrant, 5 to 10 minutes. Coconut can be toasted several hours in advance; set aside at room temperature until needed.

SIMPLE FISH GRILLING RACK

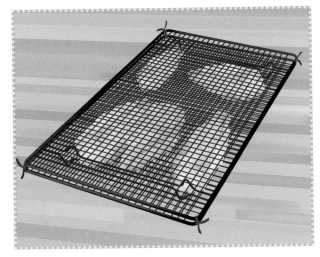

Skinless fish fillets fall apart on the grill (especially if they're thin). Here's an easy solution: Make your own fish-grilling rack from 2 wire cake-cooling racks.

Coat the racks with nonstick spray, or oil well. Arrange the fish fillets on the rack, overlapping thin portions to keep the thickness uniform. Wire the edges together in several places with thin wire (wire twist-ties from a box of plastic bags work well, although the paper will burn off during grilling). Place the rack of fish on the grate over the coals, and turn as needed to cook both sides evenly. To serve, cut the wire along one edge and open the racks like a book, loosening the fish from the rack as you open.

Herb-Rubbed Red Snapper

4 servings
Preliminary preparation: Under 15 minutes initial prep, 3 hours marinating
Grilling: Indirect medium heat, under 15 minutes
Special equipment: Hinged grilling basket, or 2 cake-cooling racks (page 58)

1 cup (240 ml/60 g) fresh parsley leaves (tightly packed)

2 fresh basil leaves

2 sprigs fresh thyme

2 sprigs fresh rosemary

2 tablespoons (30 ml) dried oregano

1 tablespoon (15 ml/9 g) kosher salt

1 teaspoon (5 ml) freshly ground black pepper

1/2 cup (120 ml) olive oil

4 boneless, skin-on red snapper fillets (about 6 ounces/170 g each)

Place parsley and basil in food processor. Strip thyme and rosemary leaves from the stems and add to processor. Add oregano, salt and pepper. Start processing and slowly drizzle in the olive oil from the top. Process until mixture is well blended. Place snapper in baking dish; cover with herb mixture. Cover dish and refrigerate for 3 hours.

When you're almost ready to cook, remove dish from refrigerator and let stand at room temperature while you prepare grill for indirect medium heat; lightly oil grilling basket. Place snapper fillets in grilling basket, or between 2 cake-cooling racks (page 58). Place on grate away from heat and cook for about 5 minutes. Turn fish, and cook for an additional 3 to 5 minutes, or until fish is just opaque. Serve immediately.

Fish-Stuffed Pepper Cups

4 servings
Preliminary preparation: Under 15 minutes
Grilling: Initial searing, followed by indirect medium-high heat, under 45 minutes

2 tablespoons (30 ml/20 g) drained capers

1/2 cup (120 ml/128 g) mayonnaise

2 teaspoons (10 ml/2 g) snipped fresh dill weed

2 teaspoons (10 ml) Dijon mustard

1/2 teaspoon (2.5 ml/3 g) salt

1 pound (454 g) boneless, skinless fish fillets at least 1/2 inch (1.25 cm) thick

2 bell peppers (for an attractive presentation, use 2 different colors)

1 teaspoon (5 ml) olive oil, approximate

2 tablespoons (30 ml/14 g) bread crumbs

2 teaspoons (10 g) butter, melted

Add capers to medium bowl and smash slightly with a fork. Add mayonnaise, dill, mustard and salt; stir to mix well. Cut fish into 1/2-inch (1.25-cm) cubes and add to mayonnaise mixture. Stir gently to blend; set aside. Carefully cut stems from peppers, removing as little of the pepper flesh as possible. Cut peppers into halves. Remove and discard seeds and pulpy veins, again removing as little of the pepper flesh as possible.

Prepare grill for indirect medium-high heat. Place peppers, cut-side up, on grate directly over heat. Brush insides of peppers with oil. Grill for about 5 minutes, or until pepper skins have colored in spots and peppers are somewhat soft. Transfer peppers to plate. Divide fish mixture evenly between the peppers. In small bowl, toss together bread crumbs and butter, then sprinkle mixture evenly over fish. Place peppers on grate away from heat. Cover grill and cook for 25 minutes; the crumb mixture should be golden and the fish cooked through.

Cedar Plank Fish

4 to 6 servings
Preliminary preparation: 8 hours soaking for plank
Grilling: Direct high heat, under 30 minutes
Special equipment: Cedar plank

This basic technique comes from the Pacific Northwest, where native peoples have used it for centuries. Salmon is the fish that is traditionally prepared on a cedar plank, but any firm, moderately oily fish works well. Be sure to get untreated cedar from the lumberyard, or purchase special cedar planks sold for cooking.

Red cedar plank, about 1/2 inch (1.25 cm) thick and large enough to hold fish in single layer

Skin-on or skinless salmon, char, halibut or trout fillets (about 2 pounds/900 g total)

2 teaspoons (10 ml) canola oil if using skinless fillets

All-Purpose Seasoning (page 118) or other seasoning of choice to taste

Soak plank for 8 hours, or overnight, in bucket of plain water (weight with brick to keep plank submerged). When you're ready to cook, prepare grill for direct high heat. Drain plank and pat dry. If using skinless fish, rub skin side with oil; place on plank, oiled-side down. If using skin-on fish, place on plank, skin-side down. Sprinkle fish generously with seasoning. Place plank on grate over heat. Cover grill and cook until fish is just opaque, 15 to 25 minutes depending on thickness of fish (the plank may catch on fire around the edges near the end, and this is okay; if fire becomes too strong, spray plank with water bottle). Serve on plank, or transfer fish to serving dish if you prefer; when you transfer fish from plank, work spatula between fish skin and flesh so skin remains on plank. Discard plank after use.

Variations

Onion Planked Fish: Use skinless fish fillets; omit oil. Place a layer of chopped green onions or sliced globe onions on soaked plank before adding fish. Place fish atop onions; season as directed. Sprinkle additional onions on top of fish; cook as directed.

Ginger Planked Fish: Omit seasoning blend. Chop together a 1-inch (2.5-cm) chunk of peeled fresh ginger-root and several strips of orange zest. Combine chopped mixture in small bowl with 1 teaspoon (5 ml) dry sherry, 1 teaspoon (5 ml) soy sauce and 1/2 teaspoon (2.5 ml) dark sesame oil. Place fish on soaked plank as directed above. Brush with ginger mixture; cook as directed.

Citrus Planked Fish: Use skinless fish fillets; omit oil and seasoning blend. Place a layer of orange and lemon slices on soaked plank before adding fish. In small bowl, combine 2 tablespoons (30 ml) thawed orange juice concentrate, and 1/2 teaspoon (2.5 ml) each of olive oil, Dijon mustard, dried oregano and salt; mix well and brush over fish. Top fish with a few additional orange and lemon slices, arranging attractively. Cook as directed.

Garlic-Cajun Planked Fish: Omit seasoning blend. In small bowl, combine 2 tablespoons (30 ml/8 g) chopped fresh parsley, 1 tablespoon (15 ml/11 g) chopped garlic and 1 1/2 teaspoons (7.5 ml) olive oil. Place fish on soaked plank as directed above. Sprinkle fish generously with any Cajun-style seasoning blend; spread garlic mixture evenly over fish. Cook as directed.

Maple-Glazed Planked Fish: Omit seasoning blend. Slice 2 green onions thinly; set aside. In small saucepan, combine 1/4 cup (60 ml) pure maple syrup, and 1 table-spoon (15 ml) each of butter, lemon or lime juice and soy sauce. Add 2 teaspoons (10 ml/10 g) minced fresh gin-gerroot, 1 teaspoon (5 ml/3 g) minced garlic and 1/4 tea-spoon (1.25 ml) hot red pepper flakes. Heat to boiling over medium-high heat; reduce heat slightly and cook until reduced by half, stirring occasionally. Place fish on soaked plank as directed above. Brush generously with maple mixture; sprinkle with green onions. Cook as directed.

- If you're cooking fillets that are at least ³/₄ inch (1.9 cm) thick or still have the skin on, you can place them directly on the grate (oil the grate or the fillets first). For an attractive presentation, put the fillet on the grate with the flesh-side down and cook until nicely marked, then rotate the fillet 90 degrees and cook a bit longer to create cross-hatch marks; turn the fillet and finish cooking.

- For thinner fillets, use a lightly oiled hinged grilling basket, or cake-cooling racks as described on page 58. Baskets and racks also work well for thicker fillets, but are almost essential for thinner fillets to keep them from falling apart.

- Fish fillets cook fairly quickly on the grill. Plan on about 10 minutes per inch (2.5 cm) of thickness for direct-heat grilling; fillets that are ½ inch (1.25 cm) thick should be cooked in about 5 minutes, while fillets that are 1½ inches (3.8 cm) thick will take about 15 minutes.

- If you like, you may brush the fish with any leftover marinade during cooking. For safety, heat the marinade to boiling after removing the fish (but before grilling); or, be sure to turn the fish, brushed-side down, after brushing to give the marinade time to cook (don't brush marinade on the top side of the fillets at the end of cooking, as it will not have time to cook properly).

- Fish is perfectly done when it is just opaque throughout. Poke a thin knife (or fork, if necessary) into the fish and separate the flakes slightly; when they are no longer translucent, immediately remove the fish from the grill.

- Medium-rare (or rare) tuna—and even salmon—is quite popular now. However, fish do have parasites, and special handling is needed to ensure safety. If you enjoy rare fish, buy special sushi-grade fish from a reliable fishmonger; or, freeze your own catch for at least 15 days in a sub-zero freezer.

Mustard-Tarragon Fish

4 servings
Preliminary preparation: 1 hour marinating
Grilling: Indirect high heat, under 30 minutes

Choose fillets that are ½ to ¾ inch (1.25 to 1.9 cm) thick for this easy dish. It's perfect for rich fish like salmon, bluefish, char or lake trout, but also works well on milder fish such as walleye, halibut or pike. Cut longer fillets into shorter pieces for individual portions; they'll be easier to handle than a long fillet.

4 skin-on salmon or other fillet portions (5 to 6 ounces/140 to 170 g each)

¼ cup (60 ml/60 g) Dijon mustard

2 tablespoons (30 ml) olive oil

2 tablespoons (30 ml/10 g) finely chopped fresh tarragon (do not substitute dried)

1 teaspoon (5 ml/2 g) coarsely ground black pepper

Rinse fillets; pat dry with paper towels. Arrange in single layer in glass baking dish, skin-side down. In small bowl, combine remaining ingredients. Divide mustard mixture evenly between fish portions, spreading over flesh to cover completely. Cover dish and refrigerate for 1 hour. Remove dish from refrigerator 15 minutes before cooking.

When you're ready to cook, prepare grill for indirect high heat. Place fish, skin-side down, on grate away from heat. Cover grill; cook until thickest portion of fish is barely opaque, 12 to 18 minutes. Remove from grill; let stand for 3 or 4 minutes before serving.

Grilled Tuna with Orange Basil Sauce

2 servings
Preliminary preparation: Under 15 minutes initial prep, 30 minutes marinating
Grilling: Direct medium heat, under 15 minutes

2 tuna fillets, 1 inch (2.5 cm) thick (about 6 ounces/ 170 g each)

Juice from 1 orange

Juice from 1 lemon

1/2 cup (120 ml) extra-virgin olive oil

6 heaping tablespoons (90 ml/15 g) finely chopped fresh basil

1/4 teaspoon (1.25 ml/.75 g) kosher salt, plus additional for seasoning

1/4 teaspoon (1.25 ml/.5 g) freshly ground black pepper, plus additional for seasoning

Place tuna fillets in zipper-style plastic bag. In mixing bowl, combine remaining ingredients and mix with a whisk. Pour mixture over tuna and marinate at room temperature for 30 minutes.

Prepare grill for direct medium heat; lightly oil grate. Shake marinade from fish, reserving marinade. Season fish with salt and pepper to taste. Place fish on grate over heat. Cook for 4 to 5 minutes per side, or until desired doneness (do not cook more than a total of 10 minutes per inch/2.5 cm of thickness). While fish is cooking, heat marinade to boiling on stovetop; cook until reduced slightly. Pour hot cooked marinade over fish to serve.

Fish Tacos

4 servings
Preliminary preparation: Under 30 minutes initial prep, 1 to 2 hours marinating
Grilling: Direct medium heat, under 15 minutes
Special equipment (optional): 2 cake-cooling racks, or thin skewers

In California, you can buy fish tacos similar to these. The fish is usually deep-fried in the tacquerias and restaurants; in this recipe, grilled fish provide a wonderful variation.

1/2 cup (120 ml) dry white wine

2 tablespoons (30 ml) freshly squeezed lime juice

2 tablespoons (30 ml) canola or olive oil

1 tablespoon (15 ml/3 g) chopped fresh cilantro

1/8 teaspoon (.6 ml) ground cumin

2 cloves garlic, minced

1 to 1 1/4 pounds (454 to 567 g) boneless, skinless marlin, mahi mahi, halibut or other firm fish (about 1 inch/2.5 cm thick)

1 1/2 cups (350 ml/105 g) finely shredded cabbage, preferably a mix of red and green

2 teaspoons (10 ml) cider vinegar or wine vinegar

1 teaspoon (5 ml/6 g) salt

1/4 cup (60 ml/60 g) mayonnaise (reduced-fat works fine, but don't use salad dressing)

3 tablespoons (45 ml) tomato-based salsa

4 flour tortillas (10-inch/25-cm size), warmed in oven or microwave just before serving

In glass dish, combine wine, lime juice, oil, cilantro, cumin and garlic; beat with fork until well blended. Cut fish with the grain into strips that are 3 or 4 inches (7.5 to 10 cm) long and roughly 1/2 inch (1.25 cm) wide. Add fish strips to wine mixture, turning gently to coat. Cover dish and refrigerate for 1 to 2 hours (but no longer, or the fish will become mushy).

Meanwhile, combine cabbage, vinegar and salt in non-reactive mixing bowl, tossing to mix well. Let stand at room temperature for about 30 minutes. Drain, rinse briefly, and drain again. In same bowl, stir together mayonnaise and salsa. Add well-drained cabbage; stir well. Cover and refrigerate until serving time.

When you're ready to cook, prepare grill for direct medium heat; oil grate well. Drain fish strips, discarding marinade. Place on grate over heat (see sidebar on page 62 for alternatives that help the fish hold together during grilling). Cook for 7 to 8 minutes total, turning carefully so each side is exposed to heat; fish should be just opaque in center. To serve, place fish strips in warmed flour tortilla, top with cabbage mixture, and roll up like a burrito.

To keep the fish from falling apart: Sandwich fish between 2 cake-cooling racks (see page 58); place wired-together racks over coals and cook for about 4 minutes on each side. Or, run thin skewers lengthwise through fish strips before placing on oiled grate; remove skewers before serving.

Salmon or Trout Niçoise

2 servings
Preliminary preparation: Under an hour
Grilling: Direct medium heat, under 15 minutes

Salmon or trout make an excellent stand-in for the tuna usually used in this updated version of a classic French dish; grilling the fish gives it a delicious flair. If you start with already-cooked beets and potatoes, prep time is reduced to about 15 minutes (bring the beets and potatoes to room temperature before using). —T.M.

Dressing

1 tablespoon (15 ml/10 g) drained capers

1/2 cup (120 ml) extra-virgin olive oil

3 tablespoons (45 ml) red wine vinegar

1 teaspoon (5 ml) Dijon mustard

Small clove garlic, pressed

Salt and pepper to taste

2 small beets

8 ounces (225 g) new red potatoes or fingerling
   potatoes

1 egg, optional

4 ounces (113 g) fresh green beans, ends trimmed

3 cups (690 ml/165 g) torn mixed salad greens

1 ripe top-quality tomato, cored and seeded, cut into 8 wedges

1/4 cup (60 ml/93 g) roasted red bell pepper strips

12-ounce (340-g) boneless, skinless salmon or trout portion*

1 teaspoon (5 ml) olive oil

Salt and pepper

10 to 12 whole black olives, preferably oil-cured

4 anchovy fillets, optional

To prepare dressing: Mash capers slightly with a fork, then transfer to small glass jar. Add remaining ingredients. Cover jar tightly and shake to blend. Set aside.

Add beets to saucepan of boiling water and cook until tender, about 35 minutes. Meanwhile, boil or steam potatoes in another pan until tender; drain and set aside to cool, then cut into quarters. Hard-boil the egg; peel while still warm and set aside to cool. Steam, microwave or boil the green beans just until tender-crisp; refresh under cold running water and drain well. When beets are tender, hold under cold running water and slip skin off (use a fork to hold a hot beet, or wear rubber gloves to protect your hands from the heat). Cut each beet into 8 wedges; set aside to cool to room temperature.

Divide greens between 2 individual serving plates. Arrange potatoes, green beans, beet pieces, tomato wedges and roasted pepper strips attractively around the edges of the plates, keeping the center clear for the salmon (there should be lettuce in the center, but none

of the other ingredients). Quarter the egg, then divide between the plates. Set plates aside.

Prepare grill for direct medium heat. Lightly oil salmon; season with salt and pepper to taste. Place on grate over heat, flesh-side down, and cook for 5 minutes, turning once to create cross-hatch grill marks. Turn fish over and cook on second side until flesh is just opaque, 5 to 10 minutes longer. Divide salmon into 2 pieces, and place onto plates in the center so salmon is surrounded by vegetables. Divide olives evenly between the 2 plates; cross 2 anchovy strips over each piece of salmon. Serve prepared dressing on the side (you may have leftover dressing, which will keep in the refrigerator for a week or longer).

*You may substitute 2 individual salmon steaks, about 5 ounces (140 g) each, for the fillet in this dish. The steaks will have skin and bones, so require additional care by the diner.

Grilled Striper with Crusty Topping

2 servings per fish portion; make as many as you wish
Preliminary preparation: Under 15 minutes initial prep, 30 minutes marinating
Grilling: Direct medium-high heat, under 15 minutes

12-ounce (340-g) portion skin-on striped bass fillet, about 1 inch (2.5 cm) thick

2 tablespoons (30 ml) dry vermouth

1 tablespoon plus 1½ teaspoons (22.5 ml/22 g) Dijon mustard

1 small shallot, minced

3 tablespoons (45 ml/21 g) Italian-seasoned bread crumbs

2 tablespoons (30 ml/20 g) crumbled feta cheese

Rinse fish; pat dry and place in glass baking dish. In small jar, combine vermouth, mustard and shallot; cover tightly and shake to blend. Pour vermouth mixture over fish. Set aside to marinate at room temperature for about 30 minutes, or refrigerate for up to 1 hour. Meanwhile, combine bread crumbs and feta in small bowl. Crumble together with a fork to break up the feta into small pieces, then rub with your fingers until the mixture is the consistency of coarse sand. Set aside.

Prepare grill for direct medium-high heat; lightly oil grate. Place fish, skin-side up, on grate over heat. Cook for about 4 minutes. Turn fish skin-side down. Spoon bread-crumb mixture over fish flesh, patting into place. Cover grill and cook until fish is just opaque; total cooking time should be 10 to 13 minutes. Let fish stand for 5 minutes before serving.

Cajun Shrimp

6 servings
Preliminary preparation: Under 15 minutes
Grilling: Direct medium heat, under 15 minutes
Special equipment: Metal skewers

1½ pounds (680 g) peeled and deveined large raw shrimp, tail on

¼ cup (60 ml) olive oil

Cajun Spice Blend

1 teaspoon (5 ml/2.5 g) onion powder

1 teaspoon (5 ml/2.5 g) garlic powder

1 teaspoon (5 ml/2 g) paprika

1 teaspoon (5 ml) ground dried oregano

½ teaspoon (2.5 ml/1.5 g) kosher salt

½ teaspoon (2.5 ml/1 g) cayenne pepper

In large bowl, combine shrimp and oil, tossing to coat well. In zipper-style plastic bag or another large bowl, mix together all spice-blend ingredients. Add shrimp, tossing to coat shrimp evenly with spices. Thread shrimp on skewers.

Prepare grill for direct medium heat; lightly oil grate. Place skewers on grate over heat. Cook until shrimp are pink and opaque, about 3 minutes per side, turning once. Serve hot.

Basil Shrimp with Pineapple

Serves 2 or 3
Preliminary preparation: Under 15 minutes initial prep, 1 hour marinating
Grilling: Direct medium heat, under 15 minutes
Special equipment: Metal or bamboo skewers

Marinade

¼ cup (60 ml) freshly squeezed lemon juice

¼ cup (60 ml) olive oil

1 tablespoon (15 ml) pineapple juice

1 tablespoon (15 ml/6 g) finely grated fresh lemon zest

2 tablespoons (30 ml/8 g) chopped fresh parsley, or 1 tablespoon (15 ml) dried

1 tablespoon (15 ml/3 g) chopped fresh basil

1 teaspoon (5 ml/3 g) kosher salt

¼ teaspoon (1.25 ml/.5 g) paprika

⅛ teaspoon (.6 ml) hot red pepper flakes

1 clove garlic, minced

12 ounces (340 g) peeled and deveined large raw shrimp

1 can (20 ounces/567 g) pineapple chunks, drained, or 1 cup (240 ml/250 g) cut-up fresh pineapple

In mixing bowl, whisk together marinade ingredients. Place shrimp in shallow dish and add marinade, stirring to coat. Cover and refrigerate for 1 hour; if using bamboo skewers, soak in water while shrimp marinates.

When you're ready to cook, prepare grill for direct medium heat. Alternate shrimp and pineapple on skewers. Place skewers on grate over heat. Cook until shrimp are pink and opaque, about 3 minutes per side, turning once.

Cajun Shrimp (left)

Grilled Shrimp with Garlic White Wine Sauce

6 servings
Preliminary preparation: Under 15 minutes
Grilling: Direct medium heat, under 15 minutes
Special equipment: Metal or bamboo skewers

1/4 cup (60 ml/40 g) chopped onion

6 cloves garlic, minced

1/4 cup (60 ml) olive oil, divided

1/3 cup (80 ml) dry white wine

2 tablespoons (30 g) unsalted butter

2 tablespoons (30 ml) lemon juice

2 tablespoons (30 ml/5 g) snipped fresh chives

1 tablespoon (15 ml) Worcestershire sauce

2 pounds (900 g) peeled and deveined jumbo raw shrimp, tail on

1 teaspoon (5 ml/2 g) cayenne pepper

Salt and freshly ground black pepper

1 tablespoon (15 ml/4 g) minced fresh flat-leaf parsley

If using bamboo skewers, soak in cold water while you prepare sauce. In skillet, sauté onion and garlic in 2 tablespoons of the oil over medium-high heat until just soft. Add wine, butter, lemon juice, chives and Worcestershire sauce. Simmer for about 3 minutes. Strain sauce; set aside and keep warm.

In nonreactive bowl, combine shrimp, remaining 2 tablespoons oil, cayenne pepper, and salt and black pepper to taste; toss to coat shrimp thoroughly. Thread shrimp on skewers.

Prepare grill for direct medium heat; lightly oil grate. Place skewers on grate over heat. Cook until shrimp are pink and opaque, 3 to 4 minutes per side, turning once. To serve, spoon some of the warm sauce onto each individual serving plate and place 4 or 5 shrimp on top of the sauce. Sprinkle with parsley and serve immediately.

Stir-Fry Alligator and Snow Peas

4 servings
Preliminary preparation: Under 30 minutes
Grilling: Direct high heat, under 15 minutes
Special equipment: Wok or large skillet

Remember to keep sleeves away from the heat, and don't slop oil into the fire. —K.F.

1 pound (454 g) alligator meat, trimmed and cut into 1/8-inch (.3-cm) slices

2 tablespoons (30 ml/15 g) cornstarch

1/2 teaspoon (2.5 ml/3 g) salt

1/2 cup plus 2 tablespoons (150 ml) peanut oil, divided

3 egg whites, lightly beaten

1 1/2 cups (350 ml/150 g) green onion bulbs (white part only), cut into 1-inch (2.5-cm) pieces before measuring

1 cup (240 ml/150 g) cut-up bok choy (1-inch/2.5-cm pieces)

1 tablespoon (15 ml/15 g) minced garlic

1/2 cup (120 ml/140 g) miso*

1 pound (454 g) snow peas

1 cup (240 ml) unsalted or reduced-sodium chicken broth

2 tablespoons (30 ml) soy sauce

2 teaspoons (10 ml) sesame oil

1 teaspoon (5 ml/5 g) minced fresh gingerroot

Place alligator meat in nonreactive bowl. Sprinkle cornstarch over meat, tossing to coat. Add salt and 2 tablespoons (30 ml) peanut oil; mix well. Mix in egg whites; let stand at room temperature for 20 minutes.

Prepare grill for direct high heat. Place wok on grate and let it get very hot. Add remaining 1/2 cup (120 ml) peanut oil to wok and let it heat up. Add alligator meat and cook, stirring constantly, for about 4 minutes. Remove alligator meat with slotted spoon and set aside.

Carefully pour off all but 1/4 cup (60 ml) oil from the wok. Add green onions, bok choy and garlic; stir-fry for about a minute. Add miso and alligator meat to the wok. Cover and let cook for 2 minutes. Add snow peas, chicken broth, soy sauce and sesame oil; stir-fry for about a minute. Add gingerroot; stir-fry for about a minute longer. Remove from heat and serve hot.

*Miso is fermented soybean paste. Look for it at natural-foods stores, health-food stores and at large supermarkets.

Tropical Shrimp and Sausage Kabobs

4 servings
Preliminary preparation: Under 30 minutes initial prep, 1 hour marinating
Grilling: Direct medium heat, under 15 minutes

Look for peeled sugar cane in the produce section of large supermarkets, or in Latin markets. Sugar cane "swizzle sticks" are easier to work with than the larger chunks that are also marketed.

One-quarter of a package (4-ounce/113-g package) sugar cane swizzle sticks

8 ounces (225 g) fresh pineapple chunks

2 skin-on Italian or other sausages (about 6 ounces/ 170 g each); venison works fine

3/4 pound (340 g) peeled and deveined raw shrimp

1/4 cup (60 ml) gold rum

2 tablespoons (30 ml) orange juice

1 tablespoon (15 ml) canola oil

1 teaspoon (5 ml/5 g) minced fresh gingerroot

1 teaspoon (5 ml/3 g) minced garlic

1/4 teaspoon (1.25 ml) hot red pepper flakes

1/4 teaspoon (1.25 ml) dried marjoram

1/4 teaspoon (1.25 ml) salt

Use large, heavy knife (such as a 10-inch/25-cm chef's knife) to cut sugar cane into skewers that are 1/8 inch (3 mm) square and about 8 inches (20 cm) long. You'll need 8 to 10; you can get 4 from each swizzle stick if you are careful (or lucky!) with your cutting. (If you can't find sugar cane swizzle sticks, use regular metal skewers.) Cut pineapple into chunks that are approximately 1/2x1x1 inch (1.25x2.5x2.5 cm). Cut sausages into 3/4-inch (1.9-cm) rounds, discarding ends. Thread pineapple, shrimp and sausage (thread sausage through the cut ends, not through the skin) alternately onto sugar-cane skewers, placing in 9x13-inch (23x33-cm) baking dish as you make each one. Combine remaining ingredients in small glass jar; cover tightly and shake to emulsify. Pour rum mixture over assembled kabobs, turning carefully to coat. Cover and refrigerate for 1 hour, turning kabobs occasionally.

When you're ready to cook, prepare grill for direct medium heat; lightly oil grate. Place kabobs on grate over heat. Cover grill and cook until sausages and shrimp are just cooked through, about 10 minutes, turning every few minutes.

Note: The sugar-cane skewers can't be completely eaten, but they are interesting to chew on; they pick up the flavor of the shrimp and sausage.

vegetarian

Portabella Mushroom Burgers <u>with</u> Basil Aioli

2 servings
Preliminary preparation: Under 30 minutes
Grilling: Direct medium heat, under 15 minutes

TIP: Grilled portabella mushrooms make a tossed salad special. Prepare a few extra mushrooms while you're making this dish, and refrigerate until needed.

2 large portabella mushroom caps (4 to 5 ounces/
    113 to 142 g each)

Marinade
1/4 cup (60 ml) balsamic vinegar
3 tablespoons (45 ml) olive oil
1 teaspoon (5 ml) dried basil
1 teaspoon (5 ml) dried oregano
1/2 teaspoon (2.5 ml) dried thyme
1/4 teaspoon (1.25 ml) kosher salt
1/4 teaspoon (1.25 ml) freshly ground pepper
1 clove garlic, finely minced

Basil Aioli
1/2 cup (120 ml/128 g) good-quality mayonnaise
    (such as Hellmann's)
1 small clove garlic, finely minced
10 to 12 large fresh basil leaves, thinly slivered
1 1/2 teaspoons (7.5 ml) freshly squeezed lemon
    juice
1/4 teaspoon (1.25 ml) kosher salt
1/4 teaspoon (1.25 ml) freshly ground pepper

2 slices cheese (1 ounce/28 g each), optional
2 split hamburger rolls
Lettuce and sliced tomatoes for serving

Cut stems off mushrooms and discard; clean caps with damp paper towels. Place smooth-side up in shallow nonreactive dish. In small bowl, whisk together marinade ingredients. Pour over mushrooms and marinate at room temperature for 15 to 20 minutes. Meanwhile, combine all aioli ingredients in another small bowl; whisk to blend and set aside.

Prepare grill for direct medium heat; lightly oil grate. Place mushrooms on grate over heat and cook for 5 to 10 minutes, or until tender, turning at least once. Top with cheese if desired during the last 2 minutes of grilling. To serve, spread the insides of split hamburger rolls with a tablespoon of Basil Aioli; top with grilled portabella, lettuce and tomatoes. Refrigerate remaining aioli for other uses.

Backyard Tofu Steaks

2 servings
Preliminary preparation: 2 to 4 hours draining, 15 minutes active prep, 1 to 3 hours marinating
Grilling: Indirect medium-high heat, under 30 minutes

TIP: Tofu readily takes on the flavors of other ingredients. Feel free to change the flavoring in the marinade to suit your taste; just be sure to use some oil and an acidic ingredient such as vinegar or lemon juice. This goes very well with grilled asparagus (page 130) and a brown-rice side dish.

1 block firm tofu (3/4 to 1 pound/340 to 454 g)
3 tablespoons (45 ml) olive oil
2 tablespoons (30 ml) freshly squeezed lemon
    juice
1 tablespoon (15 ml/4 g) chopped fresh parsley
1/4 teaspoon (1.25 ml) hot red pepper flakes
1/4 teaspoon (1.25 ml/.75 g) kosher salt
1 or 2 cloves garlic, minced

Place wire-mesh strainer (a large-diameter strainer that is wide at the bottom works best) in a mixing bowl. Gently place tofu in center. Top with a flat plate and place in the refrigerator; place a weight (such as a medium jar of pickles) on the plate and let the tofu drain for 2 to 4 hours.

When tofu has drained, discard accumulated liquid. Slice tofu in half horizontally to make 2 thinner slabs. In small glass baking dish, combine remaining ingredients, stirring with fork to blend. Add tofu slabs, turning to coat. Cover and refrigerate for 1 to 3 hours, turning several times.

When you're ready to cook, prepare grill for indirect medium-high heat; generously oil grate (the grate must be very clean to prevent the tofu from sticking). Drain tofu; place on grate away from heat. Cover grill and cook for 5 minutes. Rotate tofu 45° without flipping; re-cover and cook for 5 minutes longer. Gently flip tofu and cook for 10 minutes longer. Serve immediately.

Pizza Margherita

4 servings
Preliminary preparation: 15 minutes initial prep, plus about an hour rising for the dough
Grilling: Indirect medium-high heat, under 15 minutes

Use these general instructions to construct any sort of pizza you'd like. This one is a classic, genuine Italian pizza that you'd find in pizzerias across northern Italy; however, the Americanized version with red sauce, multiple toppings, and lots of cheese works just as well.
—T.M.

Pizza Crust*

³/₄ cup (180 ml) warm water (110°F/43°C)

1¹/₄ teaspoons (6.25 ml/3.5 g) active dry yeast (about half of a ¹/₄-ounce package)

A good pinch of sugar

2 cups (470 ml/280 g) unbleached all-purpose flour, plus additional for working dough

³/₄ teaspoon (3.75 ml/4.5 g) salt

1 tablespoon (15 ml) olive oil

2 garden-fresh medium tomatoes

8 ounces (225 g) fresh, water-packed mozzarella balls, or shredded regular mozzarella cheese

2 tablespoons (30 ml) extra-virgin olive oil

1 or 2 cloves garlic, minced

¹/₄ cup (60 ml/30 g) grated Romano or Parmesan cheese

8 fresh basil leaves, torn

To make the crust: In measuring cup, combine water, yeast and sugar; let stand until mixture appears creamy on surface and begins to form a few small bubbles, about 5 minutes. (If the mixture doesn't begin to look creamy and bubbly, discard and start over with new yeast.) Combine flour and salt in food processor fitted with metal blade; pulse a few times to mix. With machine running, add creamy yeast mixture through feed tube. Process until mixture is smooth and well mixed, then add olive oil and pulse a few times. Scrape the dough, which will be somewhat sticky, out onto work surface that has been generously dusted with flour. Knead a few times to incorporate any loose bits of flour that were not incorporated in the food processor, then divide into 2 equal portions. Shape each into a smooth ball; dust with flour. Cover with clean dishtowel; let rise for 45 minutes to an hour. Meanwhile, peel and core tomatoes; slice thinly and set on a layer of paper towels to drain. If using fresh mozzarella balls, slice about ¹/₄ inch (6 mm) thick and set aside.

After rising, place balls of dough on floured work surface and shape each into a 9-inch (23-cm) round, pressing with your fingertips and palms; work from the center to the outside edge as you shape the dough. Transfer to floured baking sheet. Let rounds stand while you heat grill.

Prepare grill for indirect medium-high heat; lightly oil grate. Place pizza rounds on grate away from heat. Grill until undersides are nicely browned and beginning to firm up. Turn with large spatula and cook until second side is browned. Transfer rounds to baking sheet. Brush tops with olive oil; scatter garlic over the top. Arrange drained tomato slices on crusts; top with mozzarella cheese, dividing evenly. Sprinkle with Romano cheese. Return pizzas to grate away from heat. Cover grill and cook until cheese melts and dough is cooked through, about 5 minutes. Scatter basil leaves over pizza before cutting; serve immediately.

*To save time, you may use a loaf of frozen bread dough, thawed, instead of the homemade dough above; cut in half and shape into 2 smaller rounds, each about 8 inches (20 cm). Proceed as directed.

Smoking Meat, Poultry & Fish

t's easy to add a bit of smoke flavoring to foods during regular grilling or barbecuing. You can simply toss a few soaked chunks of smoking wood onto the lit coals in your charcoal grill, or you might want to add a few wood chips to your gas grill. For more serious smoke, however, you need special methods and, in some cases, special equipment. Smoking is divided into four categories for this book, based on the cooking temperature: cold, cool, medium and hot.

• **Cold smoking** is used by commercial smokehouses in the production of ham, bacon and other cured, smoked meats. It takes place at temperatures below 120°F (49°C)—generally in the range of 90°F to 100°F (32°C to 38°C). Meats to be cold-smoked are almost always cured using a dry or liquid mixture containing salt and curing agents such as sodium nitrate and sodium nitrite. Because the temperatures used in cold smoking are those at which bacteria thrive, it is an advanced technique that should not be attempted at home without special equipment.

• **Cool smoking** takes place at temperatures from 140°F to 200°F (60°C to 93°C), and is used by home cooks to make jerky and smoked fish, as well as to flavor foods that will get additional cooking by another method. Box-style electric smokers (page 10) are best for this technique; a well-insulated box-style smoker helps keep the smoking

temperature at the optimal level, something that may be difficult with an uninsulated aluminum smoker. Foods to be cool smoked are typically brined (soaked in a saltwater solution; see pages 53 and 79). Brining adds moisture by changing the molecular structure of meat.

• **Medium-temperature smoking,** or barbecue smoking, is a low-and-slow method of cooking similar to that discussed in Chapter 4, Low-and-Slow Techniques; the main difference is that medium-temperature smoking includes the element of smoke, which is not always used in other low-and-slow cooking methods. Low-and-slow cooking takes place at temperatures from 175°F to 275°F (80°C to 135°C), and is perfect for less-tender cuts such as brisket and shoulder; it also works well for larger cuts such as roasts. An offset firebox smoker, steel-drum barbecue or bullet-style smoker (pages 8 and 9) is perfect for medium-temperature smoking, but you can also get great results from a covered grill (page 7) or insulated box-style smoker (page 10). Most medium-temperature smoking incorporates the use of a water pan to keep the meat moist during the lengthy cooking. Foods to be cooked at this temperature range are sometimes brined.

• **Hot smoking,** also called smoke-cooking, is done at temperatures above 275°F (135°C). The smoke flavor is less intense, because the food is exposed to the smoke for a shorter amount of time. A bullet-style water smoker is perfect for hot smoking; covered grills also work well, as do steel-drum barbecue units. Steaks and roasts that are naturally tender and have some internal marbling are best when smoked at medium to hot temperatures; the higher temperatures help develop a delicious, browned exterior while keeping the inside moist. Brining before hot smoking is optional; it firms the flesh and improves the flavor but takes longer and increases the sodium content of the food. Try a side-by-side comparison by dividing a piece of fish or meat in half; brine one half, then smoke the pieces side by side to see which you prefer.

Adjusting and Monitoring the Smoker

Because smoking often requires lengthy cooking times, it is important to keep the heat at a fairly constant level. With gas or electric equipment, maintaining even heat is fairly easy; simply keep an eye on the temperature and adjust the controls in small increments until it stabilizes. Charcoal or natural wood require a bit more finesse. If you are cooking with charcoal briquettes, add 10 to 12 every hour or so (more if you're hot smoking), dividing them evenly between each side if cooking by indirect heat in a grill. If you're using manufactured briquettes, pre-start them in a chimney starter or separate grill before adding them to the smoker; otherwise, the food may acquire an unpleasant taste as the chemicals in the briquettes burn off. Natural (lump) charcoal or natural wood can be added directly to the fire without pre-starting.

As with a charcoal grill, temperatures in a charcoal-fueled smoker can also be adjusted by regulating the airflow. Open the vents to increase the temperature; close them a bit to reduce the heat. One other key factor to maintaining the temperature is to open the

lid only when necessary. Don't open it to peek! You lose heat—and precious smoky vapors—every time the lid is opened, so keep it to a minimum. If you're using a water smoker and find that you have to add liquid to the water pan, make sure it is already boiling hot so it won't decrease the temperature in the smoker too much.

Although many smokers and grills feature thermometers built into the lid, these are not ideal for smoking. For one thing, they show the temperature at the lid, and this could vary quite a bit from the actual temperature on the cooking grate. Furthermore, the thermometers are frequently inaccurate, and become even less accurate over time. A digital cooking thermometer with a probe (below) is a much better choice. These units, which are designed for oven cooking, consist of a metal probe with a flexible, heat-proof cable that plugs into a battery-powered display unit. For oven cooking, the probe is inserted into the roast or poultry; the cable is run out the oven door and plugged into the base unit, which sits on the countertop. The base unit displays the temperature of the probe; some models incorporate an alarm that alerts the cook when the desired temperature has been reached. Polder manufactures several models that can be found in many supermarkets as well as at cookware and gourmet shops.

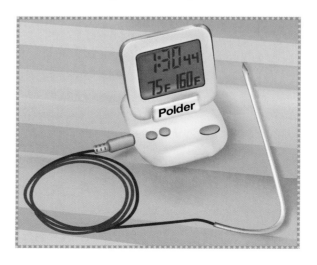

To use a digital probe thermometer to monitor smoking temperature, stick the probe through a raw half-potato so as much as possible of the tip is exposed. Place the potato on the cooking grate next to the food, and run the cable out of the smoker; plug it into the base unit, which can sit on a small table next to the smoker. (Don't expose the base unit to high temperatures.) Serious smokers have a second unit to monitor the internal temperature of the meat being smoked as well.

Types of Wood, and How to Use Them

Most hardwood can be used for smoking. Hickory is highly prized, particularly in the South, but oak, alder and maple are also highly regarded. Wood from fruit trees such as cherry and apple is said to to produce a more aromatic smoke; wood from nut trees such as walnut and pecan is also favored. In reality, the species of wood has a somewhat subtle effect on the flavor of the finished food. If you're buying wood, experiment with a few types until you determine which species you prefer; if you do a lot of smoking, consider buying wood sold for fireplaces, then cut it to smaller sizes. Make sure the wood vendor sells only quality wood, of an appropriate species; never use moldy or rotten wood for smoking. Birch should also be avoided, because it tends to spark and pop, creating too much ash. Never use wood from oleander or any poisonous plants such as poison oak.

• **If you're gathering wood** from your yard, your smoking choices will be determined by what is growing there. Save trimmings from hardwood, fruit or nut trees, and pick up any sticks that fall. The wood you gather can be used *green* (undried), or it can be set aside and allowed to dry, then split to appropriate sizes. Note that if you're removing an insect-infested or rotten tree, the wood should not be used for smoking.

• **For an electric smoker,** you must use fine wood because the hot plate that heats the smoker (and burns the wood) is generally not going to get hot enough to ignite large pieces. This is particularly true if you're cool smoking, since the hot plate will be at a fairly low temperature. Some specialty stores sell smoking sawdust, which works very well for cool smoking (The Sausage Maker, at www.sausagemaker.com is a good source). A blend containing fine chips and shavings is more common; Luhr Jensen Chips 'n Chunks is widely available at outdoor and patio stores in a variety of wood species. These fine-textured woods can be used dry; simply place the wood into the provided wood pan or box. If you're smoking at higher temperatures, you may want to dampen the wood first; see the information on page 76 for a good method.

• **For a gas grill** (or the less-common gas smoker), use medium chips, which are often available at patio stores and sporting-goods outlets; the fine chips-and-shavings mixture also works, but doesn't last as long. Wrap the chips in heavy-duty foil, making a wide, flat packet. Poke 4 to 6 holes in the top of the packet, then place the packet on the burner elements, or as directed by the grill manufacturer. The foil contains the ash so the burners don't get fouled. Note that some gas grills come with a special smoker box; add wood directly to the box rather than wrapping it in foil.

• **For charcoal grilling,** larger pieces of wood are preferred for most recipes. The fine chips-and-shavings mixture can be used if it is well soaked, but it will burn up very quickly. This is acceptable if you just want to add a bit of smoke flavor to grilled foods; in fact, this works well for any of the recipes in the Grilling chapter (pages 14–71). For more serious smoke, use larger chips or chunks; 1- to 2-inch (2.5- to 5-cm) pieces are ideal. Wood to be used for charcoal grilling should be soaked in a bucket of water before being added to the coals. Smaller chips need to soak for 30 minutes to an hour, while larger chunks should be soaked for several hours—even overnight. (Note that green wood need not be soaked; it is ready to use "as is.")

How to Dampen Smoking Sawdust or Fine Chips

Place wood in a bowl or bucket. Add ½ cup (120 ml) water per 2 cups (470 ml) of wood, stirring to mix. Cover bowl tightly with plastic wrap or foil and let stand for at least 2 hours, or as long as overnight. This allows the moisture to equalize throughout the wood.

A GALLERY OF SMOKING WOOD

Aromatic woods are popular throughout the country for the flavor they produce in the food and the aroma of the wood smoke. Popular woods and other flavor enhancers include:

• ALDER—Delicate and sweet; works well with fish, seafood and game

• APPLE—Mild, sweet and slightly fruity; works well with poultry

• ASH—Light flavor that works well with venison

• CHERRY—Similar to apple, but more robust with a darker flavor; goes well with game, red meat and poultry

• HICKORY—A strong bacon flavor that works well with pork and beef

• MESQUITE—With its slightly bitter yet honeylike flavor, it is good for beef, fish or poultry

• OAK—Lighter than mesquite; good for smoking beef and fish

• PECAN—Sweet and nutty; works well with steaks and ribs

• SUGAR MAPLE—Mellow and smoky; works well with beef and fish

• DRIED CORNCOBS—Provide a rich, mellow taste to pork, chicken and venison

• GRAPE VINE CUTTINGS—Give a rich and fruity flavor to fish and poultry

• DRIED HERB BRANCHES—Fragrant yet tangy flavor; try woody stems from rosemary, marjoram and oregano in particular

Salmon Jerky

Yield: About 1 pound (454 g) jerky
Preliminary preparation: 12 hours brining, 1½ hours drying
Recommended equipment: Bullet-style smoker or box-style electric smoker
Smoking: Cool smoking, 6 to 8 hours

This somewhat sweet jerky is chewy yet tender, and makes a fabulous appetizer or trail snack.

2 pounds (900 g) boneless, skin-on (scaled) salmon fillet, preferably 1 inch (2.5 cm) thick or thicker

⅔ cup (160 ml/135 g) sugar

¼ cup (60 ml/52 g) Morton Tender Quick (or substitute; see page 79)

1 quart (950 ml) cold water

4 cups (1 liter) smoking sawdust (220 g) or fine chips (160 g)

Slice salmon along the length (not crosswise as you would when steaking) into ¼-inch-thick (.6-cm-thick) strips; this is easiest if salmon is partially frozen. In non-reactive bowl, combine sugar, Tender Quick and water, stirring until clear. Place salmon strips in ceramic bowl or plastic container. Add brine to cover completely; weight salmon with small saucer to keep it submerged. Cover and refrigerate for 12 hours.

After salmon has brined, rinse well in cold water; pat as dry as possible with paper towels. Arrange on smoking racks that have been coated with nonstick spray. Air-dry* with the aid of a table fan until a firm sheen appears on the salmon; it should look glossy rather than wet, and should not be sticky. Turn strips and air-dry second side (the second side dries more quickly). Total drying time will be about 1½ hours. Near the end of drying time, preheat smoker to 140°F (60°C).

When salmon is dry, place racks into smoker. Fill wood pan with smoking wood. Close smoker; smoke at 120°F-140°F (49°C-60°C) until salmon is firm and almost leathery, adding more wood to pan about once per hour until all wood has been used. Total smoking time should be between 6 and 8 hours.

Note: You may run out of wood before salmon is done. For best salmon flavor, simply continue drying salmon in smoker, without any additional wood, until it is done. If you like very strongly smoked salmon, add wood as needed, but keep in mind that the smoke can overpower the salmon.

*If it is warm in the room, it is safer to place the racks, uncovered, in the refrigerator for drying. Refrigerator drying will take several hours longer.

Fish

...as much as you wish
...to 12 hours brining,

...nt: Box-style electric smoker
...g, 6 to 10 hours

...quart/liter)

...ater

1/2 c... ...nning/pickling salt (or substitute;
see sid... ...n page 79)

1/2 cup (120 ml/110 g) light brown sugar (packed)

3 tablespoons (45 ml) rice vinegar or white wine
vinegar

1 tablespoon (15 ml) mixed pickling spice

Whole dressed fish (3/4 to 3 pounds/340 g to 1.36
kg), or skin-on fillets

6 cups (1.5 liters) smoking sawdust (330 g) or fine
chips* (240 g)

In nonreactive bowl, combine brine ingredients, stirring
until salt and sugar dissolve. Place fish in glass baking
dish or other nonreactive container. Pour brine over fish;
there should be enough brine to cover fish completely
(make additional brine as needed). Refrigerate fish for 8
to 12 hours, turning once or twice if possible.

The next day, drain fish, discarding brine. Pat fish dry with
paper towels. Arrange in a single layer on smoking racks
that have been coated with nonstick spray. Air-dry with the
aid of a table fan until a firm sheen appears on the exposed
flesh, 30 minutes to 1 hour; it should look glossy rather than
wet, and should not be sticky (if you prefer, refrigerate fish
on rack, uncovered, for several hours or until skin forms).
While fish is drying, preheat smoker to 140°F (60°C).

When fish is dry, place rack into smoker. Fill wood pan with
smoking wood. Smoke at 110°F-140°F (43°C-60°C), adding
more wood about once per hour, or as needed to maintain
light smoke. Fish is done when it feels firm to the touch and
appears opaque throughout; don't smoke for too long or it
will dry out and be too strongly flavored. Small whole fish
and thin fillets will take about 6 hours; larger fish and thicker fillets could take as long as 10 hours. If fish is not done
after 8 to 10 hours, finish cooking in 150°F (65°C) oven.

*For a milder smoke flavor, use a mix of sawdust and larger
wood chunks (about 1 inch/2.5 cm across). The sawdust will
produce smoke and will help the larger chunks burn. Large
chunks alone may not burn at the lower temperatures used for
this recipe, while straight sawdust will produce quite a bit of
smoke (and therefore a stronger smoke flavor). A mix of the
two produces a light amount of smoke, which works well for
more delicate fish such as small trout.

Smoked Salmon Spread

About 2 cups

*If you've got any leftover smoked salmon, try this easy
appetizer. Smoked trout can be substituted for the
salmon. Serve the spread with pumpernickel toasts,
crackers or cucumber slices. —A. and J.C.*

8 ounces (225 g) smoked salmon

3/4 cup (180 ml/191 g) mayonnaise

1/2 cup (120 ml/115 g) sour cream

3 tablespoons (45 ml/10 g) chopped fresh dill
weed, or 1 1/2 tablespoons (22.5 ml) dried

Prepared horseradish to taste (2 teaspoons to 2
tablespoons/10 ml to 30 ml)

4 teaspoons (20 ml) freshly squeezed lemon juice

Salt and pepper to taste

Discard skin and bones from salmon and break into
pieces. Pulse salmon in a food processor until finely
chopped. Add remaining ingredients to processor and
blend well.

SALT, SMOKING AND SAFETY

Bacteria thrive and multiply at temperatures between 40°F and 140°F (4.5°C and 60°C). Traditional cold smoking is done at temperatures below 100°F (38°C), so meat to be cold-smoked is generally brined with a salt mixture containing a cure that prevents bacterial growth. Even when you're cool smoking at temperatures between 140°F and 200°F (60°C and 93°C), it's a good idea to use a curing salt blend such as Morton Tender Quick.* Canning/pickling salt or kosher salt can be used, but the chances of bacterial growth are increased somewhat. Table salt contains iodine and a free-flowing agent, and is not generally used in smoking brines; many people feel it gives the food a bitter flavor.

Canning/pickling salt is the same consistency as table salt, but it has no iodine, preservatives or free-flow agents added. Kosher salt is more coarse and packs into a measuring cup less densely, so a specific measure (by volume) of kosher salt weighs less than an equal measure of canning/pickling salt; in addition the 2 main brands of kosher salt have different flake sizes, and so measure differently by volume. Tender Quick is plain salt blended with sugar, curing agents and compounds to keep the mixture uniform; because of its formulation and granular properties, you must use more Tender Quick (by volume) than canning/pickling salt. Here is a quick reference chart to help you calculate salt substitutions when preparing brine for smoking.

BY VOLUME

Canning/ pickling salt (by measure)	Morton Tender Quick* (by measure)	Diamond Crystal kosher salt (by measure)	Morton kosher salt (by measure)
8 1/4 tsp.	1/4 cup	6 Tbsp. + 1 1/2 tsp.	Scant 1/4 cup
1/4 cup	6 Tbsp. less 1/2 tsp.	9 Tbsp. + 1 tsp.	6 Tbsp. less 3/4 tsp.
1/2 cup	3/4 cup less 1 tsp.	1 cup + 3 Tbsp.	3/4 cup less 1 1/2 tsp.

BY WEIGHT

Canning/ pickling salt (by measure)	Morton Tender Quick* (by weight)	Canning or kosher salt (by weight)
8 1/4 tsp.	52 g	55 g
1/4 cup	76 g	80 g
1/2 cup	152 g	160 g

*Morton Salt company recommends the use of its Tender Quick salt for meat, game, poultry, salmon, shad and sablefish.

Honey-Smoked Fish Chunks

6 to 8 appetizer servings
Preliminary preparation: 1 to 3 hours marinating
Recommended equipment: Box-style electric smoker
Smoking: Cool smoking, 2½ to 4 hours

Serve these tasty morsels as is, or dress them up as described in one of the variations below. Salmon or trout are the most traditional in this sort of recipe, but sea bass, opah or halibut also make interesting variations. After smoking, halibut becomes very smooth and soft, almost like pork fat, but it firms up as it cools. —T.M.

2 tablespoons (30 ml) honey

2 tablespoons (30 ml) Madeira or dry sherry

1 tablespoon (15 ml/13 g) Morton Tender Quick, or 2 teaspoons (10 ml/12 g) canning/pickling salt

½ teaspoon (2.5 ml/1.5 g) dry mustard powder

¼ teaspoon (1.25 ml/.6 g) onion powder

1 pound (454 g) boneless, skinless salmon, trout, sea bass, opah or halibut fillet* (½ to 1 inch/ 1.25 to 2.5 cm thick)

4 cups (1 liter) smoking sawdust (220 g) or fine chips (160 g)

In nonreactive bowl, combine honey, Madeira, Tender Quick, mustard and onion powder; stir well to blend. Cut fish into 1x1x½-inch (2.5x2.5x1.25-cm) pieces. Add to honey mixture, stirring gently to coat. Cover and refrigerate for 1 to 3 hours, stirring occasionally.

Preheat smoker to 150°F (65°C). Fill wood pan with smoking wood. Drain fish; arrange on smoking racks that have been coated with nonstick spray (fish pieces should not touch). Smoke at 140°F-160°F (60°C-70°C) until richly colored and just firm to the touch, 2½ to 4 hours, refilling the wood pan once each hour; if you break a chunk open, it should flake easily and appear opaque but still moist in the center. This is excellent served at any temperature—warm from the smoker, room temperature or refrigerated.

Scandinavian Tidbits: This is particularly appropriate with smoked salmon. Buy a loaf of very thinly sliced cocktail pumpernickel bread; it is often sold in small loaves that are 2 inches (5 cm) square. Or, you may find it in larger loaves that are about 4 inches (10 cm) square; cut these into quarters. Top each with a dollop of sour cream; sprinkle with a few drained capers. Top each with a smoked fish chunk. Tuck a small sprig of fresh dill alongside the fish. If you would like further garnishing, sprinkle a bit of chopped hard-cooked egg yolk, or a bit of finely minced red onion, around each fish chunk.

Cream Cheese and Fish Squares: Choose hearty wholegrain crackers that are about 2 inches (5 cm) square. Spread each with a generous spoonful of cream cheese (use chive-and-onion cream cheese for even more flavor, if you like). Top the cream cheese with a smaller spoonful of raspberry or lingonberry jam. Place a smoked fish chunk on each piece; sprinkle with minced red onion.

*To smoke leaner fish such as northern pike or walleye, add 1 tablespoon (15 ml) canola oil to marinade. Proceed as directed.

Basic Jerky Instructions

About 1 pound (454 g)
Preliminary preparation: 3 to 12 hours marinating, depending on meat used
Recommended equipment: Box-style electric smoker
Smoking: Cool smoking, 4 to 6 hours

Several marinade formulas are given below. Feel free to use whichever one suits your tastes; each will work with any of the meats listed. You may also enjoy customizing the marinade to your own tastes. Try adding spices such as cumin, mustard seeds or ginger; add sugar or syrup to a recipe that has none (or substitute one type of sweetener for another); adjust the amount of hot pepper to suit your preferences.

Jerky Marinade #1

2/3 cup (160 ml) soy sauce

1/4 cup (60 ml) Worcestershire sauce

1 tablespoon (15 ml/13 g) Morton Tender Quick, or 2 teaspoons (10 ml/12 g) canning/pickling salt

1 teaspoon (5 ml/2 g) freshly ground pepper

1 teaspoon (5 ml/2.5 g) garlic powder

1 teaspoon (5 ml/2.5 g) onion powder

1/2 teaspoon (2.5 ml/.9 g) hot red pepper flakes, optional

Jerky Marinade #2

2 cups (470 ml) cold water

1/4 cup (60 ml) maple syrup

3 tablespoons (45 ml/39 g) Morton Tender Quick, or 2 tablespoons (30 ml/38 g) canning/pickling salt

1 tablespoon (15 ml) pickling spice

1 teaspoon (5 ml/3 g) ginger

Jerky Marinade #3

2/3 cup (160 ml) soy sauce

1/4 cup (60 ml) pineapple juice

3 tablespoons (45 ml/40 g) brown sugar (packed)

2 tablespoons (30 ml/26 g) Morton Tender Quick, or 1 tablespoon (15 ml/19 g) canning/pickling salt

1 tablespoon (15 ml) pickling spice

1 small onion, sliced

Choose one of the following (easier to slice if partially frozen):

2 pounds (900 g) very lean boneless beef or venison from the round or sirloin

2 pounds (900 g) boneless, skinless turkey breast or tenderloin (best with marinade #2 or #3)

2 pounds (900 g) boneless, skinless goose or duck breast

4 cups (1 liter) smoking sawdust (220 g) or fine chips (160 g)

In nonreactive container, stir together marinade ingredients. Slice meat 1/4 inch (6 mm) thick; slice with the grain for chewy jerky, or across the grain for more tender jerky (beef or venison may be sliced up to 1/2 inch/1.25 cm thick; this makes a more substantial jerky). Add sliced meat to marinade, stirring to coat. Cover and refrigerate for 6 to 12 hours for beef or venison, or 3 to 6 hours for turkey, goose or duck; stir meat occasionally.

When ready to smoke, drain meat strips, discarding marinade. Pat dry with paper towels. Arrange in single layer on smoking racks that have been lightly coated with nonstick spray. Preheat smoker to 160°F (70°C). Fill wood pan with smoking wood. Smoke at 160°F (70°C) for about 30 minutes, then reduce smoker temperature to 120°–140°F (50°C–60°C) and smoke until meat is dry but not brittle, 4 to 6 hours, refilling the wood pan once each hour (to check for doneness, remove a strip from smoker and let cool, then twist the strip; it should bend but not break).

Note: Jerky is traditionally smoked at much lower temperatures; home cooks usually smoke at 110°F–130°F (43°C–54°C), while commercial operations use temperatures under 100°F (38°C). The USDA recommends bringing the meat to a temperature of 160°F (70°C) before drying; this kills any harmful bacteria. The use of Tender Quick helps prevent bacterial growth (see page 79), but there is not enough in this recipe to ensure complete safety. For maximum safety, therefore, it is recommended to begin smoking at a temperature of 160°F (70°C).

Slow-Smoked Venison

8 to 10 servings
Preliminary preparation: Under 15 minutes (plus wood soaking time)
Recommended equipment: Bullet-style smoker or offset firebox smoker
Smoking: Cool smoking with water pan, 8 to 12 hours

Smoked venison is a real treat served along with traditional family favorites during the holidays. If you've got plenty of venison, smoke several roasts at one time, to take advantage of the lengthy smoking procedure. The smoked roasts can be frozen for future use. —A. and J.C.

2 to 3 cups (460 to 690 ml/110 to 165 g) medium hickory or mesquite chips

1 venison roast (3 to 5 pounds/1.36 to 2.3 kg), preferably from the hindquarter, rump or loin

2 tablespoons (30 ml) olive oil

Garlic salt

Freshly ground black pepper

2 to 4 slices bacon

If using charcoal-fueled grill or smoker, soak wood chips in a bucket of water for at least an hour before starting smoker; if using electric smoker, soaking is unnecessary.

When ready to smoke, preheat smoker to 225°F (105°C). Rub roast with oil, and season liberally with garlic salt and pepper. Toss a handful of drained wood chips onto the coals, or place a handful of dry chips in firebox of electric smoker. Place filled water pan in smoker. Place roast on grate over water pan; lay several strips of bacon on top of roast. Cover smoker and cook at 200°F–225°F (93°C–105°C) for 8 to 12 hours, adding pre-started coals as necessary to maintain temperature; add wood every hour, or as needed to maintain light smoke. Roast is done when it is rich golden brown and is very tender.

Honey and Spice Smoked Nuts

8 ounces (225 g)
Preliminary preparation: Under 15 minutes (plus wood soaking time)
Recommended equipment: Box-style electric smoker, or any cool smoker
Smoking: Cool smoking, about 2 hours

If you've got extra space in the smoker when you're making something else, toss a batch of these nuts in; they can be smoked at any temperature up to 275°F (135°C). Serve them as cocktail snacks, or use to garnish salads; they're especially good with a green salad that contains blue cheese and apples.

1 tablespoon (15 ml) honey

1 teaspoon (5 ml) canola oil or olive oil

1 teaspoon (5 ml/6 g) salt

3/4 teaspoon (3.75 ml/1.5 g) ground cumin

1/4 teaspoon (1.25 ml/.5 g) cinnamon

1/4 teaspoon 1.25 ml/.5 g) cayenne pepper

8 ounces (225 g) unsalted pecan halves, filberts or other nuts (from the baking aisle)

1 to 2 cups (230 to 470 ml) smoking sawdust (55 to 110 g) or fine chips (40 to 80 g)

In microwave-safe bowl, combine honey and oil. Heat at 50% power until warm and runny, about 20 seconds. Add salt, cumin, cinnamon and cayenne; stir well. Add nuts; stir to coat.

Prepare smoker for cool heat; lightly coat smoking screen* with nonstick spray. Fill wood pan with smoking wood. Spread nuts on screen. Smoke at 150°F–175°F (65°C–80°C) for about 2 hours, or until desired level of smoke flavor has been reached. (If you smoke at higher temperatures, reduce the time, and keep an eye on the nuts to be sure they don't scorch.) Store in tightly sealed container at room temperature for up to 2 weeks; refrigerate or freeze for longer storage.

*A screen works best for smoking nuts, which would fall through the bars of most regular racks. If you don't have a screen that is suitable for smoking, place foil on top of your smoking rack before adding nuts. Stir nuts several times during smoking, and increase smoking time slightly.

Smoke-n-Roast Pheasant

3 servings
Preliminary preparation: 2 hours brining
Recommended equipment: Box-style electric smoker*
Smoking: Cool smoking, about 2 hours, followed by oven roasting for an hour

In this recipe, pheasant is cool-smoked for a nice smoke flavor, then finished in the oven. A skin-on bird will look more attractive, but a skinless bird can also be used.

Brine

2 cups (470 ml) cold water

2 cups (470 ml) apple cider

1/2 cup (120 ml/76 g) Diamond Crystal kosher salt (see page 79 for information on using other types of salt)

1/4 cup (60 ml/55 g) light brown sugar (packed)

1 teaspoon (5 ml/3 g) ginger

1 whole pheasant, or 2 pounds (900 g) cut-up parts

2 cups (470 ml/80 g) fine smoking wood chips

2 teaspoons (10 ml) canola oil, optional

In large nonreactive container, combine brine ingredients, stirring until clear. Add pheasant; weight with small saucer to keep it submerged. Cover and refrigerate for 2 hours.

Preheat smoker to 125°F (52°C). Fill wood pan with smoking wood. Drain pheasant, discarding brine; if pheasant has been skinned, pat dry and rub with vegetable oil. Place pheasant on smoking rack that has been coated with nonstick spray. Smoke at 120°F–130°F (50°C–55°C) until nicely colored, about 2 hours, refilling wood pan once.

Near the end of smoking time, heat oven to 325°F (165°C). Transfer smoked pheasant to baking dish. Bake until internal temperature reaches 165°F (74°C), 45 minutes to an hour. Remove from oven; tent loosely with foil and let stand for 10 minutes before carving.

*An electric smoker is ideal for this recipe because it's easy to control the temperature. You can prepare this in a different style of smoker; just keep the heat low and steady, and use wood that's appropriate for the smoker.

Smoke-n-Roast Chicken

4 or 5 servings

Follow recipe for Smoke-n-Roast Pheasant (above), substituting a whole chicken (3 to 4 pounds/1.4 to 1.8 kg) or equivalent in cut-up parts for pheasant. After brining, smoke for 2 1/2 hours, then oven-roast until thigh temperature reaches 170°F (77°C), 1 to 1 1/4 hours.

Smoke-n-Roast Turkey Breast

4 servings

Follow recipe for Smoke-n-Roast Pheasant, above, substituting a 3-pound (1.4-kg) turkey breast half for the pheasant. Brine for 2 1/2 hours; after brining, smoke for 2 1/2 to 3 hours, then oven-roast until temperature reaches 170°F (77°C), 1 1/4 to 1 1/2 hours.

Basic Smoked Spareribs

2 or 3 servings per slab
Preliminary preparation: 8 to 12 hours seasoning (refrigerated)
Recommended equipment: Bullet-style water smoker, covered grill or offset firebox smoker
Smoking: Medium-temperature smoking with water pan, 2¹/₂ to 4 hours

1 slab pork spareribs (about 3¹/₂ pounds/1.6 kg; see below for instructions on preparing more than 1 slab)

¹/₄ cup (60 ml) Ancho Chili Rub (page 119) or other barbecue rub from pages 118–120

8 to 12 large chunks smoking wood* (2 inches/ 5 cm square)

Barbecue sauce for serving

Begin preparation the night before you plan to cook the ribs. Peel membrane from back side of ribs (see page 26). Place ribs in large glass baking dish. Sprinkle with half the rub, then use your fingertips to rub it into the meat. Turn slab and add remaining rub to second side, rubbing in well. (If you are preparing more than 1 slab, use ¹/₄ cup/60 ml of rub per slab.) Cover dish with plastic wrap; refrigerate overnight, or for at least 8 hours.

The next day, begin soaking wood chunks* in water several hours before you plan to start cooking; remove ribs from refrigerator 1 hour before cooking. Preheat smoker to 250°F (120°C), or prepare grill for indirect medium heat. Place filled water pan in smoker or grill. Place ribs on grate over water pan. Add a few chunks of wood to coals (if using gas grill, place foil-wrapped chips on heat element; if using electric smoker, place a handful of dry chips in firebox). Cover smoker and adjust vents to maintain temperature of 200°F–250°F (93°C–120°C). Smoke-cook until meat pulls away from ends of bones, 2¹/₂ to 3 hours, adding wood and coals as necessary (if you prefer ribs that are firmer and less juicy, cook at 200°F/93°C for up to an hour longer). Cut ribs between bones; serve with barbecue sauce on the side.

To prepare more than 1 slab: Most water smokers have 2 grates above the water pan, so it's easy to prepare several slabs of ribs. If you're using a covered grill for preparing ribs, stack them on the grate over the water pan. Rearrange the slabs every 30 minutes, moving them from the top to the bottom of the stack; increase cooking time slightly to compensate for frequent opening of grill. Or, if you have a large covered grill, use a special rib rack (as shown above right), or stand the ribs between the vertical fins of an inverted meat-roasting rack.

*If you're using a gas grill or electric smoker, use 2 cups (470 ml/110 g) medium wood chips rather than chunks; soaking is unnecessary. For gas grill, wrap dry wood chips in foil as described on page 75.

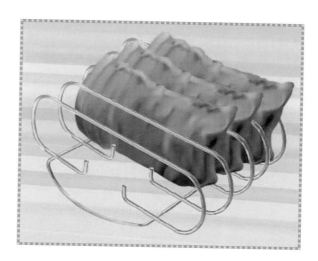

Options for Basic Smoked Spareribs

• For a bit more flavor, brush the ribs every 30 minutes with Beer Mop (or another mop of your choice). To make Beer Mop, combine 1 can (12 ounces/350 ml) beer, ¹/₄ cup (60 ml) seasoned rice vinegar or orange juice, and 1 tablespoon (15 ml) Ancho Chili Rub (page 119) or other barbecue rub in small saucepan. Heat over low heat, and keep mixture simmering between moppings. Increase smoking time slightly to compensate for frequent opening of smoker.

• For saucy ribs, brush Honey Barbecue Sauce, page 122 (or another barbecue sauce of your choice) over the ribs during the last 30 minutes of cooking.

Smoked Prime Rib of Beef

> **8 servings**
> **Preliminary preparation:** 2 to 24 hours seasoning (refrigerated), 2 hours room-temperature standing followed by 30 minutes active prep
> **Recommended equipment:** Bullet-style water smoker, covered grill or offset firebox smoker
> **Smoking:** Medium-temperature smoking with water pan, 2^1/$_2$ to 3^1/$_2$ hours

Serve this when you want to pull out all the stops for a special dinner.

4-pound (1.8-kg) boneless beef prime rib roast, excess fat trimmed

Leaves from 8 to 10 sprigs fresh flat-leaf parsley

4 cloves garlic

^{3}/$_4$ teaspoon (3.75 ml/1.5 g) coarsely ground black pepper (preferably freshly ground)

^{1}/$_2$ teaspoon (2.5 ml/1 g) finely grated fresh lemon zest

Salt

3 or 4 pieces heavy kitchen string (each about 18 inches/46 cm long), soaked in water

1 tablespoon (15 ml) olive oil

10 to 12 large chunks smoking wood* (2 inches/ 5 cm square)

Place roast in baking dish. In food processor, combine parsley, garlic, pepper and lemon zest; chop to medium-fine consistency (alternately, chop parsley and garlic by hand, then mix with pepper and lemon zest in mixing bowl). Rub parsley mixture over all sides of roast, patting in place. Cover and refrigerate for at least 2 hours, or as long as 24 hours. While meat is seasoning, soak wood in a bucket of water.*

Two hours before you want to start cooking, remove roast from refrigerator; let stand at room temperature.

After 2 hours, preheat smoker to 225°F (105°C), or prepare grill for indirect medium heat. While smoker or grill is heating, salt roast generously, then tie crosswise with heavy kitchen string. In Dutch oven, brown roast well on all sides in oil over medium-high heat.

Place filled water pan in smoker or grill; add half of the soaked wood to coals (if using gas grill, place foil-wrapped chips on heat element; if using electric smoker, place a handful of dry chips in firebox). Remove roast from Dutch oven and transfer, fat-side up, to grate over water pan (retain drippings in Dutch oven if you would like to make Yorkshire Pudding; recipe follows). Insert thermometer probe into center of roast. Close smoker and adjust to maintain 200°F (93°C) temperature. Cook until roast reaches 135°F/57°C (rare) to 145°F/63°C (medium-rare), adding remaining wood after about an hour and adding pre-started coals as necessary to maintain temperature. Total cooking time should be 2^1/$_2$ to 3^1/$_2$ hours. (If roast is done before you are ready for it, adjust smoker temperature to about 150°F/65°C and let roast remain in smoker for up to 45 minutes longer.) Transfer roast to platter; cover loosely with foil and let stand for 15 minutes before carving.

*If you're using a gas grill or electric smoker, use 2^1/$_2$ cups (580 ml/140 g) medium wood chips rather than chunks; soaking is unnecessary. For gas grill, wrap dry wood chips in foil as described on page 75.

TIP: Using heavy kitchen string, tie the roast tightly in 3 or 4 places, tying parallel to the grain—i.e., in the same direction you'd carve the roast. Tying the boneless prime rib prevents the thinner edge of meat from pulling away from the rest of the roast, yielding a more attractive—and more evenly cooked—roast.

Smoked Elk or Moose Loin

Follow recipe above, substituting 4-pound (1.8-kg) boneless elk or moose loin for beef roast. Increase olive oil to 3 tablespoons (45 ml); proceed as directed. Cooking time may be slightly less, depending on thickness of roast.

Yorkshire Pudding

6 to 8 servings
Preparation: Under an hour

This batter can be prepared an hour or two in advance if you like, but you should time the cooking so the pudding is done at the moment the prime rib is ready to serve.

Drippings reserved from browning prime rib, page 86

3/4 cup (180 ml) beef broth

3 eggs

1 cup (240 ml) milk

1 cup (140 g) all-purpose flour

1/2 teaspoon (2.5 ml/3 g) salt

Place Dutch oven, with drippings from browning roast, over medium heat. Add broth, stirring to loosen browned bits. Cook for about a minute, stirring constantly. Strain into small bowl, discarding solids. Refrigerate mixture until ready to begin cooking. Now make the batter: In mixing bowl, beat eggs with electric hand mixer or whisk until light and foamy. Add milk; beat for about 30 seconds longer. Add flour and salt; beat just until lumps disappear. Cover and refrigerate until ready to cook.

To cook, heat oven to 450°F (230°C). Place drippings mixture in 9x13-inch (23x33-cm) metal baking dish (a glass baking dish may shatter when batter is added to the pre-heated dish). Place dish in oven for 10 minutes. Carefully pour batter into heated dish. Return to oven; bake for 20 to 25 minutes, or until puffy and golden brown. Serve immediately with sliced prime rib.

Asian Smoked Quail

4 servings
Preliminary preparation: 4 to 12 hours marinating
Recommended equipment: Covered grill or any type of smoker
Smoking: Medium-temperature smoking, about 2 hours

Marinade

3/4 cup (180 ml/195 g) creamy peanut butter

3/4 cup (180 ml) water

1/2 cup (120 ml) soy sauce

1/2 cup (120 ml) Asian chili sauce

3 tablespoons (45 ml) canola oil

3 tablespoons (45 ml) lemon juice

2 tablespoons (30 ml/30 g) grated fresh gingerroot

1/2 teaspoon (2.5 ml/1 g) cayenne pepper

6 cloves garlic, minced

8 whole dressed skin-on quail

Salt and pepper

10 to 12 large chunks smoking wood* (2 inches/ 5 cm square)

Place peanut butter in mixing bowl. Gradually add water and soy sauce, stirring to blend. When mixture is smooth, add remaining marinade ingredients, stirring to blend. Place quail in glass baking dish (or zipper-style plastic bag). Add marinade, turning to coat. Cover and refrigerate for 4 to 12 hours, turning occasionally. While quail are marinating, soak wood chunks in a bucket of water.*

When you're ready to cook, preheat smoker to 220°F (104°C), or prepare grill for indirect medium heat; coat smoking racks or grate with nonstick spray. Drain quail, discarding marinade; season quail with salt and pepper to taste. Toss half of the drained wood chunks onto coals (if using gas grill, place foil-wrapped chips on heat element; if using electric bullet-style smoker, place a handful of dry chips in fire box; if using box-style electric smoker, fill wood pan with sawdust). Arrange quail, breast side down, on rack. Smoke at 200°F–220°F (93°C–104°C) for an hour. Turn quail over and add remaining wood to coals. Cook for about an hour longer, or until quail legs move freely and internal temperature is 180°F (82°C). Serve hot.

*If you're using a gas grill or electric bullet-style smoker, use 2 cups (470 ml/110 g) medium wood chips rather than chunks; soaking is unnecessary (for box-style electric smoker, use 2 cups/470 ml/110 g smoking sawdust). For gas grill, wrap dry wood chips in foil as described on page 75.

Natural wood—particularly hickory—is the fuel of choice for traditional barbecuing. Cooking devices range from offset firebox smokers, to elaborate brick units, to a variety of homemade contraptions made from oil drums, old wood stoves, commercial restaurant steamer units—even old filing cabinets. All have one thing in common, however; they're designed to cook food at relatively low temperature, using natural hardwood as the only fuel. The hardwood gives a special, woodsy flavor to the food; it's richer and more mellow than the smoke flavor of most other smoked foods, and the low-temperature cooking tenderizes tougher cuts such as brisket and pork shoulder.

With a little patience, a charcoal-fueled bullet-style smoker can be used for natural-wood barbecuing. The trickiest part is regulating and maintaining the temperature. For most barbecuing, 250°F (120°C) is the ideal temperature. In reality, temperatures inside your bullet smoker may be as high as 400°F (205°C) when you first fire it up, so you'll need to have patience while the temperature drops and a good bed of coals is created before adding the meat. Once the meat is in the smoker, you must keep a sharp eye on the temperature, and add fuel to keep the temperatures high enough—but not too high.

The type of wood you use will be determined by what grows in your area. Fireplace wood works fine, as long as it is a hardwood such as maple, oak or alder (don't use birch, however, because it tends to produce lots of ash and sparks). Wood from fruit or nut trees is fabulous; you may be able to get some trimmings from a local orchard.

Cut the wood into lengths that fit inside the burner pan of your smoker. You'll need sticks for kindling, but the bulk of the wood should be logs split as for a fireplace—typically wedges averaging 3 inches (7.5 cm) at the thickest point. Remove the water pan and racks from the smoker, then build the fire in the burner pan as though you're making a fire in a fireplace. Once your fire is going well, add a few larger chunks of wood. Let them burn down until you have a hot bed of smoldering logs; the flames should have died down so there are just a few tongues of fire. Don't rush this step; it will take at least an hour to develop a good bed of coals.

Now position the filled water pan and cooking grates (empty for now) inside the unit. Place a smoking thermometer on the top grate. Close the lid of the smoker, but leave the door open. Check the temperature after a few minutes. If it is over 300°F (150°C), close the door and any vents, and let the fire cool down a bit.

Once the temperature is in the 300°F (150°C) range, place the food on racks and close the lid. Monitor the temperature carefully, especially during the first 15 minutes or so. Open the door and vents to raise the temperature; close them to reduce it. You will eventually have to add more wood to the fire; each time you do, the temperature will spike up, but leave the door open long enough for the log to catch fire. Once it is burning, close the door as necessary to lower temperature. You can also open the lid if temperature rises too much; this lets out the heat rapidly (but it also lets out all the smoky vapors, so don't open it unless you have to).

Keep a close eye on the temperature throughout the cooking process, adding wood whenever the coal bed starts to die down or the temperature drops below 225°F (105°C). Don't open the top of the smoker except as necessary, especially once the temperature starts to drop.

Timing is imprecise with this method of cooking, due to temperature fluctuations. If you lose your bed of coals, or it is just taking too long for the meat to get done, transfer the meat to a 325°F (165°C) oven and finish cooking there; as long as the meat has been in the smoker for at least an hour, it will have that nice barbecue flavor (the longer it stays in the smoker, of course, the more flavor it will pick up). If, on the other hand, the meat becomes done more quickly than you expect, simply reduce the temperature of the smoker to about 150°F (65°C); the meat can be held at this temperature for at least an hour.

Here are basic instructions for a few foods, to get you started. Remember that part of the fun in 'cue is making variations, however, so feel absolutely free to try your own variations. Keep a notebook, listing the method you used, as well as cooking time and temperature; that way, you can replicate your barbecue success.

—T.M.

Natural-Wood-BBQ Ribs

Pork spareribs are traditional for natural-wood barbecue, but country-style ribs, pork back ribs or beef ribs can also be used (see Ribs from A to Z on page 26 for information on rib cuts). Peel the membrane from the back side of pork spareribs as shown on page 26; other ribs don't need to be peeled. Season the ribs lightly with a dry rub (pages 118–120) or salt and pepper. Place on grate in preheated smoker. Cook for 3 to 4 hours, or until the meat pulls away from the bone tips (or until country-style ribs reach 160°F/71°C); beef ribs may take a bit longer. If you like saucy ribs, brush them with barbecue sauce during the last 30 minutes of cooking; however, many purists prefer pit-smoked ribs "naked"—with the sauce on the side.

Natural-Wood-BBQ Pork Roast

Choose a well-marbled cut, such as a pork shoulder or butt roast. A roast that is made up of several separate muscles, or that has been cut open to remove the bone, works particularly well, because you can work the seasoning into the center of the roast for more flavor. Season the individual pieces, or open the boned roast and season the inside (try the Porketta mixture on page 92, or use any seasoning blend you like); then, tie the roast together with kitchen string and season the outside. Place on grate in preheated smoker. Cook for 5 to 7 hours, or until the center reaches at least 160°F (71°C). Due to the marbling, you can cook a roast like this to a higher temperature (up to 175°F/80°C); it will only become more flavorful.

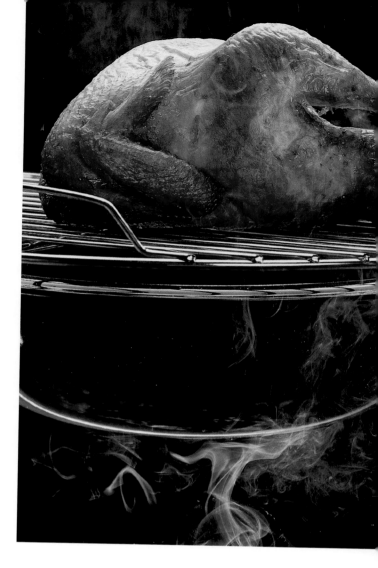

Natural-Wood-BBQ Fish

Choose whole dressed fish, fish steaks at least an inch (2.5 cm) thick, or skin-on fillets at least 3/4 inch (1.9 cm) thick. Oily fish such as salmon, trout and tuna work best. Brine the fish if you like (follow the instructions on page 78); this adds flavor and moisture, but is not necessary. Pat fish dry and rub lightly with canola oil; if it hasn't been brined, season lightly with a mild rub, seasoned salt blend, or plain salt and lemon pepper. Place on grate in preheated smoker. Cook until fish flakes, 45 minutes to 2 hours. Serve hot, warm or cold.

Natural-Wood-BBQ Chicken

Low-temperature cooking produces moist, flavorful chicken, but the skin is usually rubbery and is not eaten. For better flavor, remove the chicken skin before cooking; this way, both the smoke and any rub will directly flavor the meat. Chicken cooked on the bone is also more flavorful than boneless chicken, although either will work; bone-in chicken breasts are probably the most popular choice, but any chicken parts work fine. Finally, if you're cooking a whole chicken rather than specific parts such as breasts, it's best to cut the chicken in half; the flatter chicken halves cook more evenly than the whole chicken. Season the chicken, preferably skinless and on the bone, with a light amount of dry rub (pages 118–120) or salt and pepper. Place on grate in preheated smoker. Cook for 2 to 3 hours, or until cooked through (160°F/71°C for breasts, 170°F/77°C for thighs); bone-in chicken cooks more quickly than boneless. For saucy chicken, brush the pieces with barbecue sauce during the last 30 minutes of cooking.

Smoke-Cooked Salmon <u>with</u> Horseradish Cream Sauce

4 servings
Preliminary preparation: Under 30 minutes (plus wood soaking time)
Recommended equipment: Covered grill or any type of smoker
Smoking: Medium-temperature smoking, about an hour

1 cup (240 ml/55 g) medium smoking wood chips*

4 boneless, skin-on salmon fillets (6 ounces/170 g each), about 1 inch (2.5 cm) thick

Kosher salt and freshly ground black pepper

2 tablespoons (30 ml/5 g) snipped fresh chives

1 tablespoon (15 ml) lemon juice

³/₄ cup (180 ml/170 g) sour cream

2 tablespoons (30 ml) prepared horseradish

1 green onion (white and green parts), thinly sliced

White pepper

If using charcoal-fueled grill or smoker, soak wood chips in a bucket of cold water for at least an hour; if using gas grill or electric smoker, soaking is unnecessary. For gas grill, wrap dry wood chips in foil as described on page 75. Rinse salmon fillets; pat dry. Season with salt and pepper to taste. Sprinkle with chives and lemon juice. Set aside for about 30 minutes at room temperature, or up to an hour refrigerated, while you prepare the grill or smoker.

Prepare grill for indirect medium heat, or preheat smoker to 220°F (104°C); coat grill grate or smoking rack with nonstick spray. Toss drained wood chips onto the coals (if using gas grill, place foil-wrapped chips on heat ele-

ment; if using electric smoker, place dry chips or sawdust in firebox or wood pan). Place salmon, skin-side down, on grate or rack. Cover grill or smoker, and cook at 200°F–220°F (93°C–104°C) until salmon is cooked through, 45 minutes to an hour; salmon is done when it just flakes and is no longer translucent. While salmon is cooking, combine sour cream, horseradish and green onion in mixing bowl; stir to blend. Add salt and white pepper to taste; cover and refrigerate until ready to serve. Serve smoked salmon with a dollop of the horseradish cream sauce on the side.

*If you are using a box-style electric smoker, substitute smoking sawdust or small chips.

Smoked BBQ Chicken Wings

6 to 8 servings
Preliminary preparation: About 15 minutes (plus wood soaking time)
Recommended equipment: Covered grill or any type of smoker, disposable foil pan
Smoking: Medium-temperature smoking, about 1½ hours

The sauce can be prepared a day or two in advance; keep refrigerated until needed.

2 cups (470 ml/110 g) medium smoking wood chips*

Sauce

2 cups (470 ml) ketchup

1 cup (240 ml) cider vinegar

½ cup (110 g/1 stick) unsalted butter

½ cup (120 ml/110 g) dark brown sugar (packed)

¼ cup (60 ml) mustard

¼ cup (60 ml) Worcestershire sauce

2 tablespoons (30 ml) lemon juice

1 teaspoon (5 ml/2 g) cayenne pepper

3 pounds (1.36 kg) chicken wings or drumettes

If using charcoal-fueled grill or smoker, soak wood chips in cold water for at least an hour. If using gas grill or electric smoker, soaking is unnecessary; for gas grill, wrap dry wood chips in foil as described on page 75. In large nonreactive pan, combine all sauce ingredients, stirring to blend. Heat to boiling over medium heat, then reduce heat and cook until reduced by a third, about 15 minutes.

Prepare grill for indirect medium heat, or preheat smoker to 220°F (104°C). Place wings in disposable foil pan. Add sauce, stirring to coat evenly. Toss a handful of drained wood chips onto the coals (if using gas grill, place foil-wrapped chips on heat element; if using electric smoker, place a handful of dry chips in firebox). Place pan of wings on grate away from heat. Cover grill or smoker, and cook at 200°F–220°F (93°C–104°C) for about 1½ hours; the chicken should be cooked through and the sauce will be like a thick glaze on the wings. Serve hot.

*If you are using a box-style electric smoker, substitute smoking sawdust or small chips.

Smoke-Roasted Tomatoes

General instructions; make as much as you wish
Preliminary preparation: Under 15 minutes (plus wood soaking time)
Recommended equipment: Covered grill or any type of smoker
Smoking: Medium-temperature smoking, 2 to 3 hours

Smoke-roasted tomatoes have a rich, full flavor that works well in pasta sauces, chili or sautéed dishes. If you've got room in the smoker when you're smoke-cooking something else, toss a few tomatoes in; or, make a large batch by itself and freeze for later use. —T.M.

2 cups (470 ml/110 g) medium smoking wood chips*

Garden-ripe tomatoes (Roma tomatoes are excellent, but any kind can be used)

Olive oil (about ½ teaspoon/2.5 ml per tomato)

Finely chopped garlic (about ¼ teaspoon/ 1.2 ml per tomato)

Kosher salt and freshly ground black pepper

For charcoal-fueled grill or smoker, soak wood chips in a bucket of cold water for at least an hour; if using gas grill or electric smoker, soaking is unnecessary. For gas grill, wrap dry wood chips in foil as described on page 75.

Prepare grill for indirect medium heat, or preheat smoker to 250°F (120°C); coat grill grate or smoking rack with nonstick spray. Cut tomatoes in half across the equator (not from top to bottom). Scoop out pulpy seed mass, then hold each tomato half upside down and squeeze very gently to remove any remaining seeds (this is not necessary with Roma tomatoes). Place tomatoes, cut-side up, on grate or racks. In measuring cup, combine oil and garlic. Mix well and spoon evenly over cut sides of tomatoes. Sprinkle tomatoes with salt; grind some pepper over each one. Toss a handful of drained wood chips onto the coals (if using gas grill, place foil-wrapped chips on heat element; if using electric smoker, place dry chips or sawdust in firebox or wood pan). Smoke at 225°F–250°F (105°C–120°C) until tomatoes are somewhat shrunken and slightly darker, 2 to 3 hours; tomatoes will still be very pliable and moist. Add additional coals and wood as needed to maintain light smoke. Refrigerate in covered container for several days, or freeze for longer storage.

*If you are using a box-style electric smoker, substitute smoking sawdust or small chips.

hot smoking

Smoked Porketta Roast

5 to 7 servings
Preliminary preparation: 2 to 12 hours seasoning (refrigerated)
Recommended equipment: Bullet-style water smoker or covered grill
Smoking: Hot smoking with water pan, about 1 1/2 hours

Porketta Seasoning Mix

1 tablespoon (15 ml/9.5 g) kosher salt

1 tablespoon (15 ml/8 g) fennel seeds

1 tablespoon (15 ml/9 g) anise seeds

1 bay leaf, finely crumbled

1 tablespoon (15 ml/9 g) coarsely ground black pepper

1 tablespoon (15 ml/6 g) paprika

3/4 teaspoon (3.75 ml/1.8 g) onion powder

1/2 teaspoon (2.5 ml/.9 g) hot red pepper flakes

2 1/2- to 3-pound (1.125- to 1.36-kg) pork butt roast

2 tablespoons (30 ml) olive oil

6 cloves garlic, chopped

1 1/2 cups (350 ml/83 g) medium smoking wood chips

With mortar and pestle, crush together salt, fennel and anise seeds and bay leaf until coarse. Add remaining seasoning-mix ingredients, stirring well. Rub pork all over with oil. Sprinkle with seasoning mix and garlic, rubbing in with your fingertips. Place in zipper-style plastic bag and refrigerate for 2 to 12 hours. Near the end of this time, soak wood chips in a bucket of water for at least an hour; if using gas grill or electric smoker, soaking is unnecessary. For gas grill, wrap dry wood chips in foil as described on page 75.

When you're ready to cook, preheat smoker to 325°F (165°C), or prepare grill for hot indirect heat. Place filled water pan in smoker or grill. Add half of the soaked wood to coals (if using gas grill, place foil-wrapped chips on heat element; if using electric smoker, place a handful of dry chips in firebox). Place pork roast, fat-side up, on grate over water pan. Cover and cook at 300°F–320°F (150°C–160°C) until internal temperature of pork reaches 155°F (68°C), about 1 1/2 hours; add remaining wood after about 45 minutes and replenish coals if necessary. Transfer pork to serving platter; tent loosely with foil and let stand for 15 minutes before carving.

Pit-Style Steak

2 or 3 servings
Preliminary preparation: Under 15 minutes (plus wood soaking time)
Recommended equipment: Covered charcoal grill (can't be prepared in a gas grill)
Smoking: Hot smoking with water pan, about an hour (including grill prep)

Some rib joints also offer steaks that have been cooked in the pit. Here's a simple way to get that same flavor sensation and beautiful mahogany color at home, in your covered charcoal grill. —T.M.

1 top sirloin beef steak or venison round steak (about 1 pound/454 g), 1 1/2 inches (3.8 cm) thick

1 1/2 teaspoons (7.5 ml/3 g) Spanish Paprika Rub (page 119) or other barbecue rub

4 large sheets newspaper

10 cups (2.3 liters) natural-wood charcoal, approximate

5 or 6 large chunks dry smoking wood (2 inches/5 cm square)

3 or 4 smaller chunks smoking wood (1 inch/2.5 cm square), soaked in water for at least 1 hour

Sprinkle steak evenly on both sides with barbecue rub, rubbing in with your fingertips. Set steak aside at room temperature while you prepare grill (if you like, cover dish with plastic wrap and refrigerate for as long as 4 hours; this will provide a bit more flavor).

To prepare grill, crumple individual sheets of newspaper very tightly. Place on coal grate, confining to half of the grate (leave the other half clear for the water pan); a charcoal rail helps confine the fire area. Arrange charcoal over paper; tuck dry smoking wood chunks between charcoal pieces. Light newspaper; allow charcoal and wood to burn until flames die down, about 30 minutes.

When flames have died down, place filled water pan on other half of coal grate. Add wet smoking wood to hot coals. Place cooking grate in grill; cover and let heat for about 5 minutes. Place steak on grate over hot coals. Cook for 1 minute, then rotate 45° without flipping and cook for 1 minute longer. Flip steak and cook for 1 minute. Transfer steak to area of grate above water pan, keeping double-marked side up. Cover grill; cook for 15 to 25 minutes, until desired doneness. Remove from grill and let stand for 10 minutes before slicing.

Sweet <u>and</u> Smoky Grilled Duck

2 servings per duck
Preliminary preparation: 2 hours brining
Recommended equipment: Bullet-style water smoker or covered grill
Smoking: Hot smoking with water pan, about 1½ hours

3 cups (690 ml) apple juice

2 cups (470 ml) cold water

½ cup (120 ml/76 g) kosher salt

½ teaspoon (2.5 ml) Tabasco sauce

1 whole dressed mallard or other medium-sized wild duck, preferably skin-on

1 cup (240 ml/55 g) medium smoking wood chips

⅓ cup (80 ml) orange juice

3 tablespoons (45 ml) honey

1 tablespoon (15 ml/2 g) chopped fresh rosemary leaves, or 1 teaspoon (5 ml) crumbled dried

2 teaspoons (10 ml/4 g) paprika

½ teaspoon (2.5 ml/3 g) cracked black pepper

In nonreactive container, combine apple juice, water, salt and Tabasco; stir until salt dissolves. Cut duck in half by cutting along the breastbone and backbone; clean inside as needed. Add duck halves to apple juice mixture; weight with small ceramic plate to keep submerged. Cover and refrigerate for 2 hours. Meanwhile, if using charcoal-fueled grill or smoker, soak wood chips in a bucket of water for at least an hour; if using gas grill or electric smoker, soaking is unnecessary. For gas grill, wrap dry wood chips in foil as described on page 75.

When you're ready to cook, preheat smoker to 300°F (150°C), or prepare grill for hot indirect heat. Drain duck, discarding brine. Place filled water pan in smoker or grill.

Add half of the soaked wood to coals (if using gas grill, place foil-wrapped chips on heat element; if using electric smoker, place a handful of dry chips in firebox). Place duck halves, skin-side up, on grate over water pan. Cover and cook at 275°F–300°F (135°C–150°C) for 30 minutes. Add remaining wood and rearrange ducks, keeping skin-side up. Re-cover and cook for 30 minutes longer; meanwhile, mix orange juice, honey, rosemary, paprika and pepper in measuring cup. At the end of second cooking time (an hour total), turn ducks skin-side down and brush with orange juice mixture. Cover and cook, turning and basting every 5 minutes, for 20 minutes longer, or until desired doneness.

Hot-Smoked Chicken

4 servings
Preliminary preparation: 2 to 3 hours brining
Recommended equipment: Bullet-style water smoker or covered grill, vertical roaster
Smoking: Hot smoking with water pan, 1½ to 2 hours

For crisp skin, hot-smoke chicken at fairly high temperatures; lower temperatures cause the skin to get rubbery. The vertical roaster ensures even smoking, and produces crisp skin over the entire bird. A bullet-style smoker is perfect for this recipe, but you can use a covered grill as long as the lid is high enough to allow the chicken to stand upright.

Brine

2 quarts (1.9 liters) cold water

¾ cup (180 ml/115 g) Diamond Crystal kosher salt (see page 79 for information on using other types of salt)

½ cup (120 ml/110 g) brown sugar (packed)

1 tablespoon (15 ml) Tabasco sauce

1 tablespoon (15 ml/5 g) dry mustard powder

1 teaspoon (5 ml/3 g) ginger

1 teaspoon (5 ml/2 g) white pepper

1 whole skin-on chicken

2 cups (470 ml/150 g) smoking wood chunks* (1- to 2-inch/2.5- to 5-cm chunks)

All-Purpose Seasoning (page 118), other seasoning blend, or salt and pepper

In large nonreactive container, combine all brine ingredients, stirring until salt and sugar dissolve. Add chicken; weight with small ceramic plate to keep submerged (if necessary, add up to 1 cup/240 ml cold water to cover chicken; if you need more liquid than that, make another batch of brine). Refrigerate for 2 to 3 hours. While chicken is brining, soak wood chunks in a bucket of cold water.*

When you're ready to cook, preheat smoker to 350°F (175°C). Drain chicken and pat dry; discard brine. Season chicken liberally, inside and out, with All-Purpose Seasoning. Place chicken on vertical roaster, or use a can of beer or cola as described in Chicken on a Can (page 99); bend wings up and back so tips are behind back of bird. Add a bit more than half of the drained wood chunks to fire (if using gas grill, place foil-wrapped chips on heat element; if using electric smoker, place a handful of dry chips in firebox). Place filled water pan in smoker. Place chicken on grate and close lid. Smoke-cook at 325°F–350°F (165°C–175°C) until chicken registers 170°F (77°C) in the thigh, 1½ to 2 hours; add remaining drained wood chunks to fire an hour after starting, and replenish coals as needed. Remove chicken from smoker; let stand for 10 minutes before carving.

*If you're using a gas grill or electric smoker, use 1½ cups (350 ml/83 g) medium wood chips rather than chunks; soaking is unnecessary. For gas grill, wrap dry wood chips in foil as described on page 75.

Smoke-Roasted Potatoes

General instructions; make as many as you wish
Preliminary preparation: Under 15 minutes (plus wood soaking time)
Recommended equipment: Covered grill or bullet-style smoker
Smoking: Hot smoking, about an hour

> **TIP:** Throw a few potatoes into the smoker whenever you're smoke-cooking a roast or chicken. They make a delightful accompaniment to the smoked main course; or, refrigerate them and use them another day to make twice-baked stuffed potatoes.

1 cup (240 ml/55 g) medium smoking wood chips
Whole skin-on baking potatoes or sweet potatoes

Olive oil or canola oil (about ½ teaspoon/2.5 ml per potato)

For charcoal-fueled grill or smoker, soak wood chips in a bucket of cold water for at least an hour; if using gas grill or electric smoker, soaking is unnecessary. For gas grill, wrap dry wood chips in foil as described on page 75.

Prepare grill for hot indirect heat, or preheat smoker to 325°F (165°C). Scrub potato skins, then dry well. Prick skins in several places with a fork, then rub skins with oil to coat lightly. Add drained wood to coals (if using gas grill, place foil-wrapped chips on heat element; if using electric smoker, place dry chips in firebox). Place potatoes on grate away from heat. Cover grill or close smoker; cook at 300°F–350°F (150°C–175°C) until potatoes are tender, about an hour. Serve hot, slathered with butter if you like.

"It has long been acknowledged that the single best restaurant in the world is Arthur Bryant's Barbecue at Eighteenth and Brooklyn in Kansas City." Thus wrote humorist/food writer Calvin Trillin in a 1974 article in *The New Yorker*. This tongue-in-cheek piece sent thousands of middle- and upper-class Americans into a rough-and-tumble neighborhood in Kansas City (Missouri) to rub shoulders with the working class and eat the "world's best" pit-smoked barbecue. Soon, other local joints, such as Gates & Sons Bar-B-Q, Boyd 'N Son Barbecue, and later, Lil' Jake's and KC Masterpiece Barbecue & Grill, were "discovered," firmly ensconcing Kansas City as the Barbecue Mecca of the World.

The restaurant that became Arthur Bryant's was started in the 1920s by Henry Perry, who sold slabs of ribs for 25¢ out of an old trolley barn at 19th and Highland. Charlie Bryant, one of Perry's workers, eventually bought the operation from Perry, and hired his brother, Arthur, to help out. Arthur took over in the mid-40s when Charlie retired. The specialties of the house are pork spareribs and beef brisket—both served with soft white bread and Bryant's hallmark spicy-sweet, tomato-based barbecue sauce.

Like many 'cue enthusiasts, I've visited Bryant's, and perched at the long communal tables with my overflowing brisket sandwich in its plastic basket. Whenever I'm traveling, I love to search for good pit-smoked barbecue. I've enjoyed smoky, tender yet chewy ribs at a little roadhouse in a small Indiana town. In Tennessee, I drove into the hills to savor pulled pork at a place so far off the beaten path, the waitress had never met anyone with a Northern accent. I've ordered barbecue at restaurants, roadhouses and diners from South Carolina to Washington state. The point is, you don't have to go to Kansas City, or Memphis, or St. Louis, to enjoy good barbecue; good barbecue is where you find it.

Even before I moved to Minneapolis in the late 1970s, I'd eaten at The Market Bar-B-Que, at its original home on Glenwood Avenue in a working-class neighborhood on the north end of downtown Minneapolis. The Market was opened in 1946 by Willard and Sam Polski, who surprised the locals by serving a barbecued pork sandwich without the sauce. Willard and Sam felt that their smoky, slow-

cooked meat was good enough to be served with the sauce on the side. History proved the brothers right, and to this day, the ribs, chicken and brisket are served "naked" at The Market (with two savory, house-made sauces on the side, of course).

Like many barbecue joints, the business has stayed in the family, and is now owned and run by Willard's son, Steve, who bought the business from his dad in 1976. The Market currently has two restaurants: Minneapolis and Wayzata.

The pit, of course, is the heart of a barbecue restaurant such as The Market—and the pits at The Market are real beauties. At the bottom is the firebox, where split logs (generally a mix of red oak, apple, hickory and cherry) are burned; the food sits on heavy grates in the upper chamber. Brass-trimmed glass doors on the upper chamber allow the pit tender to monitor progress of the food; the burning wood is sprayed with a hose as needed to control the temperature and also add humidity. Glass windows allow patrons to see the pit in action. At the end of the cooking day, the pit is "fired" to burn off the day's accumulation of fat and drippings—a spectacular conflagration that heats the grate to temperatures exceeding 1000°F (538°C).

For seasoning, The Market uses a special liquid "baste." After a dip in the baste, the meat is cooked at 235°F (113°C) until it is tender and redolent with the subtle tang of hardwood. Steve takes pride in the fact that the ribs and other meats are cooked entirely in the pit—not pre-cooked and simply finished on a grill, as is the case at many other restaurants. As far as secrets, that's pretty much it; top-quality meats, seasoned just enough to accent the flavor, cooked over genuine hardwood and served with the sauce on the side. For a barbecue fan, it's worth the trip.

—Teresa Marrone

"Low & Slow" Techniques

For most people, the mention of grilling brings quick-cooked foods to mind: burgers, chops, steak and perhaps fish or chicken, prepared on a standard backyard charcoal or gas grill using relatively high heat. But there is another style of grilling—the "low-and-slow" method often referred to simply as barbecue. In addition, some backyard cooks use tools such as rotisseries and specialty roasters, or construct larger homemade grilling surfaces suitable for cooking food on a grand scale. This chapter is devoted to these special techniques.

Low-and-slow cooking is particularly suited to less-tender cuts, such as beef brisket (page 102) or pork shoulder (page 99). It also works well for larger items, such as a whole turkey (page 98) or a venison quarter (page 101); these larger cuts would burn on the outside long before the inside was cooked if exposed to the direct high heat of regular grilling. A water pan is frequently used with low-and-slow cooking; the steam helps keep the meat moist as it cooks.

For a big event, consider a pig or lamb roast. You'll need special equipment to handle a whole (or split) pig or lamb. Equipment rental centers often have drum-style rotisserie pig roasters that work well; see page 103 for instructions. A split oil drum, well cleaned and burned out, can form a good base for a large grill. You can also rig up a homemade grilling surface using an iron grid and cinder blocks; see the sidebar on page 106 for details. This large grilling surface is also useful for doing a traditional Southern clam or oyster roast (pages 104 and 105).

If you have a really large yard and don't mind digging up a part of it, you may enjoy an old-fashioned clambake (page 107); the pit that you dig can become a bonfire area for the future. Be sure to check local regulations before planning an event that involves a fire on the ground; local regulations may require a burning permit, or may prohibit this sort of event entirely.

Turkey <u>on the</u> Grill

8 to 10 servings
Preliminary preparation: 15 minutes initial prep, 1 hour room-temperature standing
Grilling: Indirect medium heat with water pan, 3½ to 4½ hours

Every Thanksgiving (and often on Easter), my brother-in-law Steve fires up the grill—no matter the weather here in Minnesota—and prepares a succulent grilled turkey for our feast. He varies his basting mixture each time, and often marinates the bird before grilling; this is a basic recipe to start from, but he would advise you to experiment freely. —T.M.

1 medium-sized whole skin-on turkey (8 to 10 pounds/3.6 to 4.5 kg)
¼ cup (55 g/half of a stick) butter, softened
1 teaspoon (5 ml) dried marjoram
½ teaspoon (2.5 ml) dried thyme
1 clove garlic, finely minced, optional
2 tablespoons (30 ml) olive oil or canola oil

Salt and freshly ground black pepper
1 cup (240 ml) chicken broth
1 cup (240 ml) white wine or apple juice
¼ cup (60 ml) soy sauce
1 tablespoon (15 ml/6 g) paprika

Remove neck and giblets from turkey and set aside for another use. Remove and discard fat inside body cavity. Rinse turkey inside and out, and pat dry with paper towels. Loosen skin over breast by working your fingertips underneath the skin, starting above the cavity. In small bowl, blend together the butter, marjoram, thyme and garlic. Spread butter mixture between skin and breast meat, using your fingertips to pack butter under the skin and smoothing from the outside. Rub outside of turkey with oil; season inside and out with salt and pepper to taste. Let turkey stand at room temperature for about an hour while you prepare grill. Also combine broth, wine, soy sauce and paprika in measuring cup or bowl.

Prepare grill* for indirect medium heat. Position filled water pan between coal banks, or away from heated area of gas grill. Place turkey, breast-side up, on grate over water pan. Cover grill and begin cooking. After about 30 minutes, baste turkey with broth mixture. Re-cover grill and continue cooking, basting every 15 minutes and replenishing coals as necessary, until turkey thigh reaches 170°F (77°C) and juices run clear; cooking time should be 3½ to 4½ hours. Transfer turkey to serving platter; tent loosely with foil and let stand for 15 to 20 minutes before carving.

*If you have a bullet-style water smoker, that will work very well for this recipe. Build a medium fire and fill the water pan; proceed as directed.

Roasted Pork Boston Butt

8 to 10 servings
Preliminary preparation: Under 15 minutes initial prep, 24 to 48 hours seasoning (refrigerated)
Grilling: Direct medium-low heat, 6 hours

This is a version of the classic dish called "pulled pork," scaled down for the average backyard cook. It's a remarkably simple process, but produces pork that is melt-in-your-mouth tender. It always gets raves and requests for the recipe. What could be easier?
—A. and J.C.

1 fresh pork Boston butt roast (8 to 10 pounds/ 3.6 to 4.5 kg)

Garlic powder

Salt and freshly ground black pepper

Prepare a dry rub using garlic powder, salt and freshly ground pepper. The amount of each depends on your preferences; however, don't be too heavy with any one because you want the flavor of the meat to come through. Season roast liberally with mixture, rubbing in with your fingers. Place rubbed roast in zipper-style plastic bag and refrigerate for 24 to 48 hours.

When you're ready to cook, prepare grill for direct medium-low heat; lightly oil grate. Place roast on grate over heat. Cook for 6 hours, adding coals as necessary to maintain 225°F-250°F (105°C-120°C) temperature, or until roast is so tender it almost falls off the bones. Turn roast every 30 minutes during cooking. Remove from heat and let it cool enough to handle. Pull or separate pork with 2 forks. Serve immediately. This is delicious served plain; or, you may serve with sauces on the side.

Chicken on a Can

4 to 6 servings
Preliminary preparation: Under 15 minutes
Grilling: Indirect medium heat, 1¼ to 2 hours

The steam from the beer makes the chicken quite moist. You can also brine the chicken (page 53) for an even juicier bird. When rubbing the chicken with the dry rub, you may wish to loosen the skin of the chicken, and rub spices under the skin.

1 large whole skin-on chicken

2 tablespoons (30 ml) olive oil

1 tablespoon (15 ml/19 g) salt

1 teaspoon (5 ml/2 g) pepper

2 tablespoons (30 ml) dry rub (see pages 118–120), or Greek or Italian seasoning blend

1 can (12 ounces/350 ml) beer

A few dashes of Worcestershire sauce

Remove neck and giblets from chicken and set aside for another use. Remove and discard fat inside body cavity. Rinse chicken inside and out, and pat dry with paper towels. Rub chicken lightly with oil, then rub inside and out with salt, pepper and dry rub.

Prepare grill for indirect medium heat; lightly oil grate. Position drip pan between coal banks, or away from heated area of gas grill. Open beer can; drink or pour off about half of the beer. Add Worcestershire sauce to beer remaining in can. Use a pointed can opener to pierce 2 additional holes in the top of the can (this step is optional, but does provide better steam). Holding the chicken upright, with the body cavity opening down, insert the beer can into the cavity. Prop the chicken on its legs and the beer can to form a tripod on the grate over drip pan. Be careful and precise making the tripod to prevent spills. Cover grill and cook chicken until the internal temperature registers 170°F (77°C) in the thigh, generally 1¼ to 2 hours. The thigh juices should run clear when stabbed with a sharp knife.

Carefully remove chicken from grill with tongs and a large metal spatula held underneath the beer can for support. The shorter the move, the better, so have a platter right next to the grill or as close as possible. Be careful not to spill hot beer on yourself. Let chicken rest for 10 minutes before carving.

The dog days of summer hold the land tight in a sweaty grip as August gives way to September. Gray darts speed across sere fields where corn has been harvested or sunflowers have been bush-hogged. Across the rural South the time is at hand for a combination backyard barbecue with a large, old-fashioned brush arbor revival, family reunion and all-day dinner. It's opening day of dove season or, as a longtime friend and fellow hunter puts it, "Christmas in September."

The occasion serves as a renewal of the timeless rites of the hunt. It's a young retriever marking its first retrieve and seeming to grin around a mouthful of feathers. It's a young hunter proudly sharing the special moment of his first successful shot at a dove with an adoring grandfather. It's family and friends getting together to swap tales, poke and prod missed shots and praise hits and to carry on a tradition that in some cases has been renewed annually for generations.

Sometimes a grand feast precedes the hunt (in most states you cannot hunt until after noon on opening day), while others celebrate with a post-hunt meal. In either instance, there will be the garden abundance of summer in great plenty—vine-ripened tomatoes, perhaps okra and watermelon rind pickles, corn-on-the-cob dripping with real butter, slices of peppers, squash casserole, golden slices of cantaloupe and wedges of ruby red watermelon so cold that beads bedeck the bright green rind. For "afters" there will be chocolate and lemon chess pies, pecan pies, cookies with raisins and black walnut or pecan pieces from last fall's gathering of nuts puckering their surfaces, layer cakes and sheath cakes, a freezer or two of homemade peach or vanilla ice cream and maybe, just maybe, that supreme treat for the Southern sweet tooth, a scuppernong pie.

Yet all these offerings form mere foot soldiers in the parade of food, and the same holds true for staples such as cathead biscuits and even pepper-laced chicken bog. For the heart of any proper dove hunt feast, the pièce de résistance if you will, comes straight from a giant barbecue outfit that might weigh hundreds of pounds and require a truck for transport.

Starting sometime late the previous afternoon or early in the evening, a whole pig will have been put in the roaster to start slow cooking, with juices pushing through the crackling skin and occasional paintbrush bastings from a bucket filled with a "secret recipe" keeping everything moist. Early the following morning, several haunches of venison, left over from deer hunts the previous fall, will take their places atop the grill flanking the pig. By the time hordes of hunters have gathered, all will be done to a turn and half a dozen volunteers will join in to "pick" the pig and place succulent morsels of meat in large bowls.

Finally the long-anticipated moment arrives when the hunt master, having covered safety rules and assigned stands, says: "It's time to eat." Those gifted with long experience will linger long and lovingly at the feast, knowing full well that it will be several hours before doves begin to fly with any degree of regularity. Meanwhile, they can sit in the shade, enjoy the food and maybe even make plans for further gustatory enjoyment after the hunt.

That comes in the form of grilled dove breasts, cooked on the same outfit where the pig and venison were roasted, and accompanied by plentiful leftovers from the earlier feasting. In the cool of the evening, with guns safely stored, glasses of chilled muscadine wine, a perfect accompaniment for the deep red meat of doves, appear. Weary sportsmen, happily tired from hours in the sun and fulfilled by another renewal of a wonderful tradition, look back on hunts past, sharing fond reminiscences and knowing full well they have been a part of something that is enduring, special and worth sustaining. For my part, it's one of the year's highlights, and I enjoy the food and festivities at least as much as I do the shooting.

—*Jim Casada*

Whole Roast Pig

100 to 125 servings
Preliminary preparation: Under 15 minutes
Grilling: Indirect low heat with water pan, 10 to 12 hours
Special equipment: Pig roaster or large grill (page 106), disposable aluminum pans or foil

(page 106)

When choosing a hog for a pig roast, figure on a pound (.5 kg) of dressed weight per person. A large roaster, made from an oil drum, is typically used; you should have at least 100 pounds of charcoal on hand. Pig roasts are often overnight affairs, with a barbecue crew watching over the pig through the night.

1 whole, dressed hog, 100 to 125 pounds (45 to 57 kg) dressed weight, prepared by the butcher for roasting (skinned but with a layer of fat remaining, or skin-on and scraped)

Baste

1 quart (950 ml) vinegar

1 cup (240 ml) lemon juice

1 tablespoon (15 ml/6 g) cayenne pepper

1 tablespoon (15 ml) Tabasco sauce

1 tablespoon (15 ml) Worcestershire sauce

1 teaspoon (5 ml) dehydrated onion flakes

2 cloves garlic, cut into slivers

For serving: barbecue sauce, mustard, buns, sliced onions and other condiments of your choice

Use a bone saw to cut the hog in half lengthwise so it will lie flat (or, have the butcher do this). Combine all baste ingredients in a large jar or other nonreactive container. Prepare a very large grill for indirect low heat. Build a drip pan from heavy-duty foil, or arrange several disposable aluminum pans between coal banks. Place a container of water in the drip pan. This serves two purposes: it minimizes any flame-ups from grease and helps keep plenty of steam inside the cooker for moist meat. Place pig halves on grate over heat, skin-side down. Cover roaster and cook at 175°F–200°F (80°C–93°C),

basting frequently and replenishing coals as necessary, until fully done; cooking time for a pig this size is generally 10 to 12 hours. The meat is ready when a meat thermometer inserted in the thickest part of the hams reaches 160°F (71°C). Pull (or shred) the meat as soon as it is cool enough to be handled. In a true "pig picking," each person pulls his own meat from the hog, but things move more quickly if the cook removes the meat from the bone and places it in several large containers, with a selection of barbecue sauces readily available.

TIP: The baste at left is vinegar-based, but others prefer bastes that are mustard- or tomato-based. An alternative, when dealing with a large group with diverse taste preferences, is to cook the hog without basting at all (the container of water and the fact that the skin serves to hold most drippings in keep the meat moist). Just have various sauces available and let each individual apply the one of his or her choice.

Roast Venison Haunch

15 to 20 servings
Preliminary preparation: Under 15 minutes
Grilling: Direct low heat, 6 to 7 hours
Special equipment: Disposable foil roasting pan

1 venison haunch (15 to 20 pounds/6.75 to 9 kg)

1 pound (454 g) sliced bacon

1 or 2 cloves garlic, cut into slivers

Salt and pepper

1/4 cup (60 ml) vinegar added to 3/4 cup (180 ml) water

Wash haunch of venison thoroughly and pat dry. Cut slits in meat across the grain, about an inch (2.5 cm) apart and an inch deep. Insert a slice of bacon and a sliver or 2 of garlic in each slit. Season venison liberally with salt and pepper. Place any remaining slices of bacon atop the venison.

Prepare grill for direct low heat. Place venison in a disposable foil roasting pan (or fashion a pan out of heavy-

duty aluminum foil). Place on grate over heat. Cover grill and cook at 175°F–200°F (80°C–93°C) until tender, basting frequently with the vinegar water and replenishing coals as necessary. Allow 20 to 25 minutes per pound cooking time. This can be placed alongside a roast pig during its final hours of cooking, timing (by weight) so that both are ready at the same time.

All-Day Beef Brisket

8 to 10 servings
Preliminary preparation: Under 15 minutes initial prep, 8 to 12 hours seasoning (refrigerated)
Grilling: Indirect low heat with water pan, 6 to 8 hours, followed by 1 hour resting time

Season the meat the night before you want to serve it, then start the actual cooking in the morning. The meat cooks slowly most of the day, and has a final resting time before it's ready to serve. —T.M.

Brisket Spice Mixture

3 tablespoons (45 ml/40 g) brown sugar (packed)

2 tablespoons (30 ml/19 g) kosher salt

2 tablespoons (30 ml/12 g) paprika

2 tablespoons (30 ml/12 g) freshly ground pepper

1 tablespoon (15 ml/7.5 g) garlic powder

1 teaspoon (5 ml/4 g) mustard seeds

1 teaspoon (5 ml/2 g) cayenne pepper

1 choice beef brisket (about 6 pounds/2.7 kg)

Buns, barbecue sauce, mustard and sliced onion for serving

Combine spice-mixture ingredients in mixing bowl; stir with fork until well mixed. Set aside 2 tablespoons of the mixture; rub remaining mixture into both sides of brisket. Place in zipper-style plastic bag and refrigerate overnight, or for 8 to 12 hours.

When you're ready to cook, prepare grill* for indirect low heat; lightly oil grate. Position filled water pan between coal banks, or away from heated area of gas grill. Rub reserved 2 tablespoons spice mixture over brisket. Place brisket, fat-side up, on grate over water pan. Cover grill and cook until brisket reaches at least 165°F (74°C), 6 to 8 hours; replenish coals (and water in pan) as necessary to maintain 200°F–225°F (93°C–105°C) temperature. When brisket is at least 165°F (74°C), remove from grill and wrap well in heavy-duty foil. Wrap a thick layer of newspaper or towels around foil-wrapped brisket; set aside at room temperature for an hour, or a bit longer. This allows the juices to equalize and also helps finish tenderizing the meat. When ready to serve, unwrap brisket carefully, pouring any juices into small bowl. Slice brisket across the grain and arrange in serving dish; pour accumulated juices over brisket and serve.

*If you have a bullet-style water smoker, it will work very well for this recipe. Build a medium fire and fill the water pan; proceed as directed.

Barbecued Turkey Legs

4 servings
Preliminary preparation: Under 15 minutes initial prep, 2 hours brining
Grilling: Indirect medium heat with water pan, 2 to 3 hours, followed by 1 hour resting time

Brine

1 quart (950 ml) cold water

1/4 cup (60 ml/70 g) canning/pickling salt

1/4 cup (60 ml/55 g) brown sugar (packed)

1 tablespoon (15 ml) pickling spice

4 skin-on turkey legs (about 12 ounces/340 g each)

3/4 cup (180 ml) prepared barbecue sauce, purchased or from the recipes on pages 122–123

In nonreactive container, combine brine ingredients, stirring until salt and sugar dissolve. Add turkey legs; weight with small ceramic plate to keep submerged. Refrigerate for about 2 hours.

When you're ready to cook, prepare grill* for indirect medium heat; lightly oil grate. Position filled water pan between coal banks, or away from heated area of gas grill. Drain turkey legs, discarding brine; pat dry with paper towels. Brush legs on all sides with barbecue sauce. Place legs on grate over water pan. Cover grill and cook until turkey legs are tender and reach an internal temperature of 170°F (77°C), 2 to 3 hours; replenish coals (and water in pan) as necessary to maintain 250°F–300°F (120°C–150°C) temperature. Remove legs from grill; brush again with barbecue sauce. Wrap well in heavy-duty foil. Wrap a thick layer of newspaper or towels around foil-wrapped turkey legs; set aside at room temperature for 45 minutes to an hour. This allows the juices to equalize and also helps finish tenderizing the legs. Serve warm.

*If you have a bullet-style water smoker, it will work very well for this recipe. Build a medium-hot fire and fill the water pan; proceed as directed.

Whole Pig in a Rotisserie Roaster

75 to 100 servings
Preliminary preparation: About an hour to prepare roaster
Grilling: Direct medium heat, 4 to 6 hours
Special equipment: Covered pig roaster with rotisserie
You will also need: 2 boxes heavy-duty foil; about 100 pounds (45 kg) charcoal; starter fluid; 2 pairs long-sleeved heavy-duty oven mitts

Check at a rental center for a covered pig roaster; most can be pulled behind your car with a trailer hitch. Make sure the rotisserie motor works properly before starting; turning is essential with this cooking method.

1 whole, dressed hog, about 100 pounds (45 kg) dressed weight, prepared by the butcher for roasting (skinned but with a layer of fat remaining, or skin-on and scraped)

1 quart (950 ml) pineapple juice

¼ cup (60 ml/30 g) chopped garlic

¼ cup (60 ml) mixed dried herb blend

3 tablespoons (45 ml/57 g) salt

2 tablespoons (30 ml/12 g) pepper

For serving: barbecue sauce, mustard, buns, sliced onions and other condiments of your choice

Secure the pig to the rotisserie spit (the butcher may be willing to do this for you); set aside on a clean surface while you prepare the roaster. Line inside of the roaster completely with foil, shiny-side up, starting at one end and overlapping foil by 3 inches (7.5 cm) as you go; this makes cleanup much easier, and is highly recommended. Add a 4- to 5-inch (10- to 12.5-cm) layer of coals along the bottom of the roaster on top of the foil. Soak coals generously with starter fluid, then light carefully. Allow to burn down until covered with gray ash before putting the pig into the roaster. Meanwhile, combine pineapple juice, garlic, herbs, salt and pepper in large jar; set aside.

It will take 2 strong people to get the spit with the pig into the roaster. Both should be wearing long oven mitts; loose sleeves and shirttails are an invitation to disaster, and must be avoided. Once the spit is securely in place, start the rotisserie motor and cover the roaster. Cook until the hams read 165°F (74°C), 4 to 6 hours; every 45 minutes, add a good amount of fresh charcoal to the fire* and baste the pig with the pineapple juice mixture (you'll have to stop the motor to check the temperature of the hams). When the pig is done, transfer the spit to a clean table that has been covered with a clean vinyl table covering, and carve there; or, if you like, carve off portions as they become done and allow the rest of the pig to continue cooking until done.

Cleanup: Allow the coals to die down completely; sprinkle them with a little water if you like, but don't use so much water that you make a puddle in the roaster. When coals are cold, roll up the foil, starting at the end you began laying it; the overlaps in the foil make it easy to roll up the ashes and waste in a fairly compact bundle. Scrape any leftover meat or fat from the spit, and soak it in a tubful of hot, sudsy water; scrub well with a steel scouring pad. Hose out any residue from the roaster, and let everything dry before returning it to the rental center. (If you return the roaster dirty, you will probably be charged an additional fee; plus, it's just common courtesy to clean it before returning it.)

*The hindquarter takes longer to cook than the forequarter, so you should pile a bit more charcoal into that area of the grill.

Whole Lamb in a Rotisserie Roaster

Follow instructions above for the whole pig, using a whole young lamb (about 50 pounds/22.7 kg dressed weight). Cooking time will be 3 to 4 hours, and the lamb will serve 30 to 40 people.

Leg-o-Lamb on a Spit

8 to 10 servings
Preliminary preparation: Under 15 minutes initial prep
Grilling: Direct high heat, about 1½ hours
Special equipment: Rotisserie

Grills with rotisseries vary in design. Some allow for the use of a drip pan; if yours is set up like this, use the drip pan to minimize flare-ups. If your rotisserie has a counterweight, use that also; it will help balance the weight of the lamb, making the rotation more smooth. —K.F.

1 butterflied, boneless leg of lamb (3 to 4 pounds/ 1.36 to 1.8 kg)

Kosher salt and freshly ground pepper

A piece of heavy kitchen string (about 4 feet/ 1.2 m long), soaked in water

½ cup (110 g/1 stick) unsalted butter

2 teaspoons (10 ml/5 g) garlic powder

Set up rotisserie, and prepare grill for direct high heat; if possible, position drip pan in area under center of rotisserie. Season butterflied leg of lamb with salt and pepper to taste, then tie into a round roast with wet kitchen string (or have the butcher tie the roast for you, then season the outside just before roasting). Place roast on rotisserie spit and secure with provided prongs. Turn motor on to begin roasting the lamb. Meanwhile, melt butter in small saucepan over medium heat; stir in garlic powder. After lamb has cooked for about 15 minutes, baste with garlic butter. Continue cooking, basting frequently, for 1¼ to 1½ hours, or until temperature is 160°F (71°C) in the thickest part of the roast. Remove the spit from the grill, then slide roast off the spit onto serving platter. Let stand for 5 minutes before carving.

Roasted Clams

Variable servings
Preliminary preparation: Under 15 minutes
Grilling: Direct high heat, under 15 minutes
Special equipment: Large grill
(see sidebar, page 106)

Once the clams have been eaten, the remaining butter and clam juice can be conserved to use with clam chowder or, better still, soak chunks of bread in it and eat on the spot. With such fare available, cholesterol counting should be momentarily forgotten.

½ cup (110 g/1 stick) butter for every 4 persons
24 to 36 live clams per person*

Prepare large grill or other fire for direct high heat; position grate over coals. This need not be anything more than a grid placed over the coals of a campfire, and any type of standard grill will work quite well. (Make sure the grate has a tight enough pattern so no clams can slip through to the fire.) Melt butter in a saucepan or other container and keep warm. Thoroughly scrub clams with a stiff wire brush and then pile them onto the grate over the heat. As the clams begin to open, usually after a couple of minutes, turn them over or redistribute them. In another minute or two they will pop wide open and at this point they should be removed from the heat. Drain any juice left in the shells into the pan of melted butter and use the mix to dunk clams.

*The number of clams depends on their size, the appetite of those who will eat them and whether they are to be a main dish or an appetizer.

Traditional Southern Oyster Roast

Variable servings
Preliminary preparation: Under 15 minutes
Grilling: Direct high heat, under 15 minutes
Special equipment: Large grill (see sidebar, page 106); 2 or 3 gunnysacks (called "tow sacks" in the South), or equivalent in burlap cloth

TIP: While use of a wet tow sack will hold more steam and make for a more succulent oyster, it is not essential. The oysters can be roasted directly without any covering.

Make sure to have gloves and an oyster knife for everyone. At old-time oyster roasts each participant in the feast was assigned his or her own "shucker." These were usually youngsters, and they took pride in two things—always having another oyster ready and in the number of these morsels their "man" consumed.
—A. and J.C.

12 to 24 live oysters per person*

Soak the tow sacks in saltwater for 15 minutes. Prepare large grill for direct high heat (make sure the grate has a tight enough pattern so no oysters can slip through to the fire). Scrub oysters with a stiff wire brush and then pile them onto the grate over the heat. Cover immediately with soaked tow sack. Cook until oysters show a hint of opening, using long tongs to turn them once. Do

Accompaniments: Tabasco or seafood sauce, saltine crackers

not overcook to the point the juice contained inside the shell evaporates. As soon as they are ready, remove from heat and eat at once. Serve while piping hot with Tabasco or seafood sauce and crackers.

*For hearty appetites, a dozen oysters amount to little more than an hors d'oeuvre.

A standard grill is too small for large-scale cooking, such as a split pig or a pile of oysters. If you have an area in your yard that is away from trees and shrubs, and you don't mind building a fire there (and if it is allowed by local code), here's how to build a large-surface grill.

You'll need a large, heavy grate (preferably cast iron or heavy steel); for a pig, 3x4½ feet (91x137 cm) is the minimum size. Don't use a grate that contains lead solder, or one that is galvanized. If you like, dig a shallow pit to hold the coals; you can also simply build your fire right on the ground, but dig away any sod first. In either case, clear an area around the edges so it is free of brush, grass or flammable materials. The fire area should be 8 inches (20 cm) smaller on all sides than the grate, to allow room for the supports.

You'll also need a number of 8-inch (20-cm) cinder blocks to support the grate; for a hotter fire, use a single layer of blocks so the grate is close to the coals, and for a cooler fire, stack blocks 2 high to raise the grate (if stacking blocks, use several for each layer, crisscrossing them for stability). Arrange the blocks at the corners of the grate, leaving the sides open so you can tend the fire; if the grate is long, put blocks in the center as well, to support the weight of the grate and food.

If you're planning to cook a split pig, you may wish to fashion a hood for the grill. Bend several 6-foot (183-cm) steel reinforcing rods into arches, and wire several straight rods crosswise to them with heavy wire. Cover the entire structure with heavy-duty foil.

For better heat reflection, line the pit or the ground with foil, shiny-side up (this is optional). Position the supports so they're ready for the grate, but don't put the grate on yet. Spread charcoal at least 2 inches (5 cm) deep over the fire area. Saturate with lighter fluid and ignite carefully. When the coals have burned down and are covered with gray ash, position the grate carefully atop the blocks, then add the food to the grate. If using a hood, place it over the cooking area. Cook as directed, replenishing the coals as necessary.

Hood

Old-Fashioned Clambake

10 servings
Preliminary preparation: 2 to 3 hours burning (plus time to dig the pit)
Cooking: About an hour in the pit
Special equipment: Shovel; long-handled hoe or heavy-duty garden rake; 4 or 5 new or very clean gunnysacks, or equivalent in burlap cloth; large, heavyweight tarp
You will also need: 20 to 30 large rocks* and a good supply of dry firewood

If you live near the ocean, substitute wet seaweed for the greens. Driftwood is the traditional fuel for a clambake, but any clean, dry hardwood works well. Logs split for a fireplace are perfect; you'll need about a quarter of a cord. Note: You will be building a large, open fire, which will deserve respect. Keep kids and pets far away, and use commonsense safety precautions. Have a hose handy, and watch to be sure flying sparks don't ignite nearby brush or grass. —T.M.

1¼ cups (290 ml/280 g) kosher salt

1 cup (240 ml/160 g) cornmeal

2 gallons (8 liters) cold water

8 to 10 pounds (3.6 to 4.5 kg) live clams

10 ears fresh corn, unhusked

3 or 4 whole skin-on chickens

Seasoned salt or garlic salt

10 baking potatoes or sweet potatoes

2 tablespoons (30 ml) canola oil

5 or 6 whole medium onions

5 live lobsters

15 pounds (6.75 kg) kale, collard greens or other edible greens

2 pounds (900 g) butter, melted

10 whole lemons, each cut into 8 wedges

Building and firing the pit: In an open area, dig a bowl-shaped pit that is 4 to 5 feet (1.2 to 1.5 meters) across and about 2 feet (60 cm) deep in the center; don't dig near trees because the fire will damage the roots (and the trees may ignite). Clear the surface around the edges so it is completely free of brush, grass, leaves or other flammable material. Arrange the rocks around the edges of the pit. Using commonsense precautions, build a fire in the pit as though building a campfire, starting with smaller kindling and gradually adding larger fuel. When the fire is going well, use the hoe to push the rocks into the center, taking care to avoid the sparks that will be kicked up. Continue adding more wood until the rocks are red- to white-hot, then let the wood burn down to glowing red-hot coals. Stay away from the fire as much as possible because even dry rocks occasionally explode; you may want to wear safety goggles. Near the end of the pit-firing, soak the gunnysacks in a bucket of water.

Preparing the food for the pit: As soon as you get the fire started, combine salt and cornmeal with water in large pot or clean bucket; stir to dissolve salt. Add clams. Refrigerate for 2 to 3 hours; this purges the clams of any grit (you could also set the pot in a tub of ice to keep it cold). Add corn to another bucket of cold water; weight it down with a clean brick and let it soak for at least an hour.

Near the end of the pit-firing time, split the chickens in half and season liberally with seasoned salt. Scrub potatoes and rub them with the oil. Peel the onions and cut off root ends.

Drain clams and scrub the shells with a stiff brush. Using live lobsters may be disconcerting to some people; kill the lobsters just before putting them into the pit, if you prefer.

Putting the food into the pit: When the fire has burned down to red-hot coals with no active flames, it is ready. Tamp down the embers with the hoe, then cover the embers and rocks with a thick layer of greens (save about half of the greens for the top layer). Quickly wring out 1 or 2 gunnysacks, then place them over the greens. Arrange potatoes, corn and onions over gunnysacks. Lay chicken halves and lobsters over vegetables; scatter clams over all.

Place remaining greens over the food in a layer. Wring out remaining gunnysacks, and use them to cover the greens. Cover all with the tarp, weighting the edges down with wood or cold rocks. Let food cook for 45 minutes, then peel back a small area of the tarp, burlap and greens and check the food. When the clams are open and the lobsters are bright red, everything should be cooked; if it is not yet done, re-cover the pit and cook for 15 minutes longer before checking again. Remove all food as soon as it is done, transferring it to serving platters or roasters. Serve with melted butter and lemon wedges.

*Choose dry rocks that are softball- to grapefruit-sized; you'll need about 100 pounds (45 kg) total. Don't collect your rocks from a river, lake or stream; they have moisture inside and may explode in the fire. Scrub the rocks to remove dirt and sand, then let them dry before using.

CHAPTER FIVE

Deep-Frying
& Boiling

Backyard deep-frying is a growing outdoor pastime. A number of special backyard turkey fryers are available, with pots ranging in size from 26 quarts (24 liters) for an 8- to 10-pound turkey (3.6- to 4.5-kg), to 60 quarts (57 liters) for a turkey up to 18 pounds (8 kg). Smaller cookers, generally 9 to 12 quarts (8.5 to 11 liters), work great for frying fish, smaller game birds, onion rings—even donuts. As an added bonus, both large and small backyard cookers can be used for a variety of specialty dishes such as booya (page 114) and fish or shrimp boils (page 115). You could even use a smaller cooker to prepare soup for a large backyard party.

In addition to the pot, the heart of an outdoor deep-fryer is the heat source. Generally, a propane burner is supported on a metal stand; a flexible hose attaches the burner to a refillable propane tank. Most commercially available turkey fryers include some sort of rack, basket or hook system for getting the turkey into—and out of—the boiling oil in the pot. Smaller backyard cookers generally come with a basket, making it easy to handle numerous pieces of food. These are great for fish or shrimp boils, as well as for deep-frying onion rings and similar foods.

A key to success in backyard frying is maintaining the oil at the proper temperature to cook the food. If the temperature drops below 340°F (170°C), the food will absorb oil and become greasy. Monitor the oil temperature with a deep-frying or candy thermometer, and adjust the propane as necessary.

Always use a quality oil with a high smoking point when deep-frying. Peanut, corn, canola and safflower oil work well. After frying, the oil can be cooled and strained through a fine-mesh strainer lined with cheesecloth, then refrigerated for another use. Discard the oil after several uses; old oil causes over-browning and may impart off-flavors to the food. Avoid cooking strong-flavored and mild-flavored foods in the same oil; if you deep-fry fish fillets and then French fries, the fries will have a fish flavor. Salt foods after cooking rather than before, when possible; salt breaks down the oil.

Turkey fryers should be used outdoors, away from any wooden decks or furniture. Remember that you will have a large pot filled with boiling oil or other liquid, so safety must be first in mind at all times. Make sure that the cooker is on a sturdy and level surface to minimize the possibility of tipping. An area of hard-packed dirt is best; oil spills will stain concrete, and wooden decking is a fire hazard. When it's time to cook, add food to the cooker carefully. Always wear long-sleeved heavy-duty cooking mitts, pants to cover your legs, and safety goggles. Keep pets and children away from the area throughout the process, and remember that the oil stays hot for a long time even after the burners are turned off. Never leave the turkey fryer unattended, and have a fire extinguisher handy.

Deep-Fried Fish

4 servings
Preparation: Under 30 minutes (plus time to heat oil)
Special equipment: Outdoor deep-fryer (at least 12 quarts/11 liters)

This recipe—a favorite of a fishing friend who is a crappie-catching wizard and loves to host fish fries—can be expanded to serve a large crowd. If you like, substitute a commercial breading mix such as Uncle Buck's Fish Batter (available at Bass Pro Shops) for the seasoned cornmeal. —A. and J.C.

3 gallons (11.3 liters) peanut oil, or as appropriate for fryer

8 whole pan-dressed* freshwater fish such as crappie, bream or small catfish

3 eggs

1 can (12 ounces/354 ml) evaporated milk

1½ cups (350 ml/240 g) cornmeal, approximate

Salt and pepper

Heat oil in turkey fryer or other outdoor deep-fryer to 350°F–375°F (175°C–190°C). Rinse fish and pat dry. In mixing bowl, beat eggs with whisk just until foamy. Add evaporated milk; beat well. Season cornmeal with salt and pepper to taste. Dip fish into milk mixture, allowing excess to drip off. Dredge in cornmeal mixture, shaking off excess. Carefully lower 2 or 3 fish into fryer. Cook until fish flakes and is golden brown outside. Place fish in a deep container (a box works well) lined with paper towels so that the tails of the fish are at the top—more grease drains this way. Cover with additional paper towels and newspapers to keep warm while you cook remaining fish.

*Skin-on, scaled, gutted, heads and fins removed (catfish don't need to be scaled).

Wright Venison Bites

10 to 12 appetizer servings
Preparation: 1 hour soaking, under 15 minutes cooking
Special equipment: Outdoor deep-fryer (at least 9 quarts/8.5 liters)

These tasty appetizer morsels are great served with ranch dressing and freshly cut vegetables.

2 to 3 pounds (1 to 1.36 kg) boneless venison steak

2 gallons (7.5 liters) peanut oil, or as appropriate for fryer

2 clean paper grocery bags

2 cups (470 ml/280 g) self-rising flour

1 cup (240 ml/160 g) white cornmeal

1 tablespoon (15 ml) dried parsley flakes

1 teaspoon (5 ml/2.5 g) garlic powder

1 teaspoon (5 ml/5 g) celery salt

1 teaspoon (5 ml/2 g) black pepper

1 teaspoon (5 ml/2 g) paprika

Cut venison into bite-sized cubes and soak in ice water for about an hour. Near the end of the soaking time, heat oil in turkey fryer or other outdoor deep-fryer to 350°F (175°C). Double up the grocery bags, then combine flour, cornmeal, parsley flakes, garlic powder, celery salt, pepper and paprika. Seal bag and shake to mix well. Drain venison in a colander; discard remaining ice. Add venison to bag with flour mixture and shake to coat. Deep-fry for 7 to 10 minutes. Serve hot.

Deep-Fried Canada Goose

8 servings
Preparation: About 15 minutes initial prep, followed by 8 to 12 hours refrigeration; under an hour cooking (plus time to heat the oil)
Special equipment: Turkey fryer

1 bottle (750 ml) chianti or other red wine

1/4 cup (60 ml) olive oil or canola oil

2 tablespoons (30 ml/38 g) salt

1 tablespoon (15 ml/15 g) Dijon mustard

2 teaspoons (10 ml) mixed dried herb blend of your choice

1 teaspoon (5 ml/2 g) pepper

Whole dressed Canada goose (about 6 pounds/ 2.7 kg), skin-on or skinless

3 to 4 gallons (11.3 to 15 liters) peanut oil, or as appropriate for fryer

Combine wine, oil, salt, mustard, herbs and pepper in large bowl; mix well. Follow instructions for deep-frying a turkey (pages 112–113), injecting goose with wine mixture. Cooking time will be about 3½ minutes per pound.

Southern Deep-Fried Quail

6 servings
Preparation: About 30 minutes
Special equipment: Outdoor deep-fryer (at least 12 quarts/11 liters)

12 whole dressed, skin-on quail

3 gallons (11.3 liters) peanut oil, or as appropriate for fryer

Cayenne pepper

Black pepper

Kosher salt

Rinse quail and pat dry; set aside at room temperature for 20 to 30 minutes while you prepare the fryer (the quail should be at cool room temperature when they go into the hot oil). Heat oil in turkey fryer or other outdoor deep-fryer to 350°F–375°F (175°C–190°C). Season quail inside and out with cayenne pepper and black pepper to taste. Carefully lower 1 or 2 quail into fryer; watch carefully for any boil-over that may occur. Cook quail until skin is golden brown, 3 to 5 minutes. Use slotted spoon to transfer quail to paper towel–lined plate; season with salt to taste and keep warm while you fry remaining quail. Serve while still hot.

Anyone who has spent much time hunting America's big-game bird, the wild turkey, quickly realizes that success in hunting this wary quarry calls for celebration. In many parts of the country turkey hunters save their birds for special occasions—a feast on the eve of opening day of the spring turkey season, as a featured item at a hunt club get-together, for the traditional Thanksgiving or Christmas dinner, or perhaps as a special treat connected with a neighborhood cookout. Whatever the event might be, rest assured that a deep-fried wild turkey, with sealed-in juiciness that cannot be obtained when the bird is cooked in any other fashion, promises culinary delight. Of course, domestic turkeys are equally scrumptious when deep-fried.

Deep-frying a turkey can be an intimidating process, primarily because it involves a lot of very hot oil and handling a hefty piece of meat as it is placed into, and removed from, the deep-fryer. Such need not be the case. The steps below provide a road map to a bird that will draw satisfying "oohs" and "aahs" from hunting buddies, neighbors or family members. Please also read the general safety and set-up information on page 109 before starting.

Preliminary preparation of the turkey (at least a day before cooking)

1. If you're processing a wild or farm-raised bird yourself, clean it well, as you would for roasting. Plucking takes more effort than skinning, but it is worth it; the skin turns a lovely rich brown, and helps retain moisture in the meat. If you're buying the bird, choose one that is 8 to 14 pounds (3.6 to 6.4 kg).

2. If the turkey has been frozen, thaw it completely and pat dry with paper towels. Always thaw frozen poultry in the refrigerator, not on the countertop, to prevent bacterial growth.

3. Make sure the body cavity is open and clear of any giblets. Turkeys to be deep-fried should not be stuffed, nor should they be trussed or have the legs tied together.

Setting up the turkey fryer (the day of cooking, or any time prior)

1. For best results, use a unit designed specifically for turkey frying. You need a very large pot for deep-frying a whole turkey; a strong, steady heat source such as a propane burner to heat the oil; and a basket, meat hook or other device to move the bird into and out of the hot oil.

2. Cooking must be done outdoors; choose a site that is level and well clear of buildings. No matter where you set up, have a fire extinguisher handy.

3. Determining in advance how much oil to use is essential. You need enough to cover the bird completely but not so much that there is danger of overflow. Place the turkey in the fryer basket if your fryer has one, then place into the empty pot. Add water to cover the turkey by 1 inch (2.5 cm). Remove the turkey and basket, then note the water level (or measure the amount of water). Dry the pot completely before adding any oil.

Seasoning the turkey (at least an hour before cooking)

1. Optional: For extra flavor and juiciness, inject the turkey with liquid seasonings or brine. Many turkey-frying units come with injection syringes; otherwise, check at a rural veterinary supply store for a livestock syringe. Many commercial turkey seasonings are available, or you can create your own. Possibilities include Italian salad dressing, a blend of lemon juice and black pepper, a standard brine (page 53) or liquid Cajun seasonings.

2. To inject the bird, fill the pump, push the tip into the meat, and withdraw it slowly while depressing the plunger. Use 3 to 5 ounces (80 to 142 ml) in each breast half, and 2 to 3 ounces (55 to 80 ml) in each leg and thigh. If you like, wrap the bird in plastic wrap and refrigerate for as long as 2 days to allow the seasoning to penetrate; or, cook the bird the same day.

3. When you're ready to cook, pat turkey dry and rub thoroughly with dry seasonings of your choice. Suggestions include seasoned salt and pepper, paprika, cayenne pepper, garlic salt, onion salt, Cajun seasonings, Italian or Greek seasonings or commercially available spice blends.

Cooking the turkey

1. Add the calculated amount of oil to the dry pot; you'll typically need 3 to 5 gallons (11 to 19 l). Peanut oil is the best for frying, as it has a high smoke point. Heat the oil to 365°F (185°C). Plan on 45 minutes to an hour to heat the oil, checking it with a deep-frying thermometer.

2. Using great care and commonsense precautions, slowly immerse the turkey in the hot oil, neck down. Commercial deep-frying pots generally come with a basket, rack or hook made for this purpose, but you can also use a pair of heavy metal coat hangers, hooking them around the legs (you might also want to tie heavy cotton string around the bony knob at the end of each drumstick before lowering it into the pot, to assist in removal; drape the string outside of the pot).

3. Cook at 340°F–350°F (170°C–175°C) for 3 minutes per pound (454 g),* or until a meat thermometer thrust deep in the thigh registers 170°F (77°C). The turkey tends to rise toward the top of the cooker or "float" when done.

*For smaller birds, plan on 3½ to 4 minutes per pound (454 g); for parts, 4 to 5 minutes.

Removing the turkey and final steps

1. If you are using propane or any type of open flame, it is best to turn it off before removing the bird. Use the same device (basket, rack, hook or coat hangers) with which the bird was lowered to remove the turkey from the cooker, exercising the same care you did when lowering it into the oil.

2. Drain the turkey well on newspapers that have been covered with paper towels, then cover with a tent of paper or wrap in foil to keep it warm.

3. Let turkey stand for 15 to 20 minutes, then carve this wonderful treat and serve immediately. Small slices can be used as appetizers or larger servings as an entrée. Remember that with wild turkeys, the meat of the legs and thighs is quite tough and sinewy. It is best set aside for use in soups, sandwiches or to make pâté.

—*Ann and Jim Casada*

Sour Cream Drop Donuts

About 3 dozen doughnuts
Preparation: Under 30 minutes (plus time to heat oil)
Special equipment: Outdoor deep-fryer (at least 9 quarts/8.5 liters)

With doughnuts, the key to a uniform product is to have all ingredients at room temperature before mixing. The flour mixture should be added in and mixed just until blended. The longer the flour mixture is stirred, the more gluten will develop in the batter and you will end up with a chewier doughnut. —K.F.

2 gallons (7.5 liters) peanut oil, or as appropriate for fryer

3 whole eggs

1¼ cups (290 ml/250 g) sugar

1 cup (240 ml/227 g) sour cream

3½ cups (810 ml/490 g) all-purpose flour

2 teaspoons (10 ml/7.4 g) baking powder

1 teaspoon (5 ml/4.3 g) baking soda

½ teaspoon (2.5 ml/1 g) cinnamon

½ teaspoon (2.5 ml/3 g) salt*

¼ teaspoon (1.25 ml/.5 g) nutmeg

Powdered sugar for dusting (about 2 cups/240 g)

Heat oil in turkey fryer or other outdoor deep-fryer to 375°F (190°C). In large mixing bowl, beat the eggs, then add sugar and beat until thoroughly mixed. Stir in sour cream. Sift together flour, baking powder, baking soda, cinnamon, salt and nutmeg. Stir flour mixture and egg mixture just until well blended. Do not overmix.

When oil in the fryer reaches 375°F (190°C), carefully drop large serving spoonfuls of dough batter into oil. Add enough to cook several at a time, but do not overcrowd fryer. Let each doughnut cook about 2 minutes per side, turning with metal slotted spoon or slotted spatula. Drain doughnuts on paper towel–lined plate. Allow oil to return to 375°F (190°C) before frying the next batch; it's important to watch over and maintain an even temperature while the doughnuts are cooking. When all doughnuts are cool, dust with powdered sugar.

*Note: The salt in this mixture is integral to the interaction of the doughnut ingredients. It will not break down the oil while deep-frying.

Wisconsin Booya

15 to 20 servings
Preparation: About 3 hours
Special equipment: Outdoor deep-fryer (at least 12 quarts/11 liters)

I first had booya at a community supper in Ladysmith, Wisconsin, where I attended college. The recipe was rather mysterious—largely because the cooks were not entirely in agreement as to what to add to the pot. (I do remember that it had a generous amount of black pepper in it.) Use this recipe as a starting point for your own creations. —T.M.

¼ cup (55 g/half of a stick) butter

¼ cup (60 ml) peanut oil

5 pounds (2.3 kg) cut-up chicken

1½ pounds (680 g) beef stew meat, cut into 1-inch (2.5-cm) cubes

½ pound (225 g) dried split peas, rinsed and picked over

5 medium onions, diced

4 pounds (1.8 kg) potatoes, peeled and diced

3 cups (690 ml/360 g) diced celery

3 cups (690 ml/390 g) diced carrots

2 cans (14.5 ounces/411 g each) whole tomatoes, undrained

1 pound (454 g) cabbage, coarsely shredded

2 cups (470 ml/330 g) frozen corn kernels, thawed

2 cans (15 ounces/425 g each) navy beans, drained and rinsed

3 tablespoons (45 ml/54 g) salt

1 to 2 tablespoons (15 to 30 ml/6 to 12 g) pepper

¼ cup (60 ml/15 g) chopped fresh parsley

In 12-quart/11-liter (or larger) pot, melt butter in oil over medium-high heat. Add chicken pieces and cubed beef; cook until chicken is browned on all sides, about 15 minutes. Add water to cover generously. Heat to boiling; adjust heat and boil very gently until chicken is tender, about 25 minutes, skimming any foam. Use long tongs to remove chicken; set aside to cool. Meanwhile, add split peas, onions, potatoes, celery, carrots and tomatoes with juices to beef and liquid in pot. Add enough water to cover mixture. Adjust heat so mixture bubbles gently. Cook for about 45 minutes, stirring frequently and

adding water if the mixture becomes too dry. During this time, remove chicken from bones, discarding bones and skin. Cut chicken into cubes, and return to pot.

When vegetables have cooked for about 45 minutes, add cabbage, corn, beans, salt and pepper; if mixture is becoming dry, add more water as needed. Cook for at least 45 minutes longer; the mixture can simmer for as long as an hour after that until you're ready to serve. Just before serving, stir in parsley; taste for seasoning and add more salt or pepper if necessary.

Crab Boil

4 to 6 servings
Preparation: Under an hour
Special equipment: Turkey fryer

About 2 gallons (7.5 liters) water

12 small red potatoes, washed

2 large onions, peeled and halved

1 whole head garlic, top sliced off

1 lemon, halved

1 lime, halved

1 cup (240 ml/290 g) salt

¼ cup (60 ml/24 g) cayenne pepper

8 ounces (225 g) kielbasa sausage

4 ears fresh corn, shucked and halved

8 to 9 pounds (3.6 to 4 kg) dressed softshell blue crabs (about 5 inches/12.7 cm across)

2 cups (470 ml/200 g) crab-boil seasoning (such as Tony Cachere's or Zatarain's)

In turkey-fryer pot, combine water, potatoes, onions, garlic, lemon, lime, salt and cayenne. Heat to boiling over medium-high heat. Stir and cover; reduce heat to a gentle boil and let cook for 15 minutes.

Add sausage, corn and crabs. Stir to mix well and let cook for 3 to 5 minutes longer. Turn off the heat. Drain as

much water from the fryer as possible; be careful, as it is boiling hot. Sprinkle crab-boil seasoning into the pot, a little at a time, turning with a long-handled slotted spoon to make sure the seasoning is mixed throughout. Cover the fryer once again and let the ingredients sit for 15 minutes longer. Serve hot.

Low Country Shrimp Boil

10 to 12 servings
Preparation: Under an hour
Special equipment: Turkey fryer, preferably with basket insert

Seafood looms large in Southern cooking, and this dish from the Carolina coast is hearty, easily prepared and ideally suited for consumption in an outdoor setting. It combines shellfish, smoked sausage, corn-on-the-cob, potatoes, celery and onions with spices. Boiled together, the result is a delightful union of flavors. —A. and J.C.

¼ cup (60 ml/24 g) Old Bay seasoning, or to taste

3 pounds (1.36 kg) smoked sausage or kielbasa, cut into 1-inch (2.5-cm) pieces

8 potatoes, cut into 2-inch (5-cm) pieces

3 onions, cut into 2-inch (5-cm) pieces

3 ribs celery, cut into 2-inch (5-cm) pieces

10 to 12 ears fresh corn, shucked and halved

5 pounds (2.3 kg) shell-on raw shrimp, heads removed

3 to 4 pounds (1.36 to 1.8 kg) whole crabs or crab legs, optional

Melted butter and seafood sauce to accompany

If fryer has a basket insert, remove basket and set aside. Fill turkey-fryer pot half full of water; add Old Bay seasoning. Heat to boiling over medium-high heat; cover the pot to speed things along.

When water is boiling, add sausage, potatoes, onions and celery (placed in basket if you have one) to pot. Boil until potatoes are tender, about 20 minutes. Add corn, shrimp and crab. Simmer for 3 to 4 minutes longer, or until shrimp turn pink. Drain and serve immediately by placing the contents atop newspapers covered with paper towels. Guests should be provided with large platters they fill from the heaping pile of goodness. Melted butter and seafood sauce complement the meal.

Great Lakes Fish Boil

6 to 8 servings
Preparation: About an hour
Special equipment: Outdoor deep-fryer (at least 9 quarts/8.5 liters) with basket insert

In a traditional fish boil, the fire is stoked at the end of cooking time so that the pot boils over and extinguishes the flames. For backyard cooking, it's much easier to just turn the burner off!

6 quarts (5.7 l) water

1 cup (240 ml/320 g) salt

6 to 8 medium potatoes

6 to 8 medium onions

3 to 4 pounds (1.36 to 1.8 kg) salmon, lake trout or steelhead steaks (scaled before steaking), 1 to 1½ inches (2.5 to 3.8 cm) thick

4 lemons, quartered

1 pound (454 g) butter, melted

Remove basket from fryer; set aside. In 9-quart/8.5-liter (or larger) pot, combine water and salt. Heat to boiling over medium-high heat; cover the pot to speed things along. Meanwhile, scrub potatoes and cut a thin slice from each end; place in fryer basket. Peel onions and cut off root ends; add to basket. Set basket aside until water boils.

When water boils, carefully lower filled basket into water. Cover and return to boiling. Cook for 20 minutes. Carefully add fish steaks to basket. Re-cover and return to boiling. Cook for 10 to 12 minutes, then check for doneness; the fish should flake easily and the potatoes should be tender. To serve, turn off heat and remove basket from fryer. Serve drained fish, potatoes and onions with lemons and melted butter.

CHAPTER SIX

Rubs, Marinades, Sauces & Butters

From the Southwest to the Far East, the flavors added by these simple preparations help turn an ordinary grilled meal into something extraordinary. Rubs are simply a blend of herbs and spices, often combined with salt and sugar. This mixture is massaged or "rubbed" into meat or poultry to add flavor; larger cuts can be refrigerated as long as overnight to allow the flavors to penetrate. When exposed to the heat of the grill, rubs form a savory crust on the meat to help seal in juices. Rubs can also be used as a quick pre-grill sprinkle for fish, which would fall apart if rubbed.

Marinades add flavor and help tenderize food; those with high salt content also act like a brine (page 53) to help keep meats juicy. Many marinades contain acidic ingredients such as lemon juice, vinegar, pineapple juice or wine. These acids help tenderize meat, but caution is warranted because if the meat is marinated too long, the acid will break down the protein fibers, making the meat mushy. When using marinades, choose a glass or Pyrex container rather than one made from aluminum or other metal; acids will react with many metals to give the food an off-flavor. Zipper-style plastic bags work well for marinating; place the food into the bag, then place bag into a baking dish or other container before adding the marinade and sealing the bag. Use enough marinade to cover the food completely, and turn or stir the food during marinating to ensure even penetration.

Sauces include both cooking sauces and table sauces; some, such as the classic "barbecue sauce," can be used both during cooking and at the table. Many barbecue sauces have high amounts of sugar, which will burn if exposed to high heat; these sauces are best brushed on for the final few minutes of cooking time, giving them just enough time to caramelize without burning. Table sauces include well-known mixtures such as tartar sauce and chutney, as well as less common but equally delicious blends featuring herbs, mustard and other savory combinations.

Flavored or compound butters are a delicious finishing touch for simple grilled foods. A T-bone steak or salmon fillet will be even more luxurious when crowned with a pat of melting flavored butter. These can be prepared in advance, formed into a log and chilled (even frozen) until needed; to serve, simply slice off a pat and add to food that is hot from the grill.

rubs

Basic Dry Rub

About 1/2 cup (120 ml)

This all-purpose rub can be used on pork ribs or chops, venison, beef, chicken or turkey. The heat of the rub can easily be adjusted to meet your needs; these proportions are medium hot. —A. and J.C.

2 tablespoons (30 ml/12 g) sweet paprika
1 tablespoon (15 ml/19 g) salt
1 tablespoon (15 ml/15 g) brown sugar (packed)
1 tablespoon (15 ml/1 g) dried Italian herb blend
1 1/2 teaspoons (7.5 ml/3 g) ground black pepper
1 1/2 teaspoons (7.5 ml/3.5 g) garlic powder
1 teaspoon (5 ml/2 g) chili powder
1/2 teaspoon (2.5 ml/1 g) ground cumin
1/2 teaspoon (2.5 ml/1.5 g) dry mustard powder
1/2 teaspoon (2.5 ml/1 g) cayenne pepper

Combine all ingredients in small mixing bowl. Blend well with fork (or your fingertips), making sure that brown sugar is well incorporated. Store at room temperature in tightly sealed glass jar.

All-Purpose Seasoning

About 1/2 cup (120 ml)

This is similar to a blend that is often called Montreal seasoning. It works great as a pre-grill sprinkle on any meat or poultry, and also makes a nice table seasoning.

1 1/2 teaspoons (7.5 ml) dried thyme
1 1/2 teaspoons (7.5 ml) dried rosemary
1 1/2 teaspoons (7.5 ml/4 g) fennel seeds
1/4 cup (60 ml/76 g) salt
1 tablespoon (15 ml/6 g) freshly ground black pepper
1 tablespoon (15 ml/7.5 g) onion powder
1 1/2 teaspoons (7.5 ml/4 g) garlic powder
1 teaspoon (5 ml/2 g) cayenne pepper
1 teaspoon (5 ml/2 g) ground coriander

In spice grinder, process thyme, rosemary and fennel seeds until very finely chopped; or, pound together with mortar and pestle until fine. Add to small jar with remaining ingredients. Cover and shake well to blend. Store at room temperature.

CUSTOMIZING RUBS, MARINADES AND SAUCES

The horizon for creativity here is limitless. If you like some zest or heat in your foods, make liberal use of various types of peppers, cumin and the like. For sauces and marinades, keep in mind the fact that lots of fruits and berries lend themselves to such uses. Peaches, apricots, blueberries, cranberries, cherries, grapes and any wild berry with hints of tartness (blackberries grow everywhere and invite picking) can be used in sauces and marinades.

Think about and experiment with various types of vinegar rather than sticking with just one. If you have a dehydrator at home and grow your own herbs, why not dry the surplus and turn it into something you can use for flavor and flair for months to come? Try leaves or cuttings from oregano, cumin, chives and basil, for example. Speaking of drying, any kind of hot peppers can be dried with ease the way folks did in yesteryear. With the arrival of the sere days of September, entire hot pepper plants would be pulled up by the roots, hung in the rafters or a barn or a similarly hot, dry place, and left to dry. After a couple of weeks, they would be dry and could be used throughout the months to come to flavor meats, dried beans and the like.

Another taste that has great versatility is mustard. In the South there are endless arguments, often quite localized, about the comparative merits of barbecue sauce based on mustard, vinegar or tomato. Of course, it is quite possible to combine the three in a marvelous marriage of flavors. Just recognize that when you do so you might be qualifying for rating as a barbecue heretic in the eyes of some. —A. and J.C.

Spanish Paprika Rub

About 1/2 cup (120 ml)

True Spanish paprika is made from special peppers that are smoked over wood fires until dry; it's available either sweet or hot. This rub contributes a subtle smoky taste to grilled meats, and works particularly well on pork or chicken. —T.M.

1/4 cup (60 ml/24 g) hot Spanish paprika*

1 tablespoon (15 ml/6 g) freshly ground black pepper

1 tablespoon (15 ml/19 g) salt

1 tablespoon (15 ml/12 g) sugar

2 teaspoons (10 ml/5 g) garlic powder

1 teaspoon (5 ml) finely crumbled dried marjoram

Combine all ingredients in small mixing bowl; blend well. Store at room temperature in tightly sealed glass jar.

*Available at The Spanish Table (www.spanishtable.com)

Ancho Chili Rub

About 1/2 cup (120 ml)

3 tablespoons (45 ml/18 g) paprika

2 tablespoons (30 ml/25 g) brown sugar (packed)

2 tablespoons (30 ml/12 g) powdered ancho chile

1 tablespoon (15 ml/19 g) salt

1 tablespoon (15 ml/6 g) freshly ground black pepper

1 teaspoon (5 ml/2.5 g) garlic powder

1 teaspoon (5 ml/2.5 g) onion powder

1/2 teaspoon (2.5 ml/1 g) ground cumin

Combine all ingredients in small mixing bowl. Blend well with fork (or your fingertips), making sure that brown sugar is well incorporated. Store at room temperature in tightly sealed glass jar.

Island-Influenced Rub

Enough for 1 pound (454 g) meat; easily increased

This recipe makes enough to flavor a pound (454 g) of steak, chops or chicken breast; it also works well on a small roast.

1 teaspoon (5 ml/3 g) cumin seeds

1 clove garlic

10 whole mixed-color peppercorns

1/4 teaspoon (1.25 ml) allspice

1x1-inch (2.5x2.5-cm) piece lime rind (green part only)

2 teaspoons (10 ml) olive oil

2 teaspoons (10 ml) lime juice

With mortar and pestle, pound together cumin seeds, garlic, peppercorns, allspice and lime rind until the texture is like sand. Add oil and lime juice; mix well with spoon.

To use: Rub mixture evenly to cover all sides of meat. Place in glass dish; cover and refrigerate for 1 to 6 hours. Grill to desired doneness.

Island-Influenced Rub

Garlic Pepper Rub

About 1/4 cup (60 ml)

This is delicious with beef, pork or venison.

2 tablespoons (30 ml/12 g) whole black
  peppercorns
2 tablespoons (30 ml/12 g) whole white
  peppercorns
1 tablespoon (15 ml/14 g) mustard seeds
1 teaspoon (5 ml/3 g) kosher salt
2 cloves fresh garlic, minced

In spice grinder, process peppercorns, mustard seeds
and salt until mixture is the texture of coarse meal; or,
pound together with mortar and pestle. Add to small
bowl with garlic and mix well. This is best used just
after making, as it does not keep well.

Rosemary Pepper Rub

About 1/2 cup (120 ml)

Try this fragrant rub on chicken, lamb, pheasant or quail.

2 tablespoons (30 ml/12 g) whole black
  peppercorns
2 tablespoons (30 ml) dried rosemary leaves
1 tablespoon (15 ml/6 g) whole white
  peppercorns
2 teaspoons (10 ml/6 g) kosher salt
1 teaspoon (5 ml) dried oregano
1/2 teaspoon (2.5 ml/1 g) cayenne pepper

In spice grinder, process all ingredients until mixture is
the texture of coarse meal; or, pound together with mortar and pestle. Store at room temperature in tightly
sealed glass jar.

Southwest Rub

About 1/2 cup (120 ml)

*Rub this salt-free blend onto beef, venison, pork, fish or
chicken for a Southwest tang.*

3 tablespoons (45 ml/18 g) whole black
  peppercorns
1 tablespoon (15 ml/6 g) whole pink peppercorns
1 tablespoon (15 ml) dried parsley flakes
1 teaspoon (5 ml/2 g) cumin
1 teaspoon (5 ml/2.5 g) onion powder
1/2 teaspoon (2.5 ml/1.5 g) chile powder
3 dried chipotle chile peppers
1 bay leaf, crumbled

In spice grinder or blender, process all ingredients until
mixture is the texture of coarse meal. Store at room temperature in tightly sealed glass jar.

Baharat (Spiced Pepper Rub)

About 1/2 cup (120 ml)

*This salt-free Arab spice blend gets its name from the
word* bahar, *which means pepper. It's particularly good
with lamb, and also goes well with venison and chicken.*

3 tablespoons (45 ml/18 g) whole black
  peppercorns
1 tablespoon (15 ml/3 g) coriander seeds
1 tablespoon (15 ml/7 g) cumin seeds
Seeds from 3 whole cardamom pods
Small piece of stick cinnamon (about 1 inch/
  2.5 cm long)
2 teaspoons (10 ml/4 g) allspice*
1 teaspoon (5 ml/2 g) nutmeg*

In spice grinder or blender, process all ingredients until
mixture is the texture of coarse meal. Store at room temperature in tightly sealed glass jar.

*Freshly ground nutmeg and allspice are much more fragrant
than pre-ground spices, and really add to the flavor of this
mixture. Look for whole nutmeg fruits and whole allspice
berries at gourmet shops; the flavor intensity may surprise you.

Herb Marinade

About 3/4 cup (180 ml)
Preparation: Under 15 minutes

We grow our own herbs and, when available, fresh is best. Today many grocery stores have fresh herbs, but there is special pleasure to be derived from a walk to the herb garden, clippers in hand, to harvest your own. —A. and J. C.

1/2 cup (120 ml) **vegetable oil or olive oil**

1/2 cup (120 ml/80 g) **chopped onion**

1/4 cup (60 ml) **lemon juice**

1/4 cup (60 ml/15 g) **chopped fresh parsley**

1 tablespoon (15 ml) **chopped fresh marjoram, or 1 teaspoon (5 ml) dried**

1 tablespoon (15 ml) **chopped fresh thyme, or 1 teaspoon (5 ml) dried**

1 teaspoon (5 ml/6 g) **salt**

1/2 teaspoon (2.5 ml/1 g) **black pepper**

1 garlic clove, minced

Stir all ingredients together in glass or ceramic bowl; use to marinate beef, venison, lamb, pork or chicken.

White Wine Marinade

About 1 1/4 cups (290 ml)
Preparation: Under 15 minutes

3/4 cup (180 ml) **vegetable oil**

1/2 cup (120 ml) **dry white wine**

1 tablespoon (15 ml) **lemon juice**

1 teaspoon (5 ml/6 g) **salt**

1/2 teaspoon (2.5 ml/1 g) **black pepper**

1 clove garlic, minced

Whisk all ingredients together in glass or ceramic bowl; use to marinate lamb, pork or chicken.

Soy-Ginger Marinade

About 1 cup (240 ml)
Preparation: Under 15 minutes

1/4 cup (60 ml) **chicken broth**

1/4 cup (60 ml) **sake (Japanese rice wine)**

1/4 cup (60 ml) **soy sauce**

2 tablespoons (30 ml) **teriyaki sauce**

2 tablespoons (30 ml/25 g) **brown sugar (packed)**

1 tablespoon (15 ml/15 g) **grated fresh gingerroot**

1 teaspoon (5 ml) **mirin***

2 cloves garlic, minced

Whisk all ingredients together in glass or ceramic bowl; let stand for 5 to 10 minutes before using to marinate beef, venison or lamb.

*Mirin is sweetened Japanese cooking wine. Look for it in the Asian section of large supermarkets, or in specialty Asian stores. If you can't find it, substitute cream sherry.

Bourbon Dipping Sauce and Marinade

About 2 cups (470 ml)
Preparation: Under 15 minutes

This is a delightfully different combination that offers the best of two worlds inasmuch as it can be used as a marinade or dip. This versatile sauce can be used on shrimp, pork, chicken, beef, venison or doves.

1 bottle (12 ounces/340 g) **chili sauce, such as Heinz**

1/4 cup (60 ml/12 g) **finely chopped chives**

1/4 cup (60 ml) **olive oil**

2 tablespoons (30 ml) **maple syrup**

2 tablespoons (30 ml) **bourbon**

2 tablespoons (30 ml) **Worcestershire sauce**

2 tablespoons (30 ml) **low-sodium soy sauce**

1 teaspoon (5 ml) **horseradish**

1 clove garlic, finely minced

Whisk all ingredients together in small bowl. Refrigerate and use as a dipping sauce or marinade.

Honey Barbecue Sauce

Special Steak Marinade

> **About 3/4 cup (180 ml)**
> **Preparation:** Under 15 minutes

Marinate beef or venison steaks for about 4 hours in this mixture, then grill to desired doneness (venison should be pink in the center). This makes enough for 4 steaks.

1/2 cup (120 ml) water

1/4 cup (60 ml) Dale's Steak Seasoning*

1 tablespoon (15 ml) Worcestershire sauce

1 tablespoon (15 ml) A-1 Steak Sauce

1 1/2 teaspoons (7.5 ml) another steak sauce, such as Heinz 57, Crosse and Blackwell or London Steak Sauce

Whisk all ingredients together in glass or ceramic bowl; use to marinate beef or venison steaks.

*Dale's Steak Seasoning is a soy sauce–based blend that is available at grocery stores and even places such as Wal-Mart; it's common throughout the South and Southeast. It really adds a special flavor, and is worth searching out. If you can't find it in your area, visit www.dalesseasoning.com.

s a u c e s

Hot Honey-Mustard Glaze

> **About 1/2 cup (120 ml)**
> **Preparation:** Under 15 minutes

Brush over poultry or pork during the last several minutes of grilling or barbecue cooking. —K.F.

1/3 cup (80 ml) honey

1/4 cup (60 ml/60 g) whole grain mustard

2 tablespoons (30 ml/22 g) minced onion

2 tablespoons (30 ml) cider vinegar

1 teaspoon (5 ml/5 g) brown sugar (packed)

1/4 teaspoon (1.25 ml) ground chile pepper, such as chipotle

In small saucepan, stir together all ingredients. Simmer over medium heat, stirring occasionally, for about 5 minutes, until slightly thickened.

Honey Barbecue Sauce

> **About 2 cups (470 g)**
> **Preparation:** Under 15 minutes

This easy sauce works well with beef, venison, pork or poultry.

1 1/2 cups (350 ml) tomato juice or V-8

1/2 cup (120 ml) honey

3 tablespoons (45 ml) canola oil

2 tablespoons (30 ml) Worcestershire sauce

1 tablespoon (15 ml) molasses

1 tablespoon (15 ml) lemon juice

1/4 teaspoon (1.25 ml) cayenne pepper

In small saucepan, combine all ingredients and heat to boiling over medium heat. Let simmer for 5 to 7 minutes, or until sauce thickens a bit, stirring frequently.

Quick Barbecue Sauce

> **About 1 1/3 cups (320 ml)**
> **Preparation:** Under 15 minutes

Try this simple but flavorful sauce on beef, venison, pork or chicken.

1 cup (240 ml) bottled chili sauce, such as Heinz (or ketchup)

1/4 cup (60 ml) olive oil

1 tablespoon (15 ml) lemon juice

1 tablespoon (15 ml) Worcestershire sauce

2 teaspoons (10 ml/4 g) sugar

3 to 4 cloves garlic, minced

Mix ingredients well.

Peach Barbecue Sauce

About 1²/₃ cups (400 ml)
Preparation: About an hour

Try this fruity, tangy sauce with pork or chicken.

1 can (15 ounces/425 g) sliced peaches in juice or light syrup, undrained

Half of a small white onion

2 cloves garlic

1 teaspoon (5 ml/5 g) minced fresh gingerroot

1 bottle (12 ounces/340 g) Heinz chili sauce

2 tablespoons (30 ml) sherry vinegar

1 tablespoon (15 ml/5 g) chili powder

¹/₂ teaspoon (2.5 ml/3 g) salt

In blender, combine peaches with juice, onion, garlic and gingerroot; process on high speed until smooth. Pour into heavy-bottomed medium saucepan. Add chili sauce, vinegar, chili powder and salt. Heat to boiling over medium-high heat, then reduce heat so mixture bubbles gently and cook for about an hour, stirring frequently. Cool and store in refrigerator for up to a month.

Wisconsin Cherry Barbecue Sauce

About 1 cup (240 ml)
Preparation: About 1 hour (plus pitting time)

This sauce uses sour pie cherries, which are grown extensively in Wisconsin. They make a delightfully tangy barbecue sauce that is particularly good on venison and duck. —T.M.

3 cups (690 ml) pitted tart cherries (about 1¹/₄ pounds/570 g before pitting)

¹/₃ cup (80 ml) orange juice

¹/₄ cup (60 ml/40 g) chopped shallot

1 tablespoon (15 ml/15 g) minced fresh gingerroot

¹/₂ teaspoon (2.5 ml/1 g) ground cumin

1 small fresh hot pepper, minced (remove seeds before mincing for milder sauce)

¹/₂ teaspoon (2.5 ml/1 g) freshly ground black pepper

¹/₃ cup (80 ml/73 g) brown sugar (packed)

2 tablespoons (30 ml/30 g) tomato paste

2 tablespoons (30 ml) white wine vinegar

1 teaspoon (5 ml/6 g) salt, or to taste

In heavy saucepan, combine cherries, orange juice, shallot, gingerroot, cumin, hot pepper and black pepper. Heat to gentle boil over medium heat; cook until most liquid has cooked away, about 20 minutes, stirring occasionally. Remove from heat and cool slightly, then purée with food mill (or process until smooth in food processor; sauce will not be as smooth). Return purée to saucepan. Add remaining ingredients. Simmer over low heat for 20 minutes; if sauce is too thin, simmer until thickened to desired consistency.

Mustard Barbecue Sauce

About 1²/₃ cups (400 ml)
Preparation: Under 45 minutes

This unusual barbecue sauce is fabulous on grilled or barbecued pork or chicken.

1 cup (240 ml/255 g) prepared yellow mustard

¹/₂ cup (120 ml) cider vinegar

¹/₃ cup (80 ml/73 g) light brown sugar (packed)

¹/₄ cup (60 ml) honey

2 tablespoons (30 ml) water

1¹/₄ teaspoons (6.25 ml) paprika

1 teaspoon (5 ml/6 g) salt

³/₄ teaspoon (3.75 ml/1.5 g) cayenne pepper

¹/₄ teaspoon (1.25 ml/.5 g) white pepper

In heavy-bottomed small saucepan, combine all ingredients. Heat over medium heat until mixture is boiling gently, whisking until smooth. Reduce heat to low and simmer gently for 30 minutes, stirring frequently.

Parsley Sauce

About ⅓ cup (80 ml)
Preparation: Under 15 minutes

A simple parsley and lemon sauce is a fabulous accompaniment to grilled steak or chicken. Sauces like this are used in many cuisines; the French call their version persillade, while the Italians make a similar mixture called gremolata that is oil-free. For a more fiery and complex version, see the Chimichurri recipe on page 126. —T.M.

¼ cup (60 ml/10 g) fresh flat-leaf parsley leaves (tightly packed)

¼ cup (60 ml) extra-virgin olive oil

½ teaspoon (2.5 ml/1 g) finely grated fresh lemon zest

¼ teaspoon (1.25 ml/1.5 g) salt

2 cloves garlic, minced

A few fresh grindings of black pepper

In blender, combine all ingredients. Process until parsley is finely chopped, scraping down sides several times. Serve at room temperature; leftover sauce may be refrigerated, tightly covered, for several days.

Tomato Topper for Burgers

4 servings
Preparation: Under 15 minutes

Yellow tomatoes offer an interesting color contrast for this recipe. This topper is excellent on venison burgers but complements beef as well. It also makes a nice, simple side dish. —A. and J.C.

1 medium red onion, thinly sliced

2 tomatoes, sliced

Dressing
2 tablespoons (30 ml) olive oil

2 teaspoons (10 ml) lemon juice

1 tablespoon (15 ml/3 g) chopped fresh basil, or 1 teaspoon dried

Salt and black pepper to taste

Soak onion in iced water for 10 to 15 minutes; drain well. Combine in dish with tomatoes. In small bowl, blend dressing ingredients with wire whisk. Pour over sliced tomatoes and red onions and toss.

Tartar Sauce

About 1½ cups (350 ml)
Preparation: Under 15 minutes

Serve with grilled fish such as salmon, tuna, trout, halibut, swordfish or crab cakes.

1 cup (240 ml/255 g) mayonnaise

2 tablespoons (30 ml/30 g) Dijon mustard

2 tablespoons (30 ml/18 g) chopped sweet pickles (drained if pre-chopped)

1 tablespoon (15 ml/10 g) minced capers

1 tablespoon (15 ml/2.5 g) finely minced fresh chives

1 tablespoon (15 ml/4 g) finely chopped fresh parsley

1 teaspoon (5 ml) freshly squeezed lemon juice

Several dashes of hot pepper sauce

Combine all ingredients in a medium bowl and mix well. Cover and refrigerate until ready to serve.

Mustard Cream Sauce

About ¾ cup (180 ml)
Preparation: Under 15 minutes

This works well as an accompaniment to beef, venison and poultry.

½ cup (120 ml/115 g) sour cream

¼ cup (60 ml/60 g) Dijon mustard

2 tablespoons (30 ml/30 g) mayonnaise

1 tablespoon (15 ml/2.5 g) snipped fresh chives

Kosher salt and freshly ground black pepper, to taste

Combine all ingredients in small bowl and mix well.

Dill Sour Cream Sauce

> **About 1/2 cup (120 ml)**
> **Preparation:** Under 15 minutes

Serve this with simple grilled fish. It also makes a nice dip for cucumbers.

1/2 cup (120 ml/115 g) sour cream

2 teaspoons (10 ml/1 g) snipped fresh chives

1 1/2 teaspoons (7.5 ml/1.5 g) snipped fresh dill weed, or 1/2 teaspoon (2.5 ml) dried

Combine all ingredients in small bowl and mix well.

Vidalia Onion Marmalade

> **About 1 1/2 cups (350 ml)**
> **Preparation:** Under 15 minutes

Serve over beef or venison steaks or burgers.

1 tablespoon (15 g) butter

2 tablespoons (30 ml) olive oil

2 large Vidalia onions, thinly sliced and separated into rings

3/4 cup (180 ml) zinfandel wine

1 teaspoon (5 ml) dried basil, crushed

1/2 teaspoon (2.5 ml/3 g) salt

1/2 teaspoon (2.5 ml/1 g) pepper

In large skillet, melt butter in oil over medium-high heat. Add onions and cook for 5 to 7 minutes, or until tender-crisp, stirring occasionally. Add wine, basil, salt and pepper. Cook until most of the liquid has evaporated, about 5 minutes longer.

Tomato Chutney

> **About 2 1/2 cups (590 ml)**
> **Preparation:** Under an hour

Use this chutney instead of ketchup on burgers or hot dogs. It also adds interesting flavors to grilled pork or chicken and makes a delicious condiment for cooked dried beans, black-eyed peas or crowder peas.
—A. and J.C.

Spice Bundle

1 small stick cinnamon

5 whole allspice

6 whole cloves

1 teaspoon (5 ml) celery seeds

1 tablespoon (15 ml) olive oil

1 medium onion, chopped

2 cloves garlic, minced

3 pounds (1.36 kg) plum tomatoes, peeled and chopped (about 4 cups/950 ml)

1/4 cup (60 ml/55 g) brown sugar (packed)

1/4 cup (60 ml) cider vinegar

3/4 teaspoon (3.75 ml/1.5 g) ground cumin

1/2 teaspoon (2.5 ml/3 g) salt

1/4 teaspoon (1.25 ml) nutmeg, preferably freshly grated

1/4 teaspoon (1.25 ml) hot red pepper flakes

1/4 teaspoon (1.25 ml) freshly ground black pepper

1/4 teaspoon (1.25 ml) chili powder

1/8 teaspoon (.6 ml) cayenne pepper

Place spice-bundle ingredients on small square of cheesecloth (or coffee filter); close and tie with kitchen string. In Dutch oven, heat oil over medium heat until hot. Add onion and cook for 5 minutes, or until golden, stirring frequently. Add garlic and cook for 1 minute longer. Add tomatoes, all other ingredients, and spice bundle. Heat to boiling, then reduce heat and simmer, uncovered, for 25 to 40 minutes, or until most of the liquid evaporates, stirring occasionally. Crush with a potato masher and test thickness; chutney should be chunky and thick. Remove spice bundle and cool before serving; refrigerate leftovers (this will keep in the refrigerator for several weeks).

Corn, Black Bean and Tomato Salsa

Corn, Black Bean <u>and</u> Tomato Salsa

About 4 cups (950 ml)
Preparation: Under 15 minutes, plus 30 minutes chilling

Serve with grilled steaks, burgers, pork or fish.

3 ears fresh corn, husked

2 cups (470 ml/360 g) seeded, diced fresh tomatoes

3 tablespoons (45 ml/12 g) chopped fresh parsley, or 1 tablespoon (15 ml) dried

2 tablespoons (30 ml) freshly squeezed lime juice

2 tablespoons (30 ml) extra-virgin olive oil

1 tablespoon (15 ml/3 g) minced fresh cilantro

1/4 teaspoon (1.25 ml) minced canned chipotle pepper in adobo sauce

1/4 teaspoon (1.25 ml) adobo sauce from pepper

1/4 teaspoon (1.25 ml/1.5 g) salt

1 can (16 ounces/454 g) black beans, drained and rinsed

1 green onion, thinly sliced

1 clove garlic, minced

Boil or microwave corn until cooked and set aside to cool; when cool, cut kernels from cobs. Combine kernels with all remaining ingredients in a medium bowl and stir to blend. Cover and refrigerate for at least 30 minutes before serving.

Argentinian Green Sauce <u>(Chimichurri)</u>

About 2/3 cup (160 ml)
Preparation: Under 15 minutes

A small spoonful of this spicy, fragrant sauce enlivens a grilled steak or lamb chop; it goes great with grilled chicken also.

1 cup (240 ml/45 g) fresh flat-leaf parsley leaves (tightly packed)

1/4 cup (60 ml/10 g) fresh cilantro leaves (tightly packed)

4 to 6 cloves garlic

2 bay leaves, optional

1 jalapeño pepper, stem end removed*

1 teaspoon (5 ml) fresh marjoram leaves, or 1/2 teaspoon (2.5 ml) dried

1/4 cup (60 ml) white wine vinegar

3 tablespoons (45 ml) extra-virgin olive oil

1/2 teaspoon (2.5 ml) salt

In food processor, combine parsley, cilantro, garlic, bay leaves, jalapeño and marjoram; pulse until finely chopped, scraping down as needed. Add vinegar, oil and salt; pulse until well blended. Serve at room temperature; leftover sauce may be refrigerated, tightly covered, for several days.

*Remove the seeds and veins if you prefer a less spicy sauce.

126

butters

Chile-Lime Butter

About 1/2 cup (100 g)
Preparation: Under 15 minutes, plus 2 hours refrigerating

Prepare this butter in advance so the flavors have time to meld. Try it on grilled fish, chicken or pork.

1 small shallot, cut into quarters

1/2 teaspoon (2.5 ml/1.5 g) kosher salt

1 small hot red pepper, finely minced

1 tablespoon (15 ml) freshly squeezed lime juice

1 teaspoon (5 ml) finely grated fresh lime zest (green part only)

1/2 cup (110 g/1 stick) unsalted butter, room temperature

With mortar and pestle, pound together shallot and salt until smooth paste forms. Transfer to small bowl; add red pepper, lime juice and zest and mix thoroughly. Add in pieces of softened butter and mix well with a fork. Place butter on waxed paper and shape into a 1-inch (2.5-cm) log; chill for at least 2 hours, or as long as a day. Slice chilled log into individual servings.

Blue Cheese Butter

About 3/4 cup (165 g)
Preparation: Under 15 minutes

Goes well on top of grilled steaks, burgers and poultry.

1/4 cup (60 ml/60 g) crumbled blue cheese

1 teaspoon (5 ml) onion powder

1 teaspoon (5 ml/2 g) freshly ground black pepper

1/2 cup (110 g/1 stick) unsalted butter, room temperature

In small bowl, combine blue cheese, onion powder and pepper. Mix thoroughly. Add in pieces of softened butter and mix well with a fork. Once all butter has been added, place in small serving bowl and serve at room temperature. If you want to chill for later use, place butter on waxed paper and shape into a 1-inch (2.5-cm) log; slice chilled log into individual servings.

Garlic Herb Butter

About 1/2 cup (110 g)
Preparation: Under 15 minutes

Goes well on top of grilled steaks, burgers, fish and poultry.

1 tablespoon (15 ml/2.5 g) snipped fresh chives

1 teaspoon (5 ml/.9 g) minced fresh basil

1 teaspoon (5 ml/1.5 g) minced fresh oregano

1 clove garlic, minced

1/2 cup (110 g/1 stick) unsalted butter, room temperature

Kosher salt to taste

In small bowl, combine chives, basil, oregano and garlic; mix thoroughly. Add in pieces of softened butter and mix well with a fork. Once all butter has been added, season with salt. Place in small serving bowl and serve at room temperature. If you want to chill for later use, place butter on waxed paper and shape into a 1-inch (2.5-cm) log; slice chilled log into individual servings.

Horseradish-Chive Butter

About 3/4 cup (165 g)
Preparation: Under 15 minutes

Use a pat of this zesty butter to top grilled steak, or rich fish such as tuna, bluefish or salmon.

3 tablespoons (45 ml) prepared plain horseradish

2 tablespoons (30 ml/5 g) snipped fresh chives

1/2 teaspoon (2.5 ml) white wine vinegar

1/2 teaspoon (2.5 ml/3 g) salt

1/2 cup (110 g/1 stick) unsalted butter, room temperature

Place paper coffee filter (or 2 paper towels) in small strainer. Add horseradish; let drain for 5 minutes, then squeeze gently to remove as much moisture as possible. In small bowl, combine drained horseradish, chives, vinegar and salt; mix thoroughly. Add in pieces of softened butter and mix well with a fork. Place in small serving bowl and serve at room temperature. If you want to chill for later use, place butter on waxed paper and shape into a 1-inch (2.5-cm) log; slice chilled log into individual servings.

CHAPTER SEVEN

Vegetables, Sides & Desserts

When the urge to grill becomes irresistible, most cooks think primarily of main-dish items—generally meat, poultry and seafood. However, grilling also works great for a tempting variety of vegetables and side dishes. Many can cook alongside the main course, while others are good enough to fire up the grill specifically to prepare them.

Cooking potatoes in a foil packet on the grill is a time-honored method. We offer several fun variations on this classic, including Peas in a Packet (page 132) and Potato Packets (page 132). You'll also find that summertime favorite, corn on the cob, as well as some intriguing new ideas such as Grill-Roasted Cauliflower (page 129), Parmesan Tomatoes (page 131) and Portabellas Au Gratin (page 135).

Finally, as a nice benefit, the grill is usually just the right temperature after the meal for cooking a delicious grilled dessert, such as Grilled Pineapple Topped with Ice Cream and Rum (page 137) or English Muffin Pies (page 137). All recipes in this chapter use the same equipment and basic techniques explained in Chapter 2, Grilling Meat, Poultry and Fish.

vegetables

Grill-Roasted Cauliflower

4 to 6 servings
Preliminary preparation: Under 15 minutes
Grilling: Indirect medium-high heat, under 45 minutes

³/₄ cup (180 ml) chicken broth

1 tablespoon (15 g) butter

1 tablespoon (15 ml/11 g) chopped garlic

¹/₂ teaspoon (2.5 ml/1.5 g) dry mustard powder

¹/₄ teaspoon (1.25 ml/.4 g) hot red pepper flakes, or to taste

1 head cauliflower

Prepare grill for indirect medium-high heat. In small skillet, combine broth, butter, garlic, mustard powder and pepper flakes; stir to blend. Heat to boiling over high heat; cook until reduced to ¹/₄ cup, 5 to 10 minutes. Meanwhile, remove any leaves from cauliflower. Cut core from underside of cauliflower head, taking care not to cut so deeply that head falls apart. Place, cut-side down, on shiny side of 18x18-inch (46x46-cm) piece of heavy-duty foil; cup foil around base of cauliflower. When broth mixture has reduced, pour evenly over cauliflower. Seal packet as shown on page 132. Place on grate away from heat. Cover and cook until just tender when pressed with gloved fingers, 25 to 40 minutes (rotate packet once or twice during cooking, but do not turn over).

Grilled Asparagus

Grilled Asparagus

4 servings
Preliminary preparation: Under 15 minutes
Grilling: Direct medium-high heat, under 15 minutes
Special equipment: Perforated grilling wok

1 pound (454 g) fresh asparagus spears

1½ teaspoons (7.5 ml) olive oil or vegetable oil

Kosher salt and freshly ground black pepper

2 tablespoons (30 ml/15 g) grated Parmesan or Romano cheese

Prepare grill for direct medium-high heat. Snap off and discard tough ends from asparagus. Place asparagus in perforated grilling wok; set wok on piece of waxed paper or a baking sheet. Drizzle oil over asparagus, tossing to coat; sprinkle with salt and pepper to taste. Place wok on grate over heat. Cook until asparagus is tender-crisp, 5 to 7 minutes, turning frequently with wooden spatula or spoon. Sprinkle with Parmesan cheese and toss to distribute cheese; serve immediately.

Parmesan Zucchini Spears

3 or 4 servings
Preliminary preparation: Under 15 minutes
Grilling: Direct medium-high heat, under 15 minutes

1½ pounds (680 g) medium-sized zucchini or yellow summer squash

2 tablespoons (30 ml) Italian-style vinaigrette dressing

Kosher salt and freshly ground black pepper

3 tablespoons (45 ml/25 g) grated Parmesan cheese

Prepare grill for direct medium-high heat. Trim ends of zucchini, then cut zucchini lengthwise into 4 spears each (6 spears if zucchini are large). Place in baking dish. Drizzle with dressing, turning to coat; use pastry brush if necessary to coat all surfaces. Sprinkle with salt and pepper to taste. Place zucchini directly on grate over heat, skin-side down to start. Cook until tender-crisp, about 10 minutes, turning zucchini to expose each side to heat. When zucchini is tender-crisp, turn skin-side down. Sprinkle each spear with a little Parmesan cheese. Cook for 2 to 3 minutes longer (covered if possible), or until zucchini is tender and cheese has melted somewhat to form a crust. Serve immediately.

Corn Roast

General instructions; make as much as you wish
Preliminary preparation: At least 30 minutes soaking
Grilling: Direct medium-high heat, about 30 minutes

In spite of what you may have heard, it is not necessary to partially husk the corn and remove the silk prior to grilling; in fact, doing so causes the corn to lose moisture during grilling. Try this easy method, and you'll see that the silk comes off easily with the charred husks. The corn is moist and flavorful, because it has been steamed with its own juices in the wet husks. —T.M.

Fresh corn ears, unhusked
Butter, salt and pepper for serving

Place corn in a bucket or sink full of water; place weights such as plates, clean bricks or whatever you can find on the corn to keep it submerged. Soak for at least 30 minutes, and as long as 2 hours. When you're ready to cook, prepare grill for direct medium-high heat. Place drained corn on grate over heat. Cook until husks char and begin to blacken and corn is tender, 20 to 30 minutes, turning corn frequently for even cooking. To check doneness, peel back a bit of husk from 1 ear and check kernels. They should be tender, and a few kernels should be browned.

To serve, hold an ear with oven mitts and peel away the burned husks (and silk). For standard serving, snap off the bunch of peeled-back husks and place the corn on a platter. For a more casual backyard affair, hand the ear of corn, with the peeled-back husks at the bottom, to a diner; the peeled-back husks can be used like a handle to hold the corn. A coffee can full of melted butter offers an easy way for diners to dip their corn, but this is practical only for a large crowd!

Grilled Vidalia Onions

6 servings; easily adjusted
Preliminary preparation: Under 15 minutes
Grilling: Direct medium heat, about an hour

6 Vidalia (or other sweet) onions
6 beef bouillon cubes
2 tablespoons (30 ml/8 g) finely chopped fresh parsley, divided
2 tablespoons (30 ml) sherry, divided
6 tablespoons (90 g) butter, cut into 6 pieces

Prepare grill for direct medium heat. Wash and peel onions. With small, narrow-pointed knife, cut a 1-inch-deep (2.5-cm-deep) hole in the top of each onion. Place each onion on the shiny side of a 12-inch-square (30.5-cm-square) piece of heavy-duty foil. Place 1 bouillon cube, 1 teaspoon (5 ml/1.5 g) parsley, 1 teaspoon (5 ml) sherry, and 1 tablespoon (15 g) butter in the hole of each onion. Seal foil tightly around each onion. Place on grate over heat and cook for 1 hour, or until fork-tender. There will be juice in the foil, so open packets carefully over a bowl to capture the juices. The juices are too good to lose and are delicious over the onion or meat. If desired, serve with an additional pat of butter and fresh parsley sprinkled on top.

Parmesan Tomatoes

4 servings
Preliminary preparation: Under 15 minutes
Grilling: Direct medium heat, under 15 minutes

4 large tomatoes
2 tablespoons (30 ml) olive oil, divided
1 clove garlic, minced, divided
2 tablespoons (30 ml/5 g) chopped fresh basil, divided
Kosher salt and freshly ground black pepper
1/2 cup (120 ml/63 g) grated Parmesan cheese

Prepare grill for direct medium heat. Cut off and discard tops and cores from tomatoes. Brush cut sides of tomatoes with olive oil and sprinkle evenly with garlic, basil, and salt and pepper to taste. Place on grate over heat. Cover and cook until almost tender, 5 to 10 minutes. Sprinkle each tomato with Parmesan cheese and cook a few minutes longer, until cheese melts and tomatoes are tender. Serve immediately.

Peas in a Packet

4 servings
Preliminary preparation: Under 15 minutes
Grilling: Direct medium heat, under 30 minutes

1 package (10 ounces/283 g) frozen green peas

1 can (3 ounces/85 g) mushrooms, drained

3 tablespoons (45 ml/35 g) finely diced onion

3 tablespoons (45 ml/27 g) finely diced ham

1 teaspoon (5 ml/1.5 g) chopped fresh parsley

2 tablespoons (30 ml) olive oil

1/2 teaspoon (2.5 ml/1 g) black pepper

1/4 teaspoon (1.25 ml/1.5 g) salt

Prepare grill for direct medium heat. Place block of frozen peas on large piece of heavy-duty foil, shiny-side up. Top with mushrooms, onion, ham and parsley. Drizzle with oil. Season with pepper and salt (adjust if ham is salty). Seal packet as shown below. Place packet on grate over heat and cook for 15 to 20 minutes, turning packet occasionally.

Potato Packets

4 servings
Preliminary preparation: Under 15 minutes
Grilling: Direct medium heat, under 30 minutes

2 tablespoons (30 ml) olive oil, divided

4 medium baking potatoes

1/2 cup (120 ml/100 g) finely diced onion, divided

1/2 to 1 teaspoon (2.5 to 5 ml/3 to 6 g) seasoned salt, divided

1 teaspoon (5 ml/2 g) freshly ground black pepper, divided

Several dashes of hot red pepper flakes

Prepare grill for direct medium heat. Tear off 4 large pieces of foil; brush the shiny side of each with a little oil. Scrub potatoes well and slice thinly. Divide potato slices evenly between prepared foil pieces. Sprinkle each batch with oil, onion, seasoned salt, black pepper and red pepper flakes. Seal packet as shown below. Place packet on grate over heat and cook for 25 to 30 minutes, or until potatoes are tender, turning packets occasionally.

HOW TO MAKE A FOIL PACKET

PLACE large piece of foil on work surface, shiny-side up. Heavy-duty foil works best; double regular-weight foil for more strength. Place food to be cooked in center of foil.

BRING long edges together over food, then roll-fold at least 3 times until foil is sealed over food (left). Leave a little room for expansion.

ROLL-FOLD the open ends tightly (right), until they form a completely sealed packet. Make sure there are at least 3 complete roll-folds on each end. Packet is now ready for grill.

UNWRAP one end to check doneness; remove packet from grill first, and open carefully to avoid steam. If food is not done, re-seal foil and return to grill.

Easy Vegetable Kabobs

Easy Vegetable Kabobs

6 servings
Preliminary preparation: Under 30 minutes
(plus time to soak skewers)
Grilling: Direct high heat, under 15 minutes
Special equipment: 6 bamboo or metal skewers

12 button mushrooms, washed, stems trimmed

12 large cherry tomatoes

3 medium red onions, peeled, quartered

3 small zucchini, cut into 1-inch (2.5-cm) chunks

1 yellow bell pepper, cored and cut into 12 chunks

3/4 cup (180 ml) Italian-style vinaigrette dressing

If using bamboo skewers, soak them in water for 30 minutes prior to starting. Thread all vegetables alternately on the skewers. Place filled skewers in shallow baking dish. Pour dressing over skewers and turn to coat evenly. Marinate at room temperature for 20 to 25 minutes, turning occasionally.

Prepare grill for direct high heat; lightly oil grate. Place skewers on grate over heat. Cook until vegetables are tender-crisp, about 8 minutes, turning once.

Salted Grilled Potatoes

Per serving; make as many as you wish
Preliminary preparation: Under 15 minutes
Grilling: Indirect high heat, under an hour

1 large baking potato

1 teaspoon (5 ml) olive oil, approximate

Kosher salt

Accompaniments: Butter, sour cream, bacon bits, chopped chives

Prepare grill for indirect high heat. Wash and dry potatoes, then pierce all over with a fork. Place a small amount of oil in the palm of your hand and coat potatoes, 1 at a time, with oil. Sprinkle each oiled potato with a generous amount of salt. Wrap each potato individually in heavy-duty foil (or a doubled layer of regular foil); use enough foil to wrap potato completely, sealing ends to trap steam. Place wrapped potatoes on grate away from heat and cook for 30 to 60 minutes, depending upon the intensity of the heat and the size of the potato. To test for doneness, insert a sharp knife into the center; potato is done when knife pierces easily. When done, unwrap potatoes, cut them open on the top and fill with accompaniments of your choice. Serve hot.

side
dishes

*Crusty Grilled
Bread with
The Works*

Hot Grilled Grits

4 to 6 servings
Preliminary preparation: Under 15 minutes, plus
overnight refrigeration
Grilling: Direct medium heat, under 15 minutes

*Grits are a traditional Southern dish that lend them-
selves to many uses. The creamy corn and garlic flavors
go well with barbecue sauces, dry rubs and fried fish. If
you like creamy grits, double the recipe and enjoy half of
the grits right after cooking. —A. and J.C.*

1 cup (240 ml) chicken broth
1/2 cup (120 ml) half-and-half
1/2 cup (120 ml) water
1/4 cup (55 g/half of a stick) butter
1 clove garlic, minced
1/2 teaspoon (2.5 ml/3 g) salt
1/4 teaspoon (1.25 ml/.5 g) freshly ground pepper
1 cup (240 ml/155 g) quick-cooking grits
3/4 cup (180 ml/85 g) shredded cheddar cheese
1 tablespoon (15 ml) olive oil
Grated Parmesan cheese, for garnish, optional

Spray 9x9x2-inch (23x23x5-cm) baking dish with nonstick spray; set aside. In large saucepan, combine broth,
half-and-half, water, butter, garlic, salt and pepper. Heat
to boiling over medium heat. Sprinkle grits into boiling
liquid, stirring constantly. Cover and reduce heat so
mixture bubbles gently; cook for 5 to 6 minutes, stirring
frequently. Remove from heat; add cheese and stir until
cheese melts. Scrape grits into prepared pan, spreading
evenly and smoothing top. Cover and refrigerate
overnight, or until well chilled and set.

When you're ready to cook, prepare grill for direct medium heat; generously oil grate. Cut grits into 3-inch (7.5-
cm) squares, or any size you like, as long as it balances
well on grate and can be turned easily. Brush grits with
oil and place on grate over heat. Cook for 4 to 5 minutes
per side, or until heated through and lightly browned.
Serve hot, sprinkled with Parmesan cheese if you like.

Crusty Grilled Bread with The Works

6 to 8 servings
Preliminary preparation: Under 15 minutes
Grilling: Indirect high heat, under 15 minutes

1 large loaf French bread
1/3 cup (70 g) butter, softened
1/3 cup (80 ml) olive oil
3 or 4 slices bacon, cooked and crumbled
2 cloves garlic, minced
1 cup (240 ml/110 g) shredded Colby cheese
1 cup (240 ml/110 g) shredded mozzarella cheese

Prepare grill for indirect high heat. Slice bread about
three-quarters of the way through, cutting vertically but
angling the cuts somewhat so each slice is wider than if
the bread were cut straight across. Place bread on doubled layer of foil that is a good bit longer than the loaf. In
small bowl, blend together butter, oil, bacon and garlic.
Spread slices with butter mixture. Mix together Colby
and mozzarella cheeses, and sprinkle between slices.
Wrap loaf well with foil. Place wrapped bread on grate
away from heat. Cover and cook for about 8 minutes, or
until cheeses melt; be careful not to burn the bread.
Remove from grill and serve immediately.

The Real Bruschetta
(Grilled Italian Garlic Bread)

4 servings
Preliminary preparation: Under 15 minutes
Grilling: Direct medium-high heat, under 15 minutes

Every time I see something called "bruschetta" on a restaurant menu, I cringe, because there are so many bad interpretations of this classic Italian dish. Here is the way that my relatives in Italy prepare it; be fore-warned that once you try it like this, you may lose your appetite for most commercially prepared stuff! (By the way, the word is generally pronounced broo-SKET-ta in most parts of Italy—not broo-SHET-ta, as it is usually called at most restaurants here.) —T.M.

Half of a loaf of day-old hearty Italian bread*
4 large cloves garlic
1/4 cup (60 ml) extra-virgin olive oil
Kosher salt

Prepare grill for direct medium-high heat. Slice bread about 1/2 inch (1.25 cm) thick. Peel garlic and cut each clove in half crosswise (not lengthwise), so you have a total of 8 shorter pieces of garlic. Place the oil in a small bowl, and have a pastry brush handy.

Arrange bread on grate over heat. Cook for 2 to 3 minutes per side, turning once or twice and rearranging on grill as necessary so all pieces cook evenly. The bread should be nicely toasted and brown, with perhaps a few lightly charred edges; watch bread carefully, as it burns easily. Remove bread from grill and, working quickly, rub each side of each toast with the cut side of a garlic clove. Brush each side of each toast with a little oil, and sprinkle 1 side with a bit of salt. Serve immediately.

*The correct loaf to use for this is hearty Italian or French country-style bread, with a dense, chewy texture and a firm crust (never try to make this recipe with soft bread; it will fall apart). Loaves typically weigh about 1 1/2 pounds (680 g). A typical slice will be about 5 inches (13 cm) across and 3 inches (8 cm) high. The loaf you use should be day-old, so it is even more firm; if you like, you can lay the slices out on the counter for a few hours to dry it out somewhat before cooking.

Zesty Pita Crisps

4 to 6 servings
Preliminary preparation: Under 15 minutes
Grilling: Direct medium heat, under 15 minutes

Make up a batch of these when you've got the grill going, then store them in a tightly sealed container for snacking. They also make a great accompaniment to salad or soup. —K.F.

4 whole-wheat pita breads
3/8 cup (90 ml) olive oil
4 cloves garlic, minced
1 teaspoon (5 ml) dried oregano
1/2 teaspoon (2.5 ml/1.5 g) kosher salt
1/4 teaspoon (1.25 ml/.5 g) cayenne pepper
1/4 teaspoon (1.25 ml/.5 g) freshly ground black pepper

Prepare grill for direct medium heat; lightly oil grate. Carefully break open the pitas. In small bowl, combine remaining ingredients, stirring to blend. Brush both sides of the pita slices with oil mixture. Place on grate over heat. Cook for 1 to 2 minutes per side, or until crisp and nicely toasted. Remove from grill and set aside to cool. Break into pieces before serving.

Portabellas Au Gratin

6 servings
Preliminary preparation: Under 15 minutes
Grilling: Direct high heat, under 15 minutes

1/3 cup (70 g) unsalted butter
2 cloves garlic, minced
6 large portabella mushroom caps
1/2 cup (120 ml/63 g) grated Parmesan cheese
1/4 cup (60 ml/30 g) grated mozzarella
3 tablespoons (45 ml/10 g) snipped fresh chives

Prepare grill for direct high heat; lightly oil grate. In small saucepan, melt butter over medium-low heat. Add garlic; cook for about 2 minutes, stirring occasionally (don't let the garlic brown). Brush tops of mushroom caps with melted garlic butter and place, top-side down, on grate over heat. Cook for about 2 minutes. Brush undersides with melted garlic butter, then turn top-side up. Cook for about 2 minutes longer. Carefully sprinkle Parmesan and mozzarella cheeses over caps; sprinkle with chives. Cook until cheese melts, then remove from grill and serve hot.

Grilled Cake with Bananas

> **4 servings**
> **Preliminary preparation:** Under 15 minutes
> **Grilling:** Direct medium heat, under 15 minutes
> **Special equipment:** Small disposable aluminum pan

You don't usually think of the grill in connection with dessert, but here's something you can do on the side of a larger unit even as you grill meat or veggies. —A. and J.C.

5 or 6 medium bananas, firm and unspotted
1/2 cup (110 g/1 stick) butter
1 cup (240 ml/220 g) brown sugar (packed)
1 teaspoon (5 ml) rum flavoring
1/2 teaspoon (2.5 ml/1 g) cinnamon
4 slices pound cake (1 inch/2.5 cm thick)
Vanilla ice cream, optional

Prepare grill for direct medium heat; lightly oil grate. Peel and slice bananas. Place butter into disposable aluminum pan; place on grate over heat and cook until butter melts, stirring frequently. Add brown sugar, rum flavoring and cinnamon; stir to blend. Add sliced bananas to brown sugar mixture. Cook until bananas are soft on the edges, 8 to 10 minutes, stirring frequently. Meanwhile, toast pound cake slices on both sides on the grill. To serve, place toasted cake slices on plates and spoon bananas and syrup over them. Top with ice cream, if you like.

desserts

Maple Apples

> **4 servings**
> **Preliminary preparation:** Under 15 minutes
> **Grilling:** Direct medium heat, under 15 minutes

Serve warm topped with ice cream for dessert. The caramel apple dip available in the produce section of most supermarkets works well for a warmed sauce to top the apples and ice cream. These apples also make a fantastic dish to serve with pork. —A. and J.C.

2 large cooking apples, such as Granny Smith, Gala, Jonathan or Braeburn
2 tablespoons (30 g) butter, melted
1/8 teaspoon (.625 ml) cinnamon
1/4 cup (60 ml) maple syrup

Prepare grill for direct medium heat; lightly oil grate. Core apples and cut into thick slices. Brush with melted butter; sprinkle with cinnamon. Place on grate over heat and brush with maple syrup. Cook, turning and basting frequently with syrup, until nicely glazed on both sides. Serve warm.

Peaches and Cream

4 servings
Preliminary preparation: Under 15 minutes
Grilling: Direct medium heat, under 30 minutes

4 firm peaches
1/2 cup (120 ml/110 g) brown sugar (packed)
3 tablespoons (45 ml) rum
1/2 teaspoon (2.5 ml/1 g) cinnamon
1 cup (240 ml) heavy cream

Prepare grill for direct medium heat. Peel peaches.* Remove and discard core; slice peaches into mixing bowl. Add sugar, rum and cinnamon, stirring to coat; adjust sugar as needed based on sweetness of peaches. Divide peach mixture between 2 large squares of foil, shiny-side up. Seal packets as shown on page 132. Place packets on grate over heat and cook for 20 to 30 minutes, or until peaches are tender and heated through, turning packets occasionally. Remove from grill and open packets carefully. It is a good idea to open into a bowl or serving dish in order to capture all the juices. Serve warm, topped with cream.

*To peel peaches, drop individually into a saucepan of boiling water and cook for 1 minute. Remove with slotted spoon and hold under cold water; the skin should slip off easily.

English Muffin Pies

4 servings
Preliminary preparation: Under 15 minutes
Grilling: Direct medium heat, under 15 minutes

4 English muffins
3 tablespoons (45 g) butter or margarine
1 can (about 20 ounces/567 g) apple, blueberry or other fruit pie filling

Prepare grill for direct medium heat. Tear off 4 pieces of foil, each about 12 inches (30 cm) square. Split English muffins. Butter the outsides generously, then place a muffin half, buttered-side down, on the shiny side of each piece of foil. Spoon about 3 tablespoons (45 ml) pie filling onto each muffin; refrigerate any remaining filling for another use. Top filled muffins with remaining buttered muffin halves, buttered-side up. Seal packets as shown on page 132. Place packets on grate over heat and cook for about 15 minutes, turning several times. The outsides of the muffins should be nicely browned. When done, remove from grill and open packets. Be careful, because the filling will be extremely hot; allow to cool for several minutes before serving.

TIP: Make and wrap the muffin pies in advance, then keep in the refrigerator while you prepare and eat dinner.

Grilled Pineapple Topped with Ice Cream and Rum

4 servings
Preliminary preparation: Under 15 minutes
Grilling: Direct medium heat, under 15 minutes

A sprinkle of toasted coconut or nuts makes a nice garnish.

1/2 cup (120 ml/100 g) sugar
1/4 teaspoon (1.25 ml/.5 g) cinnamon
4 thick slices fresh pineapple
2 tablespoons (30 g) butter, melted
1 pint (475 ml) vanilla or rum raisin ice cream
3 to 4 tablespoons (45 to 60 ml) rum (gold, dark or spiced)

Prepare grill for direct medium heat; lightly oil grate. In flat dish, stir together sugar and cinnamon. Brush pineapple with melted butter and then dip into sugar mixture, coating both sides. Shake off excess. Place on grate over heat and cook until brown and sizzling, 5 to 8 minutes per side. Serve at once, topped with ice cream and drizzled with 2 to 3 teaspoons (10 to 15 ml) of rum per serving.

Grilled Pineapple with Honey Glaze

4 servings
Preliminary preparation: Under 15 minutes
Grilling: Direct medium heat, under 30 minutes

1/4 cup (60 ml) honey
1 tablespoon (15 ml) dark rum
1 unpeeled medium pineapple, quartered, core removed
Toasted coconut, optional

Prepare grill for direct medium heat; generously oil grate. In small bowl, stir together honey and rum. Place pineapple quarters on grate over heat, with 1 of the cut sides down. Sear that side, then rotate the pineapple quarters slightly and sear the second cut side. When both cut sides are nicely seared, turn quarters rind-side down and brush cut sides with honey mixture. Cook for about 20 minutes longer, turning fruit several times. Remove from grill and sprinkle with coconut, if you like; serve warm.

Nutrition Chart

If a recipe has a range of servings, the data below applies to the greater number of servings. If the recipe lists a quantity range for an ingredient, the average quantity was used to calculate the nutritional data. If alternate ingredients are listed, the analysis applies to the first ingredient. If an ingredient cannot be accurately determined, NA is indicated.

	Calories	Fat (g)	Sodium (mg)	Saturated Fat (g)	Protein (g)	Carbohydrate (g)	Cholesterol (mg)
All-Day Beef Brisket	792	63	897	25	47	6	187
All-Purpose Seasoning	11	0	NA	0	0	2	0
Ancho Chili Rub	27	1	938	0	1	6	0
Apple-Ginger Quail	514	31	522	9	51	6	194
Apricot-Glazed Grilled Chicken Breasts	342	15	668	5	39	11	115
Argentinian Green Sauce	46	4	124	1	1	2	0
Asian Smoked Quail	714	48	1508	12	58	12	194
Backstrap in Bacon	156	7	1015	2	22	1	54
Backyard Tofu Steaks	430	33	210	5	32	10	0
Baharat	14	0	3	0	0	3	0
Barbecued Meatloaf	428	28	765	11	30	13	150
Barbecued Pork Tenderloin	279	14	385	6	25	14	85
Barbecued Turkey Legs	422	19	893	6	52	7	156
Basic Dry Rub	17	0	926	0	0	4	0
Basic Grilled Chicken	430	24	148	7	49	0	158
Basic Smoked Spareribs	860	64	1444	23	61	8	251
Basil Shrimp w/Pineapple	234	12	373	2	23	9	172
Blue Cheese Butter	79	8	40	5	1	0	23
Blue Cheese Venison Steak	331	14	565	8	46	2	169
Bourbon Dipping Sauce	31	2	192	0	0	4	0
Cajun Shrimp	167	7	270	1	23	2	173
Cedar Plank Fish	265	16	694	3	27	0	80
Chicken on a Can	346	20	1002	5	37	2	117
Chicken Under a Brick	384	24	115	6	38	0	123
Chile-Lime Butter	103	11	123	7	0	0	31
Chili Venison Burgers	341	9	868	4	27	36	95
Coconut-Basted Fish	268	11	231	8	29	13	122
Corn Roast	145	9	92	5	3	17	21
Corn, Black Bean & Tomato Salsa	51	2	89	0	2	7	0
Crab Boil	612	24	NA	8	67	40	555
Crab-Stuffed Chicken Breasts	441	24	430	8	47	7	160
Crab-Stuffed Rainbow Trout	448	22	955	9	42	18	171
Crusty Grilled Bread w/Works	414	20	606	11	12	30	47
Deep-Fried Canada Goose	540	40	562	12	41	0	147
Deep-Fried Fish	643	30	219	8	44	48	239
Dijon-Style T-Bone Steak	348	17	283	6	42	2	121
Dill Sour Cream Sauce	31	3	192	2	0	1	6
Dove Breast Appetizers	125	8	172	2	12	1	46
Easy Vegetable Kabobs	162	11	187	2	3	15	0
Elk Tenderloin w/Asian Spices	200	8	285	1	27	4	67
English Muffin Pies	253	10	371	6	5	37	23
Fabulous Fajitas	395	8	395	2	33	46	96
Fish Tacos	422	18	687	3	29	34	102
Fish-Stuffed Pepper Cups	391	30	772	6	23	6	122
Garlic Herb Butter	102	11	2	7	0	0	31
Garlic Pepper Rub	35	1	307	0	2	6	0
Great Lakes Fish Boil	928	66	1463	33	42	49	227
Greek Pheasant Skewers	269	10	68	2	34	9	94
Grilled Asparagus	46	4	48	1	4	3	2
Grilled Balsamic Chicken & Salad	801	51	1175	9	54	34	136
Grilled Cake w/Bananas	723	32	426	19	4	111	156
Grilled Goose Breast Fillets	404	22	260	11	47	0	195
Grilled Lamb Chops w/Mint Sauce	845	77	419	27	33	4	158
Grilled Lamb Loin	239	18	176	4	17	1	53
Grilled Pineapple w/Honey Glaze	122	1	2	0	1	32	0
Grilled Pineapple w/Ice Cream	350	13	113	8	3	51	45
Grilled Pork Chops	335	21	551	6	31	4	88
Grilled Shrimp w/Garlic Sauce	276	13	255	4	31	4	241
Grilled Striper w/Crusty Topping	218	6	759	2	28	9	122
Grilled Tuna w/Orange Basil Sauce	751	64	220	10	40	6	65
Grilled Vidalia Onions	240	12	992	7	5	31	31
Grill-Roasted Cauliflower	47	2	159	1	2	5	5
Grill-Roasted Rosemary Pork Loin	220	13	55	6	24	1	79
Ham Steak w/Peach Mustard Glaze	377	21	2377	6	32	14	103
Herb Marinade	85	9	196	1	0	1	0
Herbed Turkey Strips	253	12	196	1	34	1	84
Herb-Rubbed Red Snapper	423	30	1031	4	36	3	63
Honey & Spice Smoked Nuts	203	20	292	2	2	7	0
Honey Barbecue Sauce	32	1	52	0	0	5	0
Honey-Grilled Pheasant	548	33	393	11	54	6	185
Honey-Smoked Fish Chunks	113	6	218	1	11	2	33
Horseradish-Chive Butter	70	8	109	5	0	0	21
Hot Grilled Grits	266	18	534	10	7	21	43
Hot Honey-Mustard Glaze	54	0	91	0	0	13	0
Hot-Smoked Chicken	429	24	1252	7	48	3	154
Island-Influenced Rub	101	10	8	1	1	4	0

	Calories	Fat (g)	Sodium (mg)	Saturated Fat (g)	Protein (g)	Carbohydrate (g)	Cholesterol (mg)
Italian Turkey Burgers	424	22	875	9	32	23	85
Jerky Marinade #1	187	0	NA	0	14	34	0
Jerky Marinade #2	213	0	NA	0	0	54	0
Jerky Marinade #3	333	0	NA	0	12	74	0
Leg-O-Lamb on a Spit	312	25	67	12	21	0	94
Lemon Herb Chicken	273	11	233	1	39	1	99
Lemonade-Glazed Wings	219	14	458	3	15	7	45
London Broil	267	17	251	5	26	1	66
Low Country Shrimp Boil	651	34	1754	12	43	45	240
Maple Apples	154	6	60	4	0	26	16
Mustard Barbecue Sauce	29	0	211	0	0	6	0
Mustard Cream Sauce	42	4	138	2	0	0	6
Mustard-Pepper Grilled Tenderloin	221	7	671	2	33	2	84
Mustard-Tarragon Fish	363	24	453	4	31	1	92
Old-Fashioned Clambake	1904	115	1452	56	112	124	489
Oriental Chicken Breasts	282	12	83	3	35	4	97
Oven-Roasted & Grilled Chicken	422	21	598	6	46	9	137
Paprika Pork Cutlets	168	7	342	2	23	1	69
Parmesan Tomatoes	155	11	207	3	6	11	8
Parmesan Zucchini Spears	75	5	133	1	4	6	3
Parsley Sauce	101	11	118	2	0	1	0
Peach Barbecue Sauce	23	0	225	0	0	6	0
Peaches and Cream	366	22	34	14	2	43	82
Peas in a Packet	133	8	361	1	5	11	4
Pit-Style Steak	265	16	218	6	28	1	91
Pizza Margherita	575	25	574	3	22	68	48
Portabella Mushroom Burgers	385	28	557	4	7	29	7
Portabellas Au Gratin	164	13	150	8	7	6	36
Potato Packets	289	7	254	1	5	53	0
Quick Barbecue Sauce	37	3	183	0	0	4	0
Ribs in Beer	714	55	738	18	33	21	160
Roast Venison Haunch	171	6	147	2	28	0	101
Roasted Clams	284	24	295	14	14	3	99
Roasted Pork Boston Butt	602	38	159	14	59	1	219
Rolled Stuffed Turkey Breast	244	11	138	3	32	4	84
Rosemary Pepper Rub	10	0	306	0	0	2	0
Rubbed-Hot Venison Steaks	255	8	1056	2	39	5	142
Salmon Jerky	100	6	667	1	10	2	30
Salmon or Trout Niçoise	1031	82	878	13	39	40	100
Salmon w/Lemon-Dill Marinade	295	16	173	3	30	5	89
Salmon w/Parsley-Ginger Marinade	319	21	91	4	30	1	89
Salmon w/Vermouth-Maple Marinade	317	17	208	3	30	9	89
Salted Grilled Potatoes	291	5	504	1	7	56	0
Slow-Smoked Venison	227	6	108	2	42	0	109
Smoke-Cooked Salmon w/Sauce	435	29	157	10	38	3	128
Smoked BBQ Chicken Wings	421	25	953	11	19	34	85
Smoked Porketta Roast	408	29	928	10	31	3	115
Smoked Prime Rib of Beef	662	55	108	22	38	1	145
Smoked Salmon Spread	59	6	180	1	1	0	7
Smoke-N-Roast Chicken	344	19	898	5	38	2	123
Smoke-N-Roast Pheasant	487	24	1410	7	59	4	185
Smoke-N-Roast Turkey Breast	454	17	1126	5	67	3	173
Smoke-Roasted Potatoes	185	2	12	0	3	38	0
Smoke-Roasted Tomatoes	57	3	15	0	1	8	0
Sour Cream Drop Donuts	210	12	103	3	2	23	21
Southern Deep-Fried Quail	550	38	135	10	50	0	194
Southwest Rub	12	0	4	0	0	3	0
Soy-Ginger Marinade	31	0	720	0	1	5	0
Spanish Paprika Rub	19	0	922	0	1	4	0
Special Steak Marinade	8	0	449	0	1	1	0
Spiced Pork or Boar Burgers	435	24	810	8	31	22	98
Spicy Roasted Pork Ribs	1140	86	2706	27	54	37	257
Spicy Vietnamese Dipping Sauce	45	1	397	0	2	7	0
Stir-Fried Marlin & Peppers	225	11	386	2	21	10	39
Stir-Fry Alligator & Snow Peas	484	27	2297	5	36	27	55
Succulent Pork Spareribs	974	69	905	23	58	31	232
Sweet & Smoky Grilled Duck	539	31	604	10	36	28	163
Tartar Sauce	69	7	108	1	0	1	5
Teriyaki Chicken w/Mustard Sauce	183	16	879	2	2	5	13
The Real Bruschetta	280	16	332	3	5	30	0
Tomato Chutney	17	0	33	0	0	3	0
Tomato Topper for Burgers	91	7	11	1	1	7	0
Tropical Shrimp & Sausage Kabobs	344	19	773	6	30	11	178
Turkey on the Grill	526	27	592	9	66	1	200
Twice-Grilled Chicken Burritos	585	30	777	8	40	41	96
Vidalia Onion Marmalade	31	2	57	0	0	3	1
White Wine Marinade	77	8	117	1	0	0	0
Whole Fish w/Chinese Flavors	293	13	1716	2	30	10	82
Whole Pig in a Rotisserie	234	15	105	5	23	0	77
Whole Roast Pig	233	15	53	5	23	0	77
Wisconsin Booya	375	17	1303	6	25	32	71
Wisconsin Cherry Barbecue Sauce	34	0	165	0	0	8	0
Wright Sweet Venison Kabobs	527	12	1350	3	61	44	152
Wright Venison Bites	261	9	287	2	24	19	80
Yorkshire Pudding	185	12	261	6	5	14	94
Zesty Pita Crisps	240	15	390	2	4	25	0

Index

A

All-Day Beef Brisket, 102
Alligator and Snow Peas, Stir-Fry, 68
All-Purpose Seasoning, 118
Ancho Chili Rub, 119
Appetizer recipes, 30, 36, 47, 52, 77, 78, 80, 91, 111
Apple-Ginger Quail, 44
Apples, Maple, 136
Apricot-Glazed Grilled Chicken Breasts, 47
Argentinian Green Sauce, 126
Asian Smoked Quail, 87
Asparagus, Grilled, 130

B

Backstrap in Bacon, 36
Backyard Tofu Steaks, 70
Baharat (Spiced Pepper Rub), 120
Bananas, Grilled Cake with, 136
Barbecue cooking
    barbecue smoking, 73
    natural-wood barbecuing in bullet smoker, 88
    slow-roasting, 97-107
Barbecued Meatloaf, 41
Barbecued Pork Tenderloin, 22
Barbecued Turkey Legs, 102
Barbecue-Onion Burgers, 38
Barbecue units,
    choosing & fuel choices, 5-9
    temperatures, 9
Basic Dry Rub, 118
Basic Grilled Burgers with variations, 38
Basic Grilled Chicken with variations, 51
Basic Jerky Instructions, 81
Basic Smoked Spareribs, 85
Basil Shrimp with Pineapple, 67
Bass, see: Sea bass, Striped bass
Beef, 11, 13, 114
    about beef ribs, 26
    brisket, 10, 12, 73, 97, 102
    doneness (chart), 12
    ground, recipes, 38, 40, 41
    ribs, recipes, 27, 89
    roasts, recipes, 81, 86, 102
    steak, recipes, 29, 33, 34, 81, 92
    tenderloin, recipe, 22
Blue Cheese Butter, 127
Blue Cheese Venison Steak, 35

Boar Burgers, Spiced, 40
Boiling in backyard deep-fryer, 109, 114, 115
Booya, Wisconsin, 114
Bourbon Dipping Sauce and Marinade, 121
Box-style electric smokers, 10, 73
    controlling temperature, 10
    recipes using, 77-83, 87, 90, 91
    smoking wood for, 75
Bread, recipes featuring, 30, 71, 134, 135
Bream, 110
Brining, 11, 33, 47
    prior to smoking, 73, 74, 78
    technique & measurements, 53, 79
Brinkmann Corporation, 8, 9
Briquettes, charcoal, 5, 6, 74
Bruschetta, The Real, 135
BTUs (British Thermal Units), 7, 8
Buffalo, 34, 38, 40, 41
Bullet-style water smokers, 73
    fuel choices, 5, 9
    natural-wood barbecuing in, 88
    recipes using, 82-94, 102
    smoking wood for, 75
Burgers,
    judging doneness, 39
    recipes & tips, 38-41, 70
Burritos, Twice-Grilled Chicken, 51
Butters, compound, 117, 127

C

Cajun Shrimp, 67
Canadian ribs, 26
Carcinogens, 13
Carryover cooking, 11
Catfish, 11, 110
Cauliflower, Grill-Roasted, 129
Cedar Plank Fish with variations, 61
Char, 11, 56, 61
Char-Broil, 9
Charcoal, about, 5
Charcoal grills, 6
    choosing, 6, 7, 16
    controlling temperature, 7, 16, 17
    preparing for cooking, 15-17
    smoking wood for, 73, 75
Cheese-Stuffed Burgers, 38
Chicken, 10-12, 15
    breasts, recipes, 45-51, 53
    brining, 47, 53
    doneness (chart), 12
    parts, recipes, 49, 51, 52, 83, 89, 91, 114

    whole, recipes, 43, 51, 83, 89, 94, 99
Chicken on a Can, 99
Chicken Under a Brick, 43
Chile-Lime Butter, 127
Chili Venison Burgers, 40
Chimichurri, 126
Chimney starter, 16, 17
Clams, 13, 104, 107
Cobia, 57
Coconut-Basted Fish, 58
Color of meat as guide to doneness, 11, 12
Connective tissue in meat, 11
Cookshack, Inc., 10
Cool-Smoked Fish, 78
Corn, Black Bean and Tomato Salsa, 126
Corn Roast, 131
Covered grills, 6, 7, 73
Crab, 48, 55, 114, 115
Crab Boil, 114
Crab-Stuffed Chicken Breast, 48
Crab-Stuffed Rainbow Trout, 55
Crappies, 110
Crusty Grilled Bread with The Works, 134
Cures & curing, 73
    and salt types, 79
    effect on meat color, 12

D

Deep-Fried Canada Goose, 111
Deep-Fried Fish, 110
Deep-fryers & deep-frying, 5, 109
    recipes using, 110-115
    step-by-step turkey recipe, 112
Desserts, 113, 136, 137
Dieter's Burgers, 38
Dijon-Style T-Bone Steak, 29
Dill Sour Cream Sauce, 125
Direct-heat grilling, 7, 10, 11
    technique, 15, 16
Doneness of meat, poultry & fish, 11-13, 39, 62
    chart of temperatures, 12
Donuts, Sour Cream Drop, 113
Dove, 12, 52, 100
Dove Breast Appetizer, 52
Dove season, opening day feast, 100
Drip pan, 15, 19, 104
Dry-heat cooking, 11, 13

Duck
    doneness (chart), 12
    recipes, 81, 93

E

Easy Vegetable Kabobs, 133
Electric smokers, see: Box-style electric
    smokers, Bullet-style water smokers
Electric starter for charcoal, 17
Elk
    doneness (chart), 12
    recipes, 21, 22, 86
Elk Tenderloin Grilled with Asian
    Spices, 21
English Muffin Pies, 137
Environmentally friendly alternatives to
    lighter fluid, 17

F

Fabulous Fajitas, 34
Fat content of meat, poultry & fish, 13
    and cooking method, 10, 11
Firestarting gel for charcoal, 17
Fish, 10, 11, 13, 15
    accessories for grilling, 18, 58
    doneness (chart), 12
    fillets, recipes, 56, 58-65, 77, 78,
      80, 89, 90
    grilling tips, 62
    judging doneness, 13, 62
    lean vs. oily, 11
    smoked, recipes, 77, 78, 80
    steaks, recipes, 57, 64, 89, 115
    whole, recipes, 55, 78, 89, 110
    see also specific fish
Fish Boil, Great Lakes, 115
Fish grilling basket & racks, 18, 58
Fish-Stuffed Pepper Cups, 59
Fish Tacos, 63
Flank steak, 33
Flare-ups, 19, 39
Foil-packet cookery, 11, 132
    how to make a foil packet, 132

G

Game birds, 11
    doneness (chart), 12
    see also specific game birds
Garlic Herb Butter, 127
Garlic Pepper Rub, 120
Gas grills, 6
    checking for leaks, 19
    choosing, 6-8

    controlling temperature, 7, 17
    preparing for cooking, 16, 17
    smoking wood for, 75
Goose
    doneness (chart), 12
    recipes, 47, 81, 111
Grates to hold food, about, 6
Great Lakes Fish Boil, 115
Greek Pheasant Skewers, 49
Gremolata, 124
Grilled Asparagus, 130
Grilled Balsamic Chicken and Salad, 46
Grilled Cake with Bananas, 136
Grilled Goose Breast Fillets, 47
Grilled Italian Garlic Bread, 135
Grilled Lamb Chops with Mint Cream
    Sauce, 30
Grilled Lamb Loin, 23
Grilled Marinated Fish Fillets, 56
Grilled Pineapple Topped with Ice
    Cream and Rum, 137
Grilled Pineapple with Honey Glaze,
    137
Grilled Pork Chops, 33
Grilled Shrimp with Garlic White Wine
    Sauce, 68
Grilled Striper with Crusty Topping, 65
Grilled Tuna with Orange Basil Sauce,
    63
Grilled Vidalia Onions, 131
Grilling woks, 18
Grill-Roasted Cauliflower, 129
Grill-Roasted Rosemary Pork Loin, 23
Grills
    accessories, 18, 19
    choosing, 6-8
    fuel choices, 5, 6
    general techniques for grilling, 15-17
    how to build a large grill, 106
    judging grill temperature, 17
Grill screen, 18
Grits, Hot Grilled, 134
Ground meat
    doneness (chart), 12
    judging doneness, 12, 39
    red meat, recipes, 38, 40, 41
    turkey, recipe, 41
Grouper, 11, 56

H

Halibut, 11, 61, 63, 80
Ham Steak with Peach-Mustard Glaze,
    36
Health issues, 13

Heat zones, 7
Herbed Turkey Strips, 46
Herb Marinade, 121
Herb-Rubbed Red Snapper, 59
Hibachis, 6, 7
Hinged grilling basket, 18
Holland Grills, 7
Homemade grills & barbecues, 8, 97
    how to build a large grill, 106
Honey and Spice Smoked Nuts, 82
Honey Barbecue Sauce, 122
Honey-Grilled Pheasant, 43
Honey-Smoked Fish Chunks, 80
Horseradish-Chive Butter, 127
Hot Grilled Grits, 134
Hot Honey-Mustard Glaze, 122
Hot-Smoked Chicken, 94

I

Indirect-heat grilling, 7
    technique, 15, 16
Instant-read thermometer, 11, 19
Insulated electric smokehouse, 10, 73
    see also: Box-style electric smokers
Island-Influenced Rub, 119
Italian Turkey Burgers, 41

J

Jerky, 73
    recipes for, 77, 81

K

Kabobs, 15, 30
    recipes, 34, 49, 67, 69, 133
Kansas City ribs, 26
Kenmore, 7
Kettle grill, see: Covered grills

L

Lake trout, 55
Lamb
    chops, recipe, 30
    doneness (chart), 12
    ground, recipe, 38
    roast, recipe, 23, 104
    whole or split, 97, 103
Leg-o-Lamb on a Spit, 104
Lemonade-Glazed Wings, 52
Lemon Herb Chicken, 45

Liquid propane (LP), 5, 7
    see also: Gas grills
Lodge Manufacturing, 6
London Broil, 33
Low-and-slow cooking, 10, 11, 73, 97–107
Low Country Shrimp Boil, 115
Luhr Jensen, 10, 75
Lump charcoal, 5, 6, 16, 74
Lyfe Tyme, 8, 9

M

Mahi-mahi, 56, 63
Maple Apples, 136
Marbling, 10, 11
Marinades, 11, 117, 118
    and carcinogens, 13
    recipes, 22, 23, 30, 33, 34, 45, 46, 49, 52, 56, 67, 70, 121, 122
Marlin, 57, 63
Marlin and Peppers, Stir-Fried, 57
Meatloaf, Barbecued, 41
Mint Cream Sauce, 30
Moose
    doneness (chart), 12
    recipes, 22, 86
Mushroom recipes, 30, 70, 135
Mussels, 13
Mustard Barbecue Sauce, 123
Mustard Cream Sauce, 124
Mustard Dipping Sauce, 45
Mustard-Pepper Grilled Tenderloin, 22
Mustard-Tarragon Fish, 62

N

Natural gas, 5, 7
Natural-Wood-BBQ Ribs, Pork Roast, Fish or Chicken, 89
Natural-wood charcoal, 5, 6, 16, 74
Natural-wood cooking,
    barbecuing in bullet smoker, 88
    units for, 5, 8, 9
    see also: Wood
Nonreactive dish, explanation, 117
Nuts, Honey and Spice Smoked, 82

O

Offset firebox smokers, 5, 9, 10, 73
    recipes using, 82, 85-87, 90, 91
Old-Fashioned Clambake, 107

Opah, 80
Oriental Chicken Breasts, 53
Oven-Roasted and Grilled Chicken, 48
Oysters, 13, 105

P

Paprika Pork Cutlets, 32
Parmesan Tomatoes, 131
Parmesan Zucchini Spears, 130
Parsley Sauce, 124
Peach Barbecue Sauce, 123
Peaches and Cream, 137
Peas in a Packet, 132
Perch, 11, 56
Persillade, 124
Pheasant
    brining, 53
    doneness (chart), 12
    parts, recipes, 46, 49, 83
    whole, recipes, 43, 83
Pig roast, 97, 101, 103
Pineapple, Grilled,
    Topped with Ice Cream and Rum, 137
    with Honey Glaze, 137
Pit-smoked barbecue, 95
Pit-Style Steak, 92
Pizza Burgers, 38
Pizza Margherita, 71
Pizza recipes, 30, 71
Planked Fish with variations, 61
Pollo al Mattone, 43
Pork, 11
    about pork ribs, 26
    brining, 33, 53
    chops, recipe, 33
    doneness (chart), 12
    ground, recipe, 40
    ribs, recipes, 24, 27, 85, 89
    roast, recipes, 23, 89, 92, 99
    shoulder, 10, 12, 73, 92, 97
    tenderloin, recipes, 22, 32
    whole pig roast, 101, 103
Porketta Roast, Smoked, 92
Portabella Mushroom Burgers with Aioli, 70
Portabellas Au Gratin, 135
Potatoes, Salted Grilled, 133
Potatoes, Smoke-Roasted, 94
Potato Packets, 132
Poultry, 12, 53
    see also: Chicken, Game birds, Turkey
Pulled pork, 99

Q

Quail
    doneness (chart), 12
    recipes, 44, 87, 111
Quesadillas, 30
Quick Barbecue Sauce, 122

R

Rare tuna or salmon, 62
Real Bruschetta, The, 135
Red snapper, 11, 59
Rib rack, improvising, 85
Ribs, 15, 24
    about rib types & cuts, 26
    beef, recipes, 27, 89
    judging doneness, 12
    peeling pork spareribs, 26
    pork, recipes, 24, 27, 85, 89
    venison, recipe, 27
Ribs in Beer, 27
Roasted Clams, 104
Roasted Pork Boston Butt, 99
Roasters & roasting, 5, 7, 103
    slow-roasting, 97-107
Roast Venison Haunch, 101
Rolled Stuffed Turkey Breast, 44
Rosemary Pepper Rub, 120
Rotisserie or spit, 18, 97, 104
    whole pig or lamb on, 103
Rubbed-Hot Venison Steaks, 36
Rubs & seasonings, 117, 118
    recipes, 32, 36, 118-120

S

Salad recipes, 46, 64
Salmon, 11, 79
    doneness, 12, 62
    fillets, recipes, 56, 61, 62, 64, 77, 80, 90
    steaks, recipe, 64
    whole, recipe, 55
Salmon Jerky, 77
Salmon or Trout Niçoise, 64
Salsa, Corn, Black Bean and Tomato, 126
Salted Grilled Potatoes, 133
Salt in brines, about & substitutions, 53, 79
San Gennaro, Feast of, 28
Sauce recipes, 21, 30, 44, 121-126
Sausage Maker, The, 10, 75

Sausages, 15
    recipes featuring, 30, 69
Sawdust for smoking, 75, 76
Scallops, 30
Scraper for grill grate, 19
Sea bass, 11, 56, 80
Searing food on grill, 15
Seasonings, see: Rubs & seasonings
Shellfish, 13
Short ribs, about, 26
Shrimp, 13
    recipes, 30, 67-69, 115
Shrimp Boil, Low Country, 115
Slow-Smoked Venison, 82
Smoke-Cooked Salmon with
    Horseradish Cream Sauce, 90
Smoked BBQ Chicken Wings, 91
Smoked Elk or Moose Loin, 86
Smoked Porketta Roast, 92
Smoked Prime Rib of Beef, 86
Smoked Salmon Spread, 78
Smoke-n-Roast Pheasant, Chicken or
    Turkey Breast, 83
Smoke-Roasted Potatoes, 94
Smoke-Roasted Tomatoes, 91
Smokers & smoking, 73-95
    choosing, 6, 7, 9, 10
    controlling temperature, 9, 10,
      73, 74
    fuel choices & styles, 5, 6
    temperatures, 9, 10, 73
    wood for, 9, 75, 76
    see also specific smoker types
Solid fuel lighter cubes, 17
Sour Cream Drop Donuts, 113
Southern Deep-Fried Quail, 111
Southwest Rub, 120
Soy-Ginger Marinade, 121
Spanish Paprika Rub, 119
Special Steak Marinade, 122
Spiced Pepper Rub (Baharat), 120
Spiced Pork or Boar Burgers, 40
Spicy Vietnamese Dipping Sauce, 21
Steel-drum barbecue units, 8, 9, 73, 74
    see also: Offset firebox smokers
Stir-Fried Marlin and Peppers, 57
Stir-Fry Alligator and Snow Peas, 68
St. Louis-style ribs, 26
Striped bass, 11, 65
Succulent Pork Spareribs, 27
Sugar cane skewers, 69
Sweet and Smoky Grilled Duck, 93
Swordfish, 11, 57

T

Tacos, Fish, 63
Tartar Sauce, 124
Temperature
    carryover cooking, 11
    controlling in grill, 7, 16, 17
    controlling in smoker, 9, 10, 73, 74
    doneness of meat, poultry & fish
      (chart), 12
    for barbecuing or roasting, 9
    for deep-frying, 109
    for smoking, 9, 10, 73, 74
    judging grill temperature, 17
Teriyaki Chicken with Mustard Dipping
    Sauce, 45
Thai-Style Burgers, 38
Thermometer,
    digital, 74
    instant-read, 11, 19
Tilapia, 56
Tofu Steaks, Backyard, 70
Tomato recipes, 91, 124, 125, 131
Tomato Chutney, 125
Tomato Topper for Burgers, 124
Traditional Southern Oyster Roast, 105
Trailer-style barbecue units, 5, 8, 9
Tropical Shrimp and Sausage Kabobs,
    68
Trout, 11
    fillets, recipes, 55, 61, 64, 80
    whole, recipe, 55
Tuna, 11
    doneness, 12, 62
    recipes, 56, 57, 63
Turkey, 11, 12, 15
    breast, recipes, 44, 46, 49, 81, 83
    brining, 53
    deep-frying, 112, 113
    doneness (chart), 12
    ground, recipe, 41
    legs, recipe, 102
    tenderloin, recipe, 81
    whole, recipe, 98
Turkey fryers, see: Deep-fryers
Turkey on the Grill, 98
Twice-Grilled Chicken Burritos, 51

V

Vegetable recipes, 30, 70, 91, 124,
    125, 129-133, 135
Venison, 10, 11, 13
    doneness (chart), 12
    ground, recipes, 38, 40, 41
    haunch, recipe, 101
    loin, recipes, 21, 34, 36, 82
    ribs, recipe, 27

    roast, recipes, 81, 82
    steak, recipes, 34-36, 81, 92, 111
    tenderloin, recipe, 22
Vertical roaster, 99
Vidalia Onion Marmalade, 125
Vietnamese Dipping Sauce, Spicy, 21

W

Wahoo, 57
Walleye, 11, 58
Water pan, 97
    using in grill, 16
    using in smoker, 73
Water smokers, see: Bullet-style water
    smokers
Weather, effect on cooking, 10, 17
Weber-Stephens Co., 7-9
Website addresses
    Bear Mountain Forest Products, 17
    Cookshack, 10
    Dale's Steak Seasoning, 36
    Hasty Bake, 15
    The Sausage Maker, 10
    The Spanish Table, 119
White Wine Marinade, 121
Whole Fish with Chinese Flavors, 55
Whole Pig or Lamb in a Rotisserie
    Roaster, 103
Whole Roast Pig, 101
Wisconsin Booya, 114
Wisconsin Cherry Barbecue Sauce, 123
Woks for grilling, 18
Wood for smoking, 9, 73, 75, 76
    see also: Natural-wood cooking
Wright Sweet Venison Kabobs, 34
Wright Venison Bites, 111

Y

Yorkshire Pudding, 87

Z

Zesty Pita Crisps, 135
Zucchini Spears, Parmesan, 130

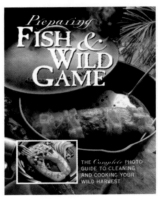